SPECULATIVE MANAGEMENT

SUNY series in the Sociology of Work and Organizations

Richard H. Hall, editor

SPECULATIVE MANAGEMENT

Stock Market Power and Corporate Change

Dan Krier

State University of New York Press

Published by
State University of New York Press, Albany

For information, address State University of New York Press,
90 State Street, Suite 700, Albany, NY 12207

Production by Judy Block
Marketing by Anne M. Valentine

HD
2741
.K75
2005

Library of Congress Cataloging-in-Publication Data

Krier, Dan, 1965–
    Speculative management : stock market power and corporate change / Dan Krier.
       p. cm. — (SUNY series in the sociology of work and organizations)
    Includes bibliographical references and index.
    ISBN 0-7914-6349-4 (alk. paper) — ISBN 0-7914-6350-8 (pbk. : alk. paper)
       1. Corporate governance—United States. 2. Corporate reorganizations—
United States. 3. Corporations—Valuation—United States. 4. Speculation—
United States. I. Title. II. Series.

HD2741.K75   2005
338.7—dc22

                    2004045337

10 9 8 7 6 5 4 3 2 1

CONTENTS

Figures and Tables   vii

Acknowledgments   xi

1. The Speculative Management of Corporate Restructuring: Introduction and Overview   1

2. Transactional Finance in Late-Twentieth-Century America   30

3. Social Intermediaries and the Wave of Internal Corporate Restructuring in the Late Twentieth Century   62

4. Financial Accounting as a Social Intermediary   91

5. Social Intermediation, Corporate Governance, and Financial Markets   125

6. The Rise of Corporate Restructuring, 1984–1990   156

7. The Reign of Restructuring, 1991–1993   184

8. The Decline and Delegitimation of Restructuring, 1994–1997   208

9. The Speculative Management of Corporate Value: Summary and Conclusions   255

Notes   271

Bibliography   291

Index   311

FIGURES AND TABLES

Table 1.1   Occupational Losers and Winners during the Era
of Restructuring: Total Employment in Selected
Occupations, 1983–1997   9

Figure 1.1   Real Hourly Wages and Weekly Earnings during
Age of Restructuring, 1970–1997   10

Figure 1.2   Productivity Gains during Era of Restructuring:
Output per Hour and Percentage Increase in
Productivity, 1970–1997   10

Figure 1.3   Income of U.S. Families during Late
Twentieth Century: Upper Limit of Each Quintile
and Lower Limit of Top 5 Percent   11

Figure 2.1   Median Net Worth of U.S. Households during the
Era of Restructuring, 1989–1998   51

Figure 2.2   Stock Holdings as a Share of U.S. Households'
Financial Assets during the Era of Restructuring,
1989–1998   52

Figure 2.3   Percentage of U.S. Households with Direct and
Indirect Holding of Stock during the Era of
Restructuring, 1989–1998   53

Figure 2.4   Financial Assets of U.S. Households as a
Percentage of their Total Assets during the Era
of Restructuring, 1989–1998   54

Figure 2.5   Median Value of Stock Holdings among U.S.
             Households with Stock, 1989–1998   55

Figure 2.6   Market Value and Number of Shares Traded on
             New York Stock Exchange during the Era of
             Restructuring, 1980–1997   56

Table 3.1   Comparison of External and Internal Corporate
             Reorganization   67

Table 3.2   Industrial Firms Selected from *Fortune* 500,
             1993   68

Table 3.3   Nonindustrial Firms Selected from
             Fortune 500, 1993   69

Table 3.4   Demonstration of the Effect of a Restructuring
             Charge on Current and Future Corporate Earnings   73

Figure 3.1   Aggregate Yearly Reorganization Charges Taken
             by Large Firms, 1984–1997   75

Figure 3.2   Intraorganizational Restructuring Charges,
             1984–1997   76

Figure 3.3   Accumulative Incidence of Restructuring among
             Industrial Firms, 1984–1997   77

Figure 3.4   Total Number of Reorganization Charges Taken
             by Companies in the the Study, 1984–1997   78

Figure 3.5   Total Value of Corporate Restructuring Charges
             Taken by Companies in the Study, 1984–1997   79

Figure 3.6   Transactional and Internal Reorganization
             Compared: Dollar Volume of U.S. Mergers,
             Acquisitions, and Divestitures and Total Number
             of Internal Restructuring Charges, 1984–1997   81

Figure 3.7 Relative Value of Charges as a Percentage of
Revenue, 1984–1997   83

Figure 3.8 Value of Reorganization Charges as a Percentage
of Profit, 1984–1997   84

Table 3.5 The Role of Social Intermediaries in Channeling
Restructuring Activity, 1984–1997   85

Figure 3.9 Reorganization Charges among 100 Industrial
Firms, 1984–1997   89

Table 4.1 Areas of Financial Accounting Subject to
Manipulation for Earnings Management   107

Table 6.1 Turbulent Financial Market Reaction to Internal
Reorganization: Stock Price Record of 40
Companies that Announced Restructuring,
1989 and 1990   173

Table 7.1 Speculative Management Teams and Restructuring:
Changes in CEO Compensation at Companies
Announcing Downsizing Reorganizations   193

Table 7.2 Top 20 Consulting Firms Worldwide as of
Year-End 1997   197

Table 8.1 "Aggressive Accounting" Targeted by the SEC
in the Fall of 1998   240

Table 8.2 Mergers Compared: 1960s, 1980s, and 1990s   250

ACKNOWLEDGMENTS

Coursework and independent study at the University of Kansas with Jack Weller, Bob Antonio, David Smith, and Mohammed El-Hodiri helped me frame this study. Dave Ekerdt, Dan Spencer, Mohammed El-Hodiri, and Eric Hanley all found me employment at the University of Kansas during critical times while working on this project. My dissertation committee—Jack Weller, Bob Antonio, David Smith, Eric Hanley, and Dan Spencer—made excellent suggestions for improving both my arguments and the expression of them. I particularly thank Bob Antonio for orienting me to economic sociology and for his thoughtful reading of an earlier draft of this document.

At the College of William and Mary, the Grants Office provided me with summer support for revisions and the Reves Center for International Studies supported travel to present selections from this manuscript at conferences in London and Amsterdam. The Thomas Jefferson Public Policy Program and the Charles Center supported travel to the New York City financial district. I have benefited from the insight and encouragement of colleagues, especially David Aday, Robert Archibald, and Gary Kreps, as well as audiences who have responded to the ideas in this study, especially students in my graduate policy seminars and participants in my courses taught through the Christopher Wren Association. I would also like to thank Richard Hall and the anonymous reviewers who made suggestions that substantially improved the manuscript.

Jack Weller transformed this project at every stage of its development. *Every* idea that is expressed in this report has been tested against his judgment, and often, reformed as a result. Jack either confirmed from among a number of variants I was using or pointed out amid my less-focused thinking some of the most vivid terms employed in this study. I reserve my deepest gratitude for Jack, who has helped me keep my intellectual bearings so that I did not lose track of the main themes and insights in the density of details.

Family and friends gave me critical aid, including my parents Richard and Shirley Krier, my brother Mike Krier, Francis and Mary McMahon, and friends John Moore, Victor Liguori, Kevin Gotham, Bill Swart, Jean VanDelinder, and Mark Worrell.

Judy Krier supported me throughout this entire project, and my daughters Adele and Johanna improved this report by lightening my mood.

Chapter 1

THE SPECULATIVE MANAGEMENT OF CORPORATE RESTRUCTURING: INTRODUCTION AND OVERVIEW

Speculators may do no harm as bubbles on a steady stream of enter-prise. But the position is serious when enterprise becomes the bubble on a whirlpool of speculation. When the capital development of a country becomes a by-product of the activities of a casino, the job is likely to be ill-done.
—John Maynard Keynes, writing on the problems with U.S. financial markets versus the less speculative British market[1]

As managers of a fund, we have an urgency. We are not short-term traders, but the urgency is still there. We have this burning in our stomach every day. It doesn't mean you buy and sell the businesses every day. But you constantly evaluate your investment, and the ur-gency is always there to hold management accountable for perfor-mance.
—Michael Price on the urgency of institutional investors[2]

You can't measure success by the interests of multiple stakeholders. You can measure success by how the shareholder fares.
—Albert J. Dunlap, CEO of Scott Paper and Sunbeam Corporation, on shareholder interests

I'm a great believer in predators.
—Albert J. Dunlap, CEO of Scott Paper and Sunbeam Corporation

That's another six hundred million. So we made a billion dollars on Sunbeam with no risk.
—Michael Price, institutional investment manager whose fund owns 20 percent of Sunbeam

[Dunlap] is persuading others that shareholder value is the be-all and end-all. But Dunlap didn't create value: He redistributed income from the employees and the community to the shareholders.
—Peter D. Capelli, Chair of Management Department at the Wharton School of the University of Pennsylvania[3]

In the fall of 2001, the stock price of Enron, America's seventh largest corporation, collapsed amid reports of deepening accounting irregularities, fictitious profits, shredded audit documents, and the suspicious suicide of a key executive. Enron struggled to avoid bankruptcy but failed. Arthur Andersen, Enron's Big Five auditor, failed as well. Enron and its most important trading partners, Dynergy, Reliant, and CMS Energy, were found to have engaged in sham accounting, including the booking of "round-trip swaps" to inflate revenues and earnings by as much as $4 billion. Congressional hearings were held after the stocks of Global Crossing and WorldCom plummeted as accounting irregularities were discovered. The widening scandal underscored an uncomfortable change in U.S. capitalism: deft manipulation of stock prices and accounting figures have displaced the efficient management of industrial production as the central concern of U.S. corporate executives.

This book chronicles changes in U.S. finance that increased the power of the stock market over corporate life, diverting focus from production to *speculative management*, the control of corporate actions and results to raise the trading price of corporate shares. This book describes how the speculative logic of the stock market was transmitted through the mediation of financial accounting, the business media, and corporate governance to encourage the dramatic restructuring of America's largest corporations in the late twentieth century. Corporate change in recent times, from hostile takeovers in the 1980s, to downsizing of U.S. firms in the early 1990s, to the spectacular failures of Enron, World-Com, and Global Crossing in the early 2000s, was closely bound to speculative trading in equity securities. Speculative management cuts across and deepens understanding of this broad spectrum of corporate change. The study's empirical focus is the episode of downsizing and corporate restructuring that peaked in U.S. corporations in the early 1990s. We begin with the consideration of a prominent example: Sunbeam Corporation.

CORPORATE RESTRUCTURING AT SUNBEAM CORPORATION

Like thousands of other workers in the 1980s and 1990s, employees of two Sunbeam Corporation factories, one in Bay Springs, Mississippi, and the other in McMinnville, Tennessee, learned in the winter of 1996 to 1997 that their plants were to be closed in a corporate restructuring.[4]

The factory in Bay Springs (pop. 2,200) manufactured wire assemblies for electric blankets and, although small, employing only 125 workers, was efficient and profitable. The workers in this plant were the kind that American management had dreamt of during the preceding two decades: workers who were nonunionized, compliant, hardworking, and satisfied with modest wages (many worked for less than $10 per hour). One 30-year veteran of the factory described life within the plant in community terms: "It was a wonderful place to work. I had good supervisors and good coworkers. To me, that plant was like one big family. I guess I spent more time there than at home. The plant had been good to me" (Byrne 1999, p. 123).

The product made in the plant, "positive temperature coefficient" wire that allowed electric blankets to adjust automatically to the temperature of the user's body, was in high demand. Because of the advantages of the wire made in Bay Springs, Sunbeam dominated the electric blanket market in the United States. Workers in Bay Springs skillfully and efficiently produced a critical component for one of Sunbeam's core products and, in the winter of 1996, could have reasonably expected to continue doing so.

Workers at Sunbeam's factory in McMinnville (pop. 11,000) also had good cause to expect continuing employment. This plant employed 700 workers in the production of Oster hair clippers. The majority were sold in retail stores, but the most profitable line was sold to professional barbers and pet groomers. The plant was one of the best in the Sunbeam portfolio. It ran virtually nonstop and at a high profit. Production was quite high: the plant produced 3.3 million retail clippers in 1996 (15,000 a day), as well as 375,000 professional trimmers and 1.2 million replacement blades (Byrne 1999, p. 129).

The McMinnville plant boasted profit margins on its products that were higher than other Sunbeam products: 38 percent margins on the retail clippers, 50 percent margins on the professional clippers, and 65 percent margins on replacement blades. In all, the plant earned $40 million a year on sales of $110 million. The Sunbeam marketing executive who was responsible for selling the clippers this factory produced characterized it thusly:

> The McMinnville facility was just a jewel. Many of the people in the assembly area had been doing their work for twenty-five or more years. They could do their jobs with their eyes closed. . . . They had a

wonderfully committed workforce. The employees had tremendous values. . . . They had flexible production. If there was a surge in demand, they knew how to deliver. (Byrne 1999, p. 135)

Byrne indicates that workers and staff at both factories expressed shock at the news of their impending closure. Both of the plants seemed well run and productive if not completely aligned with the "lean and mean" corporate rhetoric of the times. But, like hundreds of other facilities, managers conspicuously committed to production efficiency and profit closed them.

The restructuring plan that affected these plants was one of the most extreme reorganizations of the late twentieth century, calling for the removal of fully half of the corporation's staff and workers. Sunbeam's chief executive officer (CEO) Albert Dunlap, whom the media nicknamed "Chainsaw Al" for his famously ruthless reorganizations of other firms, announced the restructuring from Sunbeam's Delray Beach, Florida, headquarters. The restructuring was planned like the "invasion of Normandy," Dunlap was quoted as saying in the *Wall Street Journal*, which reported the details of the plan:

> In an effort to improve the fortunes of the ailing consumer-products company, whose reins he took as chairman and chief executive officer in July [1996], Mr. Dunlap said he would eliminate fully 50 percent of the company's 12,000 employees; sell or consolidate 39 of its 53 facilities, including 18 of its 26 factories and 37 of its 61 warehouses; divest several lines of businesses; eliminate six regional headquarters in favor of a single office in Delray Beach, Fla.; and scrap 87 percent of Sunbeam's products. [Dunlap says the plan] would save the company $225 million a year starting in 1998. He said Sunbeam would exit the businesses of making furniture, clocks, scales and decorative bedding.[5]

The plants in Bay Springs and McMinnville were 2 of the 18 factories that were to be closed as part of Sunbeam's restructuring plan. The plan called for the transfer of the production line of the Bay Springs factory, which produced components for electric blankets, to the final assembly plant in Waynesboro, Mississippi, yielding a projected savings of $200,000 in annual transportation costs. The production of the McMinnville factory was to relocate to a Sunbeam blender and waffle-iron plant in Mexico City, a move projected to reduce costs by $28 million annually (Byrne 1999, p. 133).

The downsized employees of Sunbeam Corporation had plenty of company. The late twentieth century in the United States was a period of extensive, painful industrial reorganization. One-third of the 500 largest U.S. industrial firms in 1980 ceased to exist as stand-alone companies by 1990. Employment at the 500 largest industrials fell by 25 percent during this time, from 16 million to 12 million, and half of their total products were eliminated (Useem 1996, p. 2).

During the last two decades of the century, virtually every major corporation in the United States restructured its operations. Like Sunbeam, many of these corporations initiated layoffs, plant closures, and contract renegotiations. Consultants were hired to help "turnaround managers" eliminate layers of management and "reengineer" work processes. Corporate managers presented their reorganizing plans and results to the business community, which alternately celebrated and condemned these actions. Business discourse critical of restructuring often emphasized the destruction it occasioned. But proponents claimed creative consequences. The enhanced competitiveness, long-term profitability, and efficient growth of lean, mean, reorganized firms redeemed the destructive process. As a whole, business discourse wrapped corporate restructuring in a legitimating rhetoric of competitiveness and efficiency.[6]

A best-selling business book of the early 1990s, Michael Hammer and James Champy's (1993) how-to guide to corporate restructuring, *Reengineering the Corporation: A Manifesto for Business Revolution*, justified restructuring as a necessary response to intensively competitive global product markets:

> With trade barriers falling, no company's national turf is protected from overseas competition. When the Japanese—or Germans, French, Koreans, Taiwanese, and so forth—are free to compete in the same markets, just one superior performer can raise the competitive threshold for companies around the world. . . . If a company can't stand shoulder to shoulder with the world's best in a competitive category, it soon has no place to stand at all. (P. 21)

Global competition sharply affected the consumer appliances industry in which Sunbeam operated for several reasons:

[In] few industries is competition more Darwinian than in small appliances. The barriers to making toasters and irons are low. Technological innovation is quickly knocked off by a host of competitors here and in low-labor-cost nations like China. Pricing power is almost non-existent in a retail environment dominated by giants like Wal-Mart. Even breakthrough items, such as breadmakers, quickly become low-margin commodities.[7]

Cutting costs to compete in such a world was the rationale that Sunbeam's Dunlap communicated to analysts and the business media. Dunlap argued that cost structure was Sunbeam's major problem. Two days after taking over as head of Sunbeam, Dunlap fired one of his rivals for the job and held a conference call for analysts to assess blame and outline strategy:

After a two-day review of operations, Mr. Dunlap diagnosed Sunbeam as having excess capacity, high costs and irrational product lines. He said that while the company had strong brands and some solid products, it built new production capacity based on sales growth that never materialized. "We've got too many people, too many products, too many facilities and too many headquarters," Mr. Dunlap said during the conference call. He said management teams will start studying the operations more closely on Monday and begin announcing specific changes. . . . "We're going to look at everything," he said. Mr. Dunlap plans to centralize the company's sprawling divisions and offices, which now remain largely autonomous. "[Autonomy] is nonsense," he said. "The last thing we need is for people to be setting up empires."[8]

And so Sunbeam joined the ranks of major U.S. corporations that implemented drastic restructuring programs. Although painful to local communities and workers, restructuring held out the promise of gains for the surviving company, its managers, and its owners. In the legitimating rhetoric of restructuring's proponents, restructuring improves production efficiency, product quality, and profits in an era of tough global product market competition; restructuring is possibly the only way for U.S. industry to survive. In business discourse of the late twentieth century, restructuring might be ruthless, but it was definitely good production management.[9]

Corporate restructuring meant different things at different points in the late twentieth century.[10] Business media emphasized plant closings and deindustrialization in the 1970s and early 1980s, takeovers in the late 1980s, and downsizing and reengineering in the 1990s. Deindustrialization crystallized as a coherent corporate strategy in the early 1980s (Bluestone and Harrison 1982).[11] Deindustrialization generally involved disposal or divestment of "noncore" lines of business. Production facilities U.S. corporations owned in the industrial Northeast and Midwest were closed and production shifted to new factories built in the southern United States, Mexico, South America, and Asia to exploit low-wage rates in those regions.

In the technical jargon of the academic finance literature, deindustrialization was a form of asset restructuring whereby a corporation strategically exited lines of business and entered others, changing the portfolio of businesses under corporate control (Donaldson 1994, Rock and Rock 1990). Although asset restructuring changed a firm's portfolio, capital restructuring altered the firm's capital structure, often by increasing the financial leverage—ratio of debt to equity—of the firm. Debt for equity swaps, stock repurchase plans, leveraged buyouts (LBOs), and leveraged recapitalizations redistributed cash to shareholders and forced the firm's management to deploy assets more efficiently. Capital restructuring was not oriented toward production improvements, but toward nonoperational matters, especially accounting profits.

During the 1980s, corporate restructuring became a euphemism for the external, transaction-based business reorganizations known as corporate takeovers. Using complicated forms of financing, competing groups of financiers and managers struggled with each other for the control and the spoils of U.S. corporations. The operational consequences of these reorganizations were often catastrophic: many of the companies taken over were subsequently broken up, their assets and subsidiaries sold off to pay the overwhelming debt burden the winning bidders incurred.

Many scholars of U.S. capitalism confirmed the crisis framing of restructuring found in business discourse, viewing it as an epoch-making response to the challenge of aggressive global competition. Scholars drew attention to many facets of restructuring. Some emphasized the transformation of industrial production systems to inject flexibility and rapid adaptability (Harvey 1989, Piore and Sabel 1984). Some focused on broad changes in the legitimating culture of management that encouraged the abstract control of firms in terms of financial measurements (Brewster Stearns and Allan 1996; Davis, Diekmann, and Tinsley 1994; Davis and Stout 1992; Fligstein 1985, 1990, 2001). Some emphasized concentration of corporate ownership by institutional investors that forced managers to restructure corporations to advance long-term shareholder interests (Useem 1996).

Prechel (1997, 2000) and Prechel and Boies (1998) describe and explain late-twentieth-century restructuring of the legal form of U.S. corporations from organizations of divisions to subsidiaries. Subsidiaries, unlike divisions, have an identity and capital-raising capacity that is legally separate from the parent company. During the 1980s, many firms adopted a *multilayered subsidiary form*, essentially a holding-company structure that enabled greatly intensified embedding of U.S. corporations in financial markets. Parent companies were able to generate capital through security issues of their subsidiaries. The multilayered subsidiary form (MLSF) also facilitated corporate spin-offs, divestitures, and acquisitions. Transactional restructuring greatly facilitated the subsidiarization of U.S. industry.

During the early 1990s, the term *corporate restructuring* jumped off the business pages to enter the popular lexicon in the sense used in this book. In the early 1990s, corporate restructuring referred to *internal reorganization* of a corporation's existing lines of business, production processes, operations, and bureaucratic structure. In the media and popular usage, corporate restructuring ceased to be a synonym for corporate takeovers and became synonymous with employee downsizing and layoffs for the express purpose of boosting the productivity and profitability of the corporation. This form of restructuring included the fleetingly fashionable and broadly discussed form of reorganization known as *business process reengineering* (or *simply reengineering*). Internal reorganization altered a firm's interior organizational structure and processes within the continuing businesses of the firm. These intraorganizational changes aimed to increase corporate efficiency, to help firms become, in the words of an executive announcement, "leaner, tougher minded, more competitive." Table 1.1 and Figures 1.1, 1.2, and 1.3 present some of the social and economic consequences of corporate restructuring.

TABLE 1.1
Occupational Losers and Winners during the Era of Restructuring: Total Employment in Selected Occupations, 1983–1997

	1983	1997	Change in Employment
Big Losers during the Age of Restructuring			
Typists	906	555	–39%
Computer operators	597	385	–36%
Computer equipment operators	605	392	–35%
Weighers, measurers, and checkers	79	53	–33%
Farm workers	1,149	796	–31%
Telephone operators	244	173	–29%
Communications equipment operators	256	185	–28%
Pressing machine operators	141	102	–28%
Extractive occupations	196	145	–26%
Textile sewing machine operators	806	607	–25%
Secretaries, stenographers, and typists	4,861	3,692	–24%
Textile, apparel, and furnishings machine operators	1,414	1,083	–23%
Secretaries	3,891	3,033	–22%
Telephone installers and repairers	247	197	–20%
Payroll and time keeping clerks	192	155	–19%
Stock and inventory clerks	532	454	–15%
Forestry and logging occupations	126	108	–14%
Bookkeepers, accounting, and auditing clerks	1,970	1,735	–12%
Financial records processing	2,457	2,196	–11%
Statistical clerks	96	89	–7%
Bank tellers	480	446	–7%
Big Winners during the Age of Restructuring			
Adjusters and investigators	675	1,701	152%
Insurance adjusters, examiners, and investigators	199	434	118%
Data entry keyers	311	664	114%
Securities and financial services sales	212	429	102%
Kitchen workers, food preparation	138	278	101%
Correctional institution officers	146	284	95%
Data processing equipment repairers	98	190	94%
Sales-related occupations	54	91	69%
Cashiers	2,009	3,007	50%

Source: U.S. Bureau of Labor Statistics, Employment and Earnings, monthly. Obtained from Statistical Abstracts Online. 2001.

FIGURE 1.1
Real Hourly Wages and Weekly Earnings during Age of Restructuring, 1970–1997

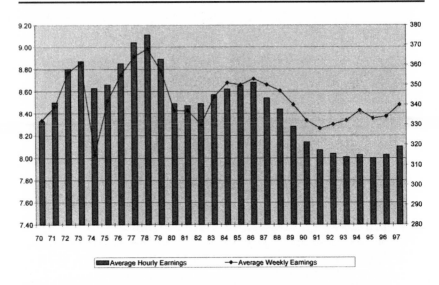

Source: U.S. Bureau of Labor Statistics. 2001. Obtained from Statistical Abstracts Online.

FIGURE 1.2
Productivity Gains during Era of Restructuring:
Output per Hour and Percentage Increase in Productivity, 1970–1997

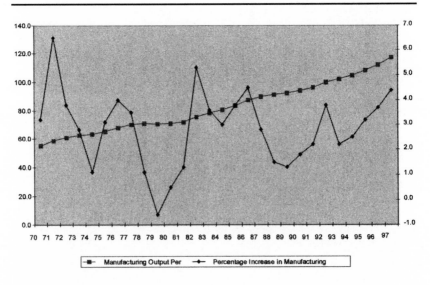

Source: U.S. Bureau of Labor Statistics. 2001. Obtained from Statistical Abstracts Online.

FIGURE 1.3
Income of U.S. Families during Late Twentieth Century:
Upper Limit of Each Quintile and Lower Limit of Top 5 Percent
(in constant 1998 dollars)

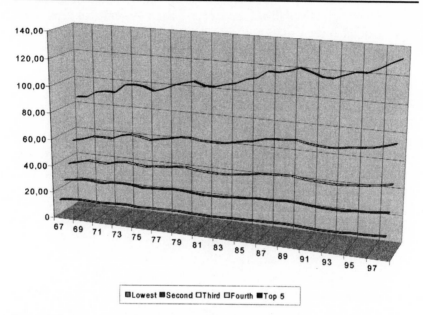

Source: U.S. Census. 2001. Obtained from Statistical Abstracts Online.

AMERICAN STEEL: RESTRUCTURING AS PRODUCTION MANAGEMENT

Wide acceptance of corporate restructuring as good production management rested, in part, on successful turnarounds of firms in struggling industries. U.S. industrial corporations faced severe problems in the last decades of the twentieth century. The combination of economic stagnation and high inflation in the macroeconomic environment of the 1970s and early 1980s was one challenge that constrained profits. New global competitors that sold product at much lower costs was another. These problems were especially acute in basic industries such as steel because added to cost pressures were imperatives to improve quality. Industrial purchasers of steel, especially automobile manufacturers, demanded higher quality steel and imposed demanding quality controls on suppliers. Restructuring the production process to achieve greater quality and efficiency became a prime management imperative.

Sociologist Harlan Prechel has studied corporate restructuring in the steel industry (Prechel 1990, 1994, 2000). One part of his research is an intensive case study of American Steel, a pseudonym for an integrated steel manufacturing and distribution firm that underwent an extensive reorganization between 1980 and 1992. An early phase of American Steel's restructuring focused on production improvements to achieve greater product quality and profitability, primarily through improvements in the corporation's cost accounting and information management systems. The reorganization began with the collection of highly detailed cost accounting data that allowed management to identify product costs and profitability at a high level of precision. The cost accounting system tracked more than 50,000 cost points. Restructuring decisions were tied to these data. Poorly performing products and the facilities that manufactured them were identified and closed down. Fully 30 percent of production capacity was eliminated through this process. This stage of American Steel's reorganization realigns the firm to its product and labor markets, and as such, is good production management.

The data were also used to analyze remaining production processes to identify areas where work process reorganization could yield additional cost savings. Consultants were employed to retune the corporate culture on decision accountability and cost management. The cost data allowed managers to track inventories better, for example, significantly reducing inventory carrying costs (no small matter when interest rates were high) and material shortages (Prechel 2000, p. 185–6).

The accounting system was further employed to provide cost and quality control information for each discrete managerial decision. The system could track the effect of small variations in production procedures on product quality and product cost. This allowed for the identification of optimal procedures and the centralization of production process controls in a manufacturing decision center. As stated in a corporate document, this highly sophisticated management information system allowed management to "increase accountability at each level and enlarge decision-making responsibility throughout the organization" (Prechel 2000, p. 192). The restructuring further coordinated the manufacturing process through the implementation of an "operations control center" that used computer technology to implement statistical quality control and statistical process control. Computer-aided manufacturing and computer-integrated manufacturing were further used to optimize production processes, maximize efficiency, and ensure quality. This technological infrastructure enabled American Steel to cut its inventory by more than 90 percent, thereby reducing the amount of working capital required (Prechel 2000, p. 198).

This information infrastructure also enabled a restructuring of the organizational hierarchy at American Steel. The new information system altered the management function by assessing costs precisely, tracking managerial performance, maintaining consistent quality, and selecting optimal production processes. The system allowed for (and in some degree required) a thinning of the ranks of middle management. The information system centralized the design and conception of production, eliminating the need for autonomous, information-rich middle managers. Simultaneously, the information system allowed for the decentralization of responsibility for executing production. As a result, American Steel reduced the layers of lower and middle management by 50 percent during its restructuring (from eight layers to four), and cut 28 percent of its managers (Prechel 2000, p. 200).

The restructuring of American Steel led to a sharp turnaround in corporate profitability in the late 1980s.[12]

American Steel's reorganization conforms to images of restructuring as good production management such as those found in Hammer and Champy's (1993)book. The important role information technology played at American Steel to integrate work processes, provide highly detailed cost data, and closely monitor production processes conforms closely to Hammer and Champy's recommendations (p. 83–101). So too is American Steel's integration of computers into decision-making to select optimal processes that reduce production bottlenecks and quality problems. American Steel's decision to eliminate 30 percent of its products and production facilities in the restructuring not as crude cost cutting, but as part of a transformation of the managerial and production process for greater efficiency, quality, and profit.

SUNBEAM REVISITED: RESTRUCTURING AS SPECULATIVE MANAGEMENT

The production-efficiency rhetoric surrounding the restructuring of Sunbeam Corporation indicated that its restructuring would follow a formula similar to that of American Steel. Dunlap stated that "management teams," not unlike those at American Steel, would "study" the operations of Sunbeam to identify production and organizational improvements. Consultants observed Sunbeam's processes and developed an integrated restructuring plan. Sunbeam's managers expressed concern about low-cost global competitors and their focus on reducing costs to increase competitiveness, which mirrored the restructuring objectives of American Steel. The decision to close the Bay Springs and McMinnville factories, saving transportation and labor costs, appears consistent with similar decisions at American Steel.

Despite apparent similarities between the restructuring of Sunbeam and American Steel, significant differences appear. Sunbeam's restructuring was justified with efficiency rhetoric, but few, if any, organizational changes Dunlap's management team made were refinements based on a close accounting of the costs of production processes. Dunlap's justifications also used other themes that had come to dominate business discourse in the late twentieth century. These themes focused on corporate shareholders: shareholder rights, shareholder value, and the price of corporate stock. A "shareholder value" orientation did not conspicuously feature in American Steel's reorganization[13] but predominated in Sunbeam's. The restructuring of Sunbeam Corporation focused on increasing the price of Sunbeam's stock.

Dunlap was named Sunbeam's CEO in the summer of 1996, just months after he published a ghostwritten book, *Mean Business: How I Save Bad Companies and Make Good Companies Great*, about his restructuring and downsizing philosophy. In this book, and in subsequent public statements about Sunbeam, Dunlap exalted the rights of shareholders and enthusiastically advocated the managerial pursuit of maximum shareholder value (stock prices). Dunlap told reporters on the day of his appointment to Sunbeam, "If I make a lot of money here [at Sunbeam]—which I certainly intend to do—then the shareholders will make a lot. . . . I'm in lockstep with the shareholders."[14] The following quotations from *Mean Business* illustrate both the broad legitimacy of shareholder rights in business rhetoric in the late twentieth century and the special salience of shareholder values in Dunlap's (1996) restructuring philosophy:

> In corporate circles, the world's most abused minority is the shareholder. Barely tolerated, not respected. . . . That's why a company's No. 1 responsibility is not to the customer but to the shareholder. It

doesn't mean that the customer is not of the utmost importance. But when you adopt the attitude of shareholder value first, then the way you spend the corporation's money becomes a function of how you spend money on behalf of the shareholder. (P. 193)

It's the shareholder's company, not the CEO's. If the shareholders lose value, the CEO doesn't deserve to gain! Talk about mixed-up priorities. The risk of buying a share of stock is enormous. It's not like buying a U.S. Treasury certificate, which is guaranteed. When someone buys a share of stock, he or she may lose some or all of that money. That's why executives of a company must respect that investment and treat it as an awesome responsibility. (P. 194)

Shareholders own the companies in which they invest. That means the employees—executives included—work for the shareholders. Let me put it in perspective. If you own a house, do you let the gardener tell you when you should sell your house? Does your auto mechanic say, "Oh, no, you can't sell your car!" Stock ownership is the only situation where someone who doesn't own the asset usually gets away with telling the owner what to do. (P. 195)

The stock price drives me. You can fool the market for a short period of time, but you can't fool it forever. . . . Wall Street is always trying to understand if what has been announced constitutes normal earnings or good earnings. Can they be sustained? Will they grow? (P. 256)

At Scott, I endeavored to be the most shareholder-friendly CEO in America. . . . How does a CEO become shareholder-friendly? For starters, he or she must be a shareholder. (P. 196)

Dunlap's compensation for becoming CEO of Sunbeam was heavily weighted toward equity-based compensation. Although he did receive a $1 million annual salary, the bulk of his compensation was in the form of huge grants of stock. Dunlap received *1 million shares* of restricted stock on his appointment. He also received stock options to purchase an additional *2.5 million shares*. He was also allowed to purchase $3 million in stock from the corporate treasury on the day before his appointment was announced so that he could profit immediately from any increase in value from his appointment.[15] All of

Sunbeam's senior managers were granted substantial blocks of stock options and Dunlap forced many to make large open-market stock purchases. The result was that the vast majority of Sunbeam's management compensation came through stock price appreciation. Dunlap also transformed how the members of Sunbeam's board of directors were compensated, shifting from a mostly cash compensation plan to an all stock compensation plan. Each director was granted 1,500 shares per year. "I want directors who are as committed to shareholder value as I am," Dunlap said.[16] The predominance of equity compensation meant that "the executives and directors of Sunbeam are now shareholders in the company and will have an increased commitment to improving shareholder value."[17]

Like most corporate stock compensation plans, Sunbeam placed restrictions on when executives could exercise their stock options. In other words, a period of time had to elapse between the time when the stock options were granted and when an executive could actually obtain and sell the stock. This period often extended several years into the future and served as a means of discouraging short-term tactics to raise the stock price temporarily. At Sunbeam, however, each contract contained a clause that allowed executives to exercise their options immediately if a change of ownership occurred. If Sunbeam were to be acquired by or merged with another firm, Dunlap and the other Sunbeam executives could instantly cash out their stock options.[18]

This was precisely the mechanism that Dunlap employed to pocket about $100 million from the 1994 to 1995 restructuring of Scott Paper. Dunlap's restructuring activity at Scott Paper roughly tripled the stock price in 18 months, and when he sold the company to rival Kimberly-Clark, his restricted options for 750,000 shares of stock became immediately exercisable. In Dunlap's long career of turning around more than a dozen companies, the restructuring activity usually ended in the company being sold. Although business rhetoric in the late twentieth century often championed stock compensation plans because they created long-term incentives in management, the reality at Sunbeam (and many other companies) was that stock options encouraged aggressive, short-term management action to boost share prices. Dunlap and other stock-compensated managers at Sunbeam expected to restructure the firm massively, drive up its stock price, then sell the firm, cash in their stock options, and walk away wealthy.[19]

At Sunbeam, as at Scott Paper and many other companies in the late twentieth century, corporate restructuring could affect the price of company stock. Restructuring was both a practice of production management and of speculative management (actions oriented toward financial markets and security values). One business media analyst, trying to make sense of Dunlap's conspicuous cutting, sees these actions as largely aimed at increasing stock prices:

> But why would Dunlap and his team choose to accentuate the supposed severity of the downsizing, in the face of a storm of criticism from the likes of then-Secretary of Labor Robert Reich and editorialists around the country? Maybe because Chainsaw Al wants to impress his most important constituent—Wall Street—as the meanest man in the valley, the cost-slasher nonpareil. The stock market pays a lot more for predators than for pussycats.[20]

In retrospect, the restructuring plan to close 18 of Sunbeam's factories, including the plants in Bay Springs and McMinnville, cut in half the workforce, and cut nearly 90 percent of the firm's product lines was poor production management.

Byrne reports that the plant at Bay Springs was closed primarily to save shipping costs. The Bay Springs product would no longer have to be shipped the 40 miles to the final assembly plant in Waynesboro. Additionally, one would expect that the cost of leasing and maintaining the building could be saved. Support staff, plant managers, maintenance crews, and other sundry employees could all be eliminated when the factory was consolidated with Waynesboro.

But the reality was that Sunbeam actually saved very little from closing this plant. Sunbeam did not own the 59,000-square-foot Bay Springs plant; the county government owned it and leased it to Sunbeam without rent. Sunbeam not only paid no rent on the building, but also paid no taxes; the county had long ago waived them to encourage Sunbeam to stay in the community. Furthermore, the Bay Springs facility employed many skilled workers running precision machinery—the wires had to be inundated with radiation during the manufacturing process, for example. Replacing these workers in Waynesboro would be difficult and would require expensive training. The annual expected cost savings from closing the plant: $200,000. The cost of relocating the

plant: $8 million to $10 million. The move made little economic or production sense, which the mayor of Bay Springs noted:

> It doesn't take a genius to figure out it would take thirty to thirty-five
> years to get the payback to save $200,000 a year. If you can't make
> a profit in a free building with no taxes, how are you going to make a
> profit in an $8 million building in Waynesboro? (Byrne 1999, p. 121)

Closing the McMinnville plant made even less sense from the
standpoint of production management. Even the consulting-firm partner
whose team designed the restructuring plan admitted that the plant was
very well run from a production standpoint:

> It was a good business. It ran by itself. It was doing well from that
> point of view. You could leave it alone, and it would be perfect. But
> you could get much more money out of it by moving . . . much more
> income for Sunbeam if you moved the easy part down to Mexico.
> (quoted in Byrne 1999, p. 132)

The restructuring plan projected cost savings of some $28 million
of annual cost savings from the transfer of the McMinnville plant to
Mexico. These savings came entirely from reductions in labor costs. In
fact, relocating to Mexico City, to a plant that had been manufacturing
blenders and waffle irons, would actually increase most other costs of
producing clippers. Manufacturing these products required more skilled
workers and precision manufacturing than did blenders and waffle irons.
The McMinnville plant ran so efficiently that it could fill customer orders in one day (which meant that Sunbeam did not have to maintain an
inventory of clippers). The plant operated to high quality standards and
boasted a low warranty return rate. Furthermore, like at Bay Springs,
Sunbeam had worked out extremely favorable terms on the lease of the
McMinnville plant, paying just $29,000 a year for a nearly 170,000-
square-foot plant (Byrne 1999, 131).

Finding and training workers in Mexico City to produce at this
level proved difficult. Sunbeam brought 100 workers from Mexico City
to McMinnville so that workers who were being eliminated in the restructuring could train their replacements. The last job some of the
McMinnville workers completed was to crate their factory's machinery

onto trucks for transport to Mexico. One Sunbeam executive described the Mexico City plant as a poorly run, outmoded facility that lacked the productivity and quality of the McMinnville plant:

> There was trash all over the place. Few of the workers could speak English. There was no communication. It was just chaos. It was absolutely crazy. It was brutal. You had no planners, no systems. They couldn't get trucks in because there wasn't a traffic department to control it. There was no pride among the employees. When you have people making $5 a week, they don't care. (quoted in Byrne 1999, p. 137)

The production efficiency of the Mexico City plant was well below that of McMinnville. The assembly line frequently was idled because of material shortages. The facility ran out of storage space and had to rent three additional warehouses. Quality was low, as was the volume of production because the plant produced only a quarter of its projected capacity during its first months. "The lost production destroyed profits, wrecked market share, alienated customers and consumed great amounts of organizational energy" (Byrne 1999, p. 138).

From the standpoint of production management, closing these plants in this manner made little sense. Some executives at Sunbeam carried on a stealth campaign to delay or block the closing of these plants because they needed their products and because they were profitable, efficient facilities. So why were they targeted for shutdown in the first place? In Byrne's account, Dunlap designed the restructuring plan to impress Wall Street analysts. The magnitude of the restructuring plan, the amount of annual savings and the size of the job cuts, Dunlap determined before his hired team of Coopers and Lybrand consultants ever opened a laptop. He wanted to tell analysts he was cutting half the workforce, so half were cut. He wanted to tell analysts that the restructuring would result in annual savings of $225 million, so costs of this magnitude were cut. He wanted to boast of having only 100 employees in the corporate headquarters, so 208 people were fired (Byrne 1999, p. 110–17). The restructuring decisions at Sunbeam were made to maximize their impact on stock analysts, not on production efficiency.

From a production management standpoint, the restructuring of Sunbeam was a disaster. The company has not been profitable since the restructuring began. Early, glowing accounting figures that reported record income under the Dunlap regime were later found to be fabricated and were restated to reflect deep losses. The losses continued in the following years. But for a period of time between 1996 and 1998, the restructuring plan at Sunbeam was very effective speculative management. The price of Sunbeam stock increased from roughly $12 when Dunlap was appointed CEO in summer 1996 to a high of $53 in the winter of 1998. By the fall of 2000, the shares were virtually worthless, trading at less than a dime a share.[21]

The reorganizations of Sunbeam and American Steel are examples of two very different orientations to corporate restructuring: production and speculation. The two cases match most closely in the shared emphasis on production efficiency in management's rhetoric. The two cases diverge most sharply in the substance and objectives of their restructuring activities.

This study conceptualizes the orientation of restructuring to financial markets and seeks to understand how restructuring actions were geared to influence financial actors and affect stock prices. Restructuring was a practice of speculative management—managerial action oriented toward financial markets. This study seeks to supplement interpretations of restructuring that focus on production efficiency and develop an appreciation for speculative management as a characteristic and important aspect of late-twentieth-century American capitalism.

SPECULATIVE MANAGEMENT IN CORPORATE RESTRUCTURING

> *Knowing how to simplify one's description of reality without neglecting anything essential is the most important part of the economist's art.*[22]
> —James S. Duesenberry

> *It is not enough to construct an abstract model and provide an explanation of how it operates; it is just as important to demonstrate the explanatory effectiveness of such a model as applied to historical realities.*[23]
> —Celso Furtado

This study constructs and focuses a model of speculative management to interpret a *particular, historically limited* social object: the late-twentieth-century wave of U.S. corporate restructuring.[24] This model was formed and refined using an ideal type methodology that the work of Max Weber (1949, 1978) inspired.[25] Research conducted under this logic develops one-sided, logically integrated heuristic concepts to understand empirical social objects.[26] Ideal type concepts are "ideal": they are mental constructs. These concepts do not represent averages or categories of empirical social phenomena. Instead, they are selectively constructed conceptual models that are simpler, more integrated, and more self-consistent than the empirical social objects that they help define. To Weber (1949), an ideal type is an analytical accentuation of certain elements of reality:

> An ideal type is formed by the one-sided *accentuation* of one or more points of view and by the synthesis of a great many diffuse, discrete, more or less present and occasionally absent *concrete individual* phenomena, which are arranged according to those one-sidedly emphasized viewpoints into a unified *analytical* construct. In its conceptual purity, this mental construct cannot be found empirically anywhere in reality. It is a utopia. (P. 90)

This study is intended to conceptualize a particular complex reality, the late-twentieth-century wave of corporate restructuring, from one standpoint, speculative management. The model and concepts formed in this study are deliberately one-sided. The speculative management model is designed to aid in the comprehension of financial market orientations and speculative interests in this particular reorganization wave. The model developed in this study is not an exhaustive interpretation. Other selective accounts of restructuring from other standpoints reveal features that speculative management does not. Speculative management is not the whole story of restructuring. It does, however, reveal important features of late-twentieth-century restructuring that are difficult to appreciate from production-centered standpoints.

This research attempts to unify several decisive aspects of a wave of corporate restructuring and the late-twentieth-century U.S. capitalist context in which it occurred with an underlying logic or imagery (Weller 2000) of speculative management. This study aims to develop a complex conceptualization of corporate restructuring that unites tendencies in several elements of late-twentieth-century firms and their capitalist context. These tendencies and elements include: corporate governance and control, secondary financial markets, equity securities valued as capitalized earnings, financial accountancy, and the business media.

Complex, multidimensional ideal types, including the speculative management model of restructuring developed here, are still one-sided in the sense that they are constructed to reveal features of social reality from a particular point of inquiry. The elements unified into complex types do not deplete the essential features of a particular social object because other features would come into view from other points of view. Some features of late-twentieth-century corporate restructuring, such as product-market and production-efficiency orientations, are better brought into view with other, more production-centered models. Speculative management is not intended as a comprehensive replacement or substitution for other models, but it is intended to augment understanding of restructuring by providing an optic that allows the role of financial and speculative interests to be viewed clearly.

A provisional description of speculative management in corporate restructuring is expressed here:

> Late-twentieth-century restructuring of American corporations was to a significant extent undertaken by managers to realize pecuniary gains. Restructuring was calculated to influence the market valuation of corporate stock in mass, secondary stock markets. Restructuring was, therefore, a practice of speculative management. Corporations were connected to these markets by social intermediaries that enabled, structured and constrained the manipulation of market value in restructuring.

In addition, this study constructs, refines, and employs several concepts to interpret aspects of corporate restructuring and late-twentieth-century financial markets. The most important of these are:

Speculative management (contrasts with *production management*): Corporate actions oriented toward secondary stock markets with the intention of influencing the trading price of corporate equity shares (stock). Many corporations express speculative management in terms of maximizing shareholder value. The concept also contrasts with investor capitalism, as an image of the primary orientation of late-twentieth-century U.S. capitalism.

Internal reorganization (contrasts with *transactional reorganization*): intraorganizational restructuring as a business event.

May include downsizing, reengineering, or streamlining. Synonymous with *corporate restructuring* in the early 1990s. When initiated to generate reorganizer's profit, a type of pecuniary reorganization based on accounting accruals rather than an external transaction.[27]

Transactional reorganization (contrasts with *internal reorganization*): extraorganizational restructuring from a business reorganization deal. May include takeovers, acquisitions, divestitures, mergers, and more complicated transactions such as equity carve-outs. Synonymous with *corporate restructuring* in the 1980s. When initiated to generate promoter's or reorganizer's profit, a type of pecuniary reorganization.

Pecuniary reorganization: A disruptive event that triggers a reevaluation of corporate securities and thereby generates reorganizer's profit. There are two types: transactional reorganization (mergers and spin-offs) and internal reorganization (corporate restructuring).

Reorganizer's profit (compares to *promoter's profit*): Increase in the trading price of a firm's securities due to a pecuniary reorganization. Represents an increase in the market value, or shareholder value, of the firm (fictitious capitalization). Comparison term is promoter's profit (Hilferding 1910, Veblen 1904), which represents the increase in value of a privately held firm on listing on a public securities market. Whereas a promoter's profit emerges from initial public offerings (IPOs) on primary markets, a reorganizer's profit arises from pecuniary reorganization and is captured on secondary markets. Reorganizer's profit accrues almost entirely to owners of record before the reorganization is announced.[28]

Conceptions of aggressively good management: Prevailing views among financial market participants, corporate executives, and the business media of the managerial practices that are most likely to maximize shareholder value (trading price of corporate stock). Management consultants specialize in the marketing of innovative conceptions of aggressively good management.

Social intermediaries (compares with *financial intermediary*): Social institutions that connect corporations to secondary stock markets. This study focuses on three structures: corporate governance structures, financial accounting, and the business media (including print, broadcast, and electronic media). Comparison is to financial intermediaries that link firms to primary financial markets.

Not only the overall model, but also the focused concepts developed in this study are ideal types rather than empirical categories.[29] Transactional reorganization (for example, mergers and divestitures) and internal reorganization (for example, reengineering and downsizing) are two selective, one-sided logics for restructuring. Speculative management (practices aimed directly at manipulating stock values on financial markets) and production management (practices aimed directly at operations and performance on product markets) are both selective, one-sided renderings of executive orientation. Concrete instances of corporate restructuring exhibit a blend of orientations and practices and different forms of restructuring were taking place at different firms at the same time.

An assumption of this study is that restructuring activity in the late twentieth century was sufficiently oriented to financial markets to warrant a speculative management interpretation. Evidence is presented to demonstrate that a speculative management interpretation of restructuring is plausible and that such an interpretation effectively explains the inflection points of the rise, reign, and decline of the late-twentieth-century restructuring wave. Some sectors (aerospace, computer chips, steel) appear to have been less oriented to financial markets and reorganized to a production logic rather than a speculative logic. The management-information-system–based internal reorganization of American Steel is close to the type of restructuring as production management.[30] Byrne's (1999) account of Sunbeam's restructuring conforms closely to the type of restructuring as speculative management.

THE SCOPE OF EMPIRICAL INVESTIGATION

This study began in 1994 with an empirical investigation into corporate restructuring that examined how managers communicated these activities to shareholders and the financial community in news releases and shareholder reports. The information herein is based on a deeper and more systematic investigation that inspected a sample 100 of the largest industrial U.S. firms and an array of 67 other very large firms in financial services, diversified services, transportation, utilities, and retail. The aim was to track the wave of restructuring as it passed through corporate America from 1984 to 1997.

Empirical materials were gathered and analyzed that allowed for the refinement of the speculative management model of corporate restructuring. Materials were sought to address several related research questions: Why did the stock market reward firms that announced large losses due to restructuring activities with an increase in market value of the firm's shares? How were firms communicating restructuring activities to shareholders and the financial public? What information was available to the investing public to enable them to view restructuring activities? What connecting structures make it possible for corporations and financial markets to assess and influence each other mutually?

Primary materials that illuminated management presentations of restructuring plans to shareholders of the firm and to the financial public were especially important to this research. These materials included corporate annual reports and Securities and Exchange Commission (SEC) filings, financial and business media archives, corporate news releases, trade publications, and numerous other sources. Because restructuring initiatives frequently generated significant costs for firms, financial statements of firms and regulatory filings revealed how these costs were recognized.

Rules and procedures of financial accounting constrain management presentations of financial information, so pronouncements of accounting standards-setting boards and business discourse about them were examined in accounting trade publications, professional training materials, and the financial media. The public documents of accounting rule-making bodies, particularly meeting minutes of the Emerging Issues Task Force (EITF) of the Financial Accounting Standards Board (FASB) and public response forums, available via the Internet, were especially useful. The investigation of financial patterns of restructuring and financial accounting relies heavily on my professional training and experience as an auditor.

Additional materials revealed how financial publics processed the restructuring activities of firms.[31] Financial media archives were greatly used for this purpose. Publications and statements by investor

organizations and major financiers were also used. Electronic information media, such as Lexis-Nexis and Dow Jones Interactive facilitated
the search for specific information. Additionally, the Internet sites of
large corporations became a useful source of information because they
are often geared toward investor relations. Many sites contain the annual report to shareholders, news release archives, SEC filing archives,
and so on, which made obsolete, for some purposes at least, the maintenance of a physical archive of annual reports.

Other critical information formerly available only in archives became instantaneously available via the Internet in the 1990s. The SEC
and FASB each maintain information-rich Web sites that facilitated this
research. Internet investing Web sites, such as BigCharts.com, allowed
for the generation of graphs of stock performance, summaries of analyst
earnings projections, and other financial information.

The ideal type method employed in this study calls for the empirical refinement of concepts and models through interpretive contact with
a wide range of materials. The construction and refinement of ideal type
concepts, in Weber's work especially, requires the confrontation of comparative and historical materials: Kahlberg (1994) describes Weber's
concepts as "historically saturated." The ideal types in this study have
been formed and refined in conjunction with a selective inquiry into the
structure and dynamics of U.S. markets for corporate securities and the
relationship of these markets to the industrial factories and plants that
underlie the securities traded on them. Sociologists have not thoroughly
researched this area of American life (the secondary security markets).
American corporate finance was compared with the financial systems
of continental Europe to form an image of its unique features. American
finance was also studied historically (genetically) to conceptualize how
it came to be so structured.

Comparative study pointed to the dominating secondary stock
market as a characteristic feature of U.S. finance. Financial markets in
Europe, until quite recently, have lacked a strong, active secondary stock
market and are much closer to the image of markets portrayed in the
socioeconomic literature. Historical and comparative study helped to establish limits to the concepts employed in this study and aided in their
refinement.

Methodical study provided only a part of the source material
drawn on for this study. The speculative management model of corporate restructuring was formed and tested against a much wider set of

empirical materials than are cited herein. I majored in business administration as an undergraduate, worked for a time as an auditor for a Big Six accounting firm, and later as a research director for a business consulting firm. While a graduate student in sociology, I continued to read widely on business matters, completed coursework in economics, and taught in an organizational behavior department. I have been a daily reader of financial and business news for more than a decade and have maintained a clipping file on restructuring and financial speculation. As much as possible, I immersed myself in relevant materials that were examined from many angles, giving me the opportunity to come across inconvenient facts that forced me to refine my thought.

Consistent with the concept-forming purpose of this study, the empirical materials presented in this report were selected to illustrate vividly and communicate the interpretation of speculative management in restructuring, not to prove the argument.

OVERVIEW

The study investigates and interprets financially oriented corporate restructuring in the late twentieth century, developing and supporting the position that downsizing restructuring (internal reorganization) of the kind characteristic of the 1980s and 1990s receded from the corporate landscape by the end of the 1990s. This was especially true of leading firms and of industrial (as opposed to financial or medical) firms. During the 1990s bull market, the financial news buzzed with stories of corporate reorganization, but these stories described mergers, acquisitions, and other transactional restructuring more often than "downsizing" packaged as a corporate event. The exceptions, including Coca-Cola's announcement of the elimination of 20 percent of its workforce in early 2000, were greeted more with indifference or aversion than cheers. Rather than boosting stock market valuation, Coke's year 2000 downsizing caused a drop in its stock price.[32]

Chapters 2 through 8 present the interpretation of corporate restructuring as speculative management. Chapter 2 provides some historical financial context for the emergence of internal reorganization as a management practice in the 1980s. Chapter 3 presents findings from an extensive investigation of more than 2,000 annual reports to shareholders and SEC filings for 167 very large U.S. firms. Corporate restructuring (internal reorganization) emerged as a management practice intimately tied to corporate takeovers in the very early 1980s and spread slowly among the firms in the study throughout the rest of the decade. Corporate restructuring sharply increased in both frequency and magnitude during the early 1990s as corporations became unable to pursue external reorganization and focused their speculative management activity internally instead. Corporate restructuring activity fell sharply in 1994 when accounting regulators constrained the use of internal reorganization as a mechanism to manipulate corporate financial statements. Corporate restructuring declined further in the late 1990s as financial markets ceased to view internal reorganization as a good management practice.

In each of the three phases of the "wave" of restructuring (the rise, reign, and decline), institutions that connect firms to secondary equity markets (stock markets), conceptualized herein as *social intermediaries*, were found to be important for channeling speculative management interests into and out of corporate restructuring. The three social intermediaries discussed here: corporate governance structures, financial accounting and the business media (including print, broadcast, and electronic media) contributed to the emergence of internal reorganization as a discrete management strategy, helped support restructuring as a good management practice during its reign and contributed to the decline in restructuring. Chapter 4 conceptualizes financial accounting and the business media as social intermediaries. Chapter 5 considers issues of corporate control and theories of markets from a standpoint sensitive to social intermediaries and speculative management. Chapters 6 through 8 analyze the rise, reign, and decline of restructuring using detailed illustrative material selected from annual reports, shareholder communications, and business media articles. The speculative management view of corporate change is summarized and concluded in Chapter 9 with a brief comparison of the speculative management perspective to others currently employed in the study of corporate restructuring.

Late-twentieth-century corporate managers and business reorganizers represented restructuring to business constituencies as production management, an effort to increase the efficiency of industrial corporations. This study develops a view of corporate restructuring as speculative management engaged in to increase the trading price of corporate securities. Although other studies have brought into view how restructuring was used to increase corporate profits from increased industrial efficiency, this study highlights how restructuring was used to capture profits from increased stock values.

This book explains the historically limited episode of corporate change that swept through U.S. corporations in the late twentieth century and moves toward a broad interpretation of the structure and dynamic of the U.S. market for financial securities that enables financiers to capture gains through pecuniary reorganizations of their business.

Chapter 2

TRANSACTIONAL FINANCE IN
LATE-TWENTIETH-CENTURY AMERICA

*If I were to describe the new rules of the '90's it would really proba-
bly start and finish with the power of the financial markets to really
control the destiny, the strategy of the corporation.*
> —Stephen Roach, economic analyst for Morgan Stanley, early guru of
> the voluntary restructuring movement, who turned negative on
> restructuring in 1996.[1]

*Well, Wall Street loves anything that gets a stock price up. So, if firing
people gets a stock price up, it's good. Hiring people gets the stock
price up, that's good. They don't care.*
> —A stock trader, Sloan, on management action oriented toward financial
> markets.[2]

*Sometimes the market is like running with the bulls in Pamplona. That
means you just get in there for a minute, and then you get out of the
way fast before you get gored.*
> —A stock trader, Longman, on market timing.[3]

*The biggest investment bankers get hired "to complete a deal, irre-
spective of whether the deal actually adds value or destroys value for
the acquirer."*
> —Raghavendra Rau, Purdue University finance professor, on why the clients
> of large banks do not fare well after a merger is consummated.[4]

This chapter places corporate restructuring in the context of changes in
late-twentieth-century U.S. financial markets (Harrison and Bluestone
1988, Harvey 1989, Jameson 1998, Jensen 1989). During the late twentieth century, finance moved from the periphery of managerial capitalism to the center of what some call investor capitalism (Useem 1996),
and others view in terms of changing conceptions of firm control (Fligstein 1990, 2001). In this chapter, suggestive materials that highlight
features of three trends in late-twentieth-century finance are reviewed.
The first set of materials focuses on *financial deregulation*, broadly

conceived, that ended the stable form of corporate finance characteristic of the mid-twentieth century and created the active money market that underlie corporate finance in the late twentieth century.

The second set of materials highlights the structure and process of transactional finance, brought about by the transformation of the source of financial institution revenue away from stable relationships to disruptive transactions. Transactional finance was characterized by an active "market for corporate control" (Jensen 1989). Beginning in the late 1970s and escalating into the 1980s, hostile takeovers, management buyouts, and other deals proliferated. Transactional reorganization created an infrastructure of deal-makers, brokers, and speculators with extensive experience in the extraction of profit from business reorganization.

The third set of materials features another aspect of transactional finance in the 1980s: the injection of *shareholder interests* into the management of corporations. Maximizing stock prices, the practical meaning of shareholder value, became the primary goal of corporate control teams in the final decades of the twentieth century.

In this study, transactional finance remains a rough-hewn, rather than a finely polished, ideal type concept. This chapter will sensitize the reader to the U.S. financial environment of the late twentieth century. This chapter works toward an orienting conception of transactional finance that was a crucial environment for corporate restructuring.

TRANSACTIONAL FINANCE AND FINANCIAL DEREGULATION

Many informed commentaries on late-twentieth-century industrial restructuring recognize that financial deregulation was a contributing factor to the decline of mid-twentieth-century American capitalism (Baskin and Miranti 1997, Bluestone and Harrison 1982, Harvey 1989).[5] Most often associated with banking and interest-rate reforms of the late Carter administration (continued and intensified with abandon during the early Reagan administration), financial deregulation embraced broader changes that transformed corporate finance.

Economic historian, Robert Sobel (1987), summarizes the rapid changes in the financial environment of corporations:

> Six of the more important alterations, roughly in order of their appearance, have been: (1) the breakdown of old relationships and the fading

of the "Old Guard", (2) the maturing of institutional investing and the appearance of block trading, (3) the emergence of what for the American context was hyperinflation in 1973–1974 and again in 1979–1980, and its decline afterwards, (4) the rise of options creation and trading in its many manifestations, (5) the appearance of negotiated commissions, and finally, (6) the internationalization of markets and the steady crumbling of remaining political barriers to investment. (P. 22)

The last of these changes, the globalization of financial markets, profoundly altered the financial environment of U.S. corporations. The emergence of the Eurodollar or international money market in the early 1960s created opportunities for firms to raise capital on a global scale, significantly loosening the constraint national money supplies impose. The Eurodollar market, and the Eurobond market (which deals in bonds denominated in Eurodollars), is described as:

> . . . a pool of stateless money. . . . The first Eurodollars had come into being after World War II, when the Soviet Union, wary of reprisals by American authorities [American government was seizing Russian assets] deposited its dollars at the Banque Commerciale pour l'Europe du Nord in Paris and in London's Moscow Narodny Bank. In time, Euro came to signify any currency held outside its country of origin. . . . By the mid-1980s, this free-floating unregulated market . . . would swell to $2.5 trillion in deposits. (Brooks 1984, p. 115)

Large commercial banks were among the first to take advantage of global money markets, actively purchasing money rather than passively waiting for deposits. Eventually industrial corporations began floating securities directly on them as well. During the mid- to late twentieth century, the "market for money" developed in other forums as well. Chernow (1990) describes the origin of *certificates of deposit* (CDs) and their consequences:

> In 1961, George Moore and Walter Wriston of First National City figured out how to circumvent the regulatory cap on interest rates. By law, banks couldn't pay interest on deposits held under thirty days. But by selling "negotiable certificates of deposits" that matured in more than thirty days, banks could pay interest. These CDs could also be traded. . . . Their use sparked a revolution in the way commercial

banks operated, freeing them from reliance on deposits. Bankers no longer had to wait for deposits and were liberated from both companies and consumers. Now they could roam the world and raise money by selling CDs in overseas wholesale markets. The new system was known as managed liabilities. (P. 538)

Also significant during this time was the development of the Federal Funds market, through which banks lend each other excess reserves short term. The combined impact of the Eurodollar market, negotiable CDs, and the Fed funds market permanently altered the business of banking from a "deposit to a money-purchase business":

> The business acquired a new speculative cast as banks built up huge, diversified investment portfolios. . . . The old fashioned banker lunched with corporate treasurers to make sure they kept deposits at the bank. But traders were a lean, hyperthyroid breed who spent days on the telephone, riveted to the changing prices. (Chernow 1990, p. 539)

The emergence of the Eurodollar market created a fluid, global capital market that was not just unregulated, but was largely incapable of regulation. This undermined existing state regulation of finance, especially New Deal–era financial reforms, and threatened state capability to introduce new regulations to maintain stable financial systems.

The emergence of international money markets had profound effects on banking and finance by creating opportunities for investors to obtain higher returns than those available from savings deposits, which made obtaining deposits difficult for banks. Investment bankers were forced to find alternative sources of capital. The money market served this purpose, enabling investment banks literally to purchase capital when needed. International money markets also provided a new mechanism to capture profits. By trading in money, purchasing it wholesale, and lending it out again retail, the money market helped augment bank profits. The Eurodollar or Eurobond market, the international stateless unregulated money market, opened up the potential for vast trading operations.

The high returns available in money markets led corporate finance officers to withdraw noninterest-bearing retainer deposits characteristic of *relationship banking*. During the mid-twentieth century U.S. finance was structured around enduring relationships between investment banks and their corporate clients. Corporations did not shop for banking services on an ad hoc basis, but relied on the banker with whom they had cultivated a relationship. Compensating balances cemented the relationship between investment bank and corporate client, serving as a sort of retainer of the banks services:

> Wall Street banks financed their operations—especially a practice called compensating balances. In exchange for a loan, companies would leave up to 20 percent of the money behind in interest free deposits. By paying such tribute, the borrowers preserved the banking relationship and received free services, such as the right to consult the bank economist or have a merger arranged. Compensating balances also guaranteed credit during times of scarcity, an assurance that reflected historic corporate anxiety about maintaining a constant flow of capital. This setup bound Wall Street banks to their customers in an intimate relationship and gave banks free cash to lend at high spreads. It was a wonderful racket. In these fading days of relationship banking (1950s), profits seemed almost guaranteed, producing a pleasant but stolid generation of bankers. (Chernow 1990, p. 494–95)

Banks were willing to maintain these large noninterest-earning balances in investment bankers' control in part because both inflation and interest rates were low. When interest rates began to rise, clients withdrew their money, and with it, a major source of income for banks. Financiers lost another source of funds as a result of late-twentieth-century rule changes. The elimination of brokerage commissions—the traditional businesses of underwriting securities—meant that underwriting became less profitable for financial institutions. At the same time, speculative profits from bank "trading" departments grew. The financial services side of investment banking decreased in importance at the same time that the speculative side increased. This represents a shift from banks as important financial intermediaries in primary security markets to becoming speculative operators on secondary security markets.

Until the early 1970s, the business of investment bankers was primarily directed toward underwriting new securities issues. Erwin Miller, professor at the Wharton School of Finance and Commerce, University of Pennsylvania, describes the function of investment banking in 1967:

In its strict sense, investment banking is that business which has as its function the flotation of new securities, both debt and equity, to the general public (including institutions) for the purpose of acquiring funds for clients that are private firms or public bodies. . . . In essence [investment banking is] intermediation in the public new issues market for all types of issues. (quoted in Brooks 1984, p. 34)

During the mid-twentieth century, the full round of investment bank activities were oriented toward primary securities markets and the flotation of new issues rather than trading in existing issues. In the late twentieth century, the primary security market ceased to be the focus of investment banks as the secondary market rose in importance.

Financial deregulation aided in the transformation of stable, mid-twentieth-century corporate finance into an active market for capital. Approximating the classical ideal of a free market, stateless globalized money markets altered the process and structure of corporate finance.

TRANSACTIONAL FINANCE AND THE MARKET FOR CORPORATE CONTROL

The changes in financial institutions previously discussed deeply affected late-twentieth-century corporate finance, but changes in domestic financial policy also contributed to the shift to transactional finance. The deregulation of U.S. finance begun in the 1970s accelerated in the 1980s. Politically effective mobilization of business interests substantially weakened some of the most powerful regulations that had shaped U.S. capitalism during the Fordist era (Akard 1992). The transparency of the changed political climate was apparent:

This meant that the Glass-Steagall [Banking] Act [of 1933] would become a dead letter—the regulatory wall between investment and commercial banking that had been created in 1933 would be ignored. So would the antitrust laws. The SEC would have its budget slashed annually. The Boeskys, Icahns, and Milkens of the world were given to know that, as far as Washington was concerned, almost anything was acceptable. The carefully regulated zoo of the 1950s was to be reconstituted as a jungle. (Sobel 1993, p. 83)

In 1982 under Rule 415, firms no longer had to wait 20 days after filing a security offering before floating it, but instead were able to get preauthorization for a large block of securities and then take these off the shelf at any moment. Investment bankers bid against each other to get this business (Brooks 1984). The major change from this rule is that it took much of the profit out of underwriting (and decreased due diligence) by making underwriting far more competitive. In this scenario, an investment banker "bought the deal"; that is, the banker assumed the entire risk for any interest rates or market fluctuations from the time the deal was closed until the securities were placed. This transformed underwriting into essentially a transaction game—a trading game. Huge losses and huge gains were possible due to the bought deal. This helped spur the shift from traditional investment and commercial banking toward "trading," constituting a switch from relationship banking to transaction banking.[6]

During the late 1960s, merger and acquisition departments formed at most leading investment banks. This further spurred the development of transactional finance because these departments earned revenue from the completion of transactions. Merger and acquisition departments often worked under contingent contracts: fees for financial services could be collected only when a deal was completed. Additionally, investment banks began to participate in *risk arbitrage*—purchasing securities that are potential merger targets to profit from appreciation when merger is announced. By the 1980s many of the largest investment banks had begun risk arbitrage operations on a grand scale. Robert Rubin, later Secretary of Treasury under President Clinton, headed risk arbitrage at Goldman Sachs during the 1980s.

Louis Lowenstein (1991) comments on the increased trading in late-twentieth-century U.S. security markets:

> They're buying and selling at a much more rapid rate than they did a few years ago. Since 1960 the rate of turnover, not just absolute number of shares but the rate of turnover on listed shares, has gone up 5005 percent. Whatever Keynes was concerned about [in the 1930s] was a shadow of the pace of turnover today. (P. 130)

The rise of trading departments at large investment banks corresponded to the rising power of deal-makers committed to generating transactions for fees at large financial institutions. The first real trader at Morgan Stanley was Ralph Leach who came to Morgan Stanley after its merger with Guaranty Trust in 1958. Leach was a pioneer in trading for profits, first with the Fed funds market, later with Treasury securities and municipal debts (investment banks had been prohibited from purchasing industrial securities after the Glass-Steagall Banking Act of 1933). Leach began taking large speculative positions in Treasury securities that would commit a large portion of the entire firm's assets. In the early 1960s the emerging "transactional" bankers were beginning to make their presence felt in the old culture of investment banking (whose profits from traditional businesses were beginning to unravel anyway):

> Soon the tenth floor of Morgan's building at 15 Broad Street had scores of frenetic young traders taking positions in T-bills, negotiable CDs, foreign exchange, and Fed funds. Before long, Leach oversaw $1 billion of market transactions daily. The rise of bought money, negotiable CDs, and daring trading would have an enduring effect on banking. Bankers formerly had been preoccupied with the "asset" side of the business—that is, making loans. Now the liability side— the money on which loans were based—took on equal importance. . . . This new environment . . . elevated the trader to unaccustomed eminence. (Chernow 1990, pp. 540–41)

The formerly déclassé activity of trading suddenly emerged as the most profitable side of investment banking. Increasingly, traders and deal-makers would assume power over the largest investment firms in the United States. Throughout the 1950s and into the 1960s, the relationships between bankers and their corporate clients began to unravel and with it, the stable system of finance that characterized America at midcentury. In its place grew a system of finance that generated income through trades and transactions, in essence, a transactional financial system that required instability to generate profit.

Deregulation also provided opportunities for business reorganizers to realize speculative gains from the manipulation of assets in the business portfolio of large diversified firms. In actions that closely mirrored the financial deals of the 1960s, the 1980s reversed conglomerate growth. Speculative gains—in the form of reorganizer's profits— were captured when conglomerates were stitched together during the 1960s, and they were generated again when conglomerates were unbundled during the 1980s. By the end of the 1980s, an active market for corporate control (Jensen 1989)—in this book perhaps reconceptualized as a market for reorganizer's profits—replaced investment-oriented corporate shareholding. Rather than passive long-term owners, active speculative traders of corporate ownership dominated financial markets. Arbitrageurs, white knights, and corporate raiders realized gains through shrewd trading of corporate ownership rather than through long-term holding of corporate assets. Corporate raiders realized their gains by buying shares of a company, reorganizing it (often by dismantling its operations), and reselling the assets at a profit. The search for capital gains and the trading mentality that accompanied this search grew to be a widespread justification for financial market participation during this period. Apologists for takeovers claimed that these financial transactions forced improvements in the efficiency of America's industrial production. Certainly, the reported profits of many reorganized firms increased in the period after restructuring, but whether this is clear evidence of improved efficiency or rather evidence of speculative management is a matter of some dispute.

The macroeconomic conditions of the 1970s and early 1980s created a unique opportunity for the growth of takeovers.[7] High interest rates lowered the "discounted present value" of future earnings, depressing stock prices. High inflation boosted the value of underlying assets. This meant that the market capitalization of many corporations (the total value of all outstanding equity securities of the firm) was less than the book value of the firm (the recorded historical cost of assets less liabilities that served as a rough proxy for the asset value of the firm). It also meant that the market capitalization was much less than the current economic net worth of the firm:

> In 1966, the book value of corporate assets for the Standard & Poor's 500 was around half the price of their shares, and it actually fell somewhat by the end of the decade. As stock prices declined and the value of underlying assets rose, the direction was reversed. At the beginning of the 1980s, the S&P book value was 90 percent of market value. In July 1984, S&P estimated that nearly 30 percent of all industrial stocks listed on the NYSE [New York Stock Exchange] were selling below tangible book value. In a few cases, someone might have purchased all of a company's shares and, assuming this was done at market value, own a company whose treasury had more cash than was expended on the takeover. (Sobel 1993, p. 122)

The rise of transactional finance corresponded with increased external, transactional reorganization in the late 1970s and 1980s. The volume of takeovers generated enormous fees for investment bankers but the bulk of the gains from takeovers went to those who owned shares immediately before takeovers were announced:

> During the 1980s, more than a third of the *Fortune* 500 were acquired, merged or taken private. . . . Bankers and their allies took in some $60 billion in fees, but stockholders did even better. According to Harvard Business School professor Michael Jensen, between 1976 and 1990, stockholders' gains due to takeovers and restructurings came to more than $650 billion. (Sobel 1993, p. 121)

Trading departments (risk arbitrage) at investment banks focused on the capture of a significant portion of these increased values.

> As takeovers grew in popularity, they attracted individuals who hoped to profit by taking positions in the stock that was about to be put into play. The possession of information available to those concocting the deal was a valuable commodity, a fact obvious to all involved. "Risk arbitrageurs" would take positions in likely takeover candidates, knowing they would profit should there be a contest for control. (Sobel 1993, p. 109)

The great bull market of the 1980s was sensitive to takeover news and rumors. The big movers on the New York Stock Exchange (NYSE) during many trading days were shares of firms involved in potential takeovers.

To facilitate the ready buying, selling, combining, and managing of business units, many corporations legally restructured their divisions into subsidiary corporations, leading to a neo-holding company structure, the MLSF, which enabled takeovers and acquisitions by reducing the capital necessary for acquisitions because subsidiaries required majority, not complete, ownership. By acquiring subsidiaries with subsidiaries, corporate parents leveraged their existing finance capital and used their subsidiaries to raise additional funds in financial markets (Prechel 1997, 2000; Prechel and Boies 1998).

Transactional reorganization greatly boosted the returns of transactional financiers. The rise of transactional reorganization, including leveraged buyouts, mergers, and acquisitions corresponded to the unraveling of relationship banking under regulated finance. The former system encouraged economic stability and steady accumulation, the new system requires disruption and reorganization to capture profit. Transactional finance represented an unraveling of stability and an insertion of risk and volatility into the financial system. Temporally, the collapse of managerial finance occurred before the collapse of Fordist production.

SPECULATIVE INSTRUMENTS OF TRANSACTIONAL FINANCE: JUNK BONDS AND CORPORATE STOCK

The currency that funded the external reorganizations of the 1980s was the junk bond:

> Corporate bonds are rated by rating agencies, such as Standard and Poor's and Moody's. Those companies with the strongest balance sheets and credit history, the elite of corporate America, are rated triple A. When they issue bonds in order to raise debt capital, the interest those bonds pay is not much higher than that of risk-free U.S. treasury bonds. These are known as "investment grade" companies . . . [a bond] downgraded because of a perceived deterioration in the company's condition trades at a discount from its face, or par, value. Below investment grade bonds are rated [Ba1] or lower by Moody's, BB+ or lower by Standard and Poor's, or are unrated. (Bruck 1988, p. 27)

Michael Milken virtually created the junk bond market, composed of below-investment-grade bonds that sold at a deep discount to triple A bonds, sometimes as low as ten cents on the dollar. In a section in his book on Milken, "The Academic Foundations of Milkenism," Sobel describes Milken's discovery in 1967 of a relatively unknown 1958 book by a finance professor named W. Braddock Hickman, *Corporate Bond Quality and Investor Experience*. Hickman's central research finding, as it relates to Milken, was that a portfolio of low-rated bonds would outperform a portfolio of high-rated bonds: the increased return far outweighed the added risk of default and bankruptcy. "Issues in the high-quality classes had the lowest default rates, promised yields, and loss rates; but the returns obtained by those who held them over long periods were generally below those on low-grade issues" (cited in Sobel 1993, p. 65). In addition, Hickman found that financial markets tended to deeply discount low-rated bonds when the issuing company appeared to be close to default. At such moments these bonds are real bargains. Milken also relied on a 1947 study by another professor, O. K. Burrell, who found that the spread (difference in price and effective yield) between high- and low-rated bonds increased during times of business pessimism and decreased during times of business optimism. Thus, in a market downturn, the value of low-rated bonds plummets far more than high-rated bonds and conversely, in times of improving economic conditions, low-rated bonds will increase in value far more than high-rated bonds. Burrell found that bonds rated BAA appreciated 75.8 percent in value between June 1932 and December 1934 (a period of improved economic outlook), whereas bonds rated AAA only appreciated 19.9 percent (Sobel 1993, pp. 65–69).

From the perspective pursued in this study, the significance of Milken's junk bond empire lies not in the undisputed fact that junk bonds helped fund takeovers and hence were essential for spurring the restructuring episode. What is essential is that low-rated securities have much greater price variability on secondary security markets than high-rated bonds.[8] High-rated bonds essentially track government bonds, and their value is influenced primarily by overall macroeconomic conditions. But the value of low-rated bonds is primarily influenced by microeconomic factors: the creditworthiness and likelihood of default of the issuing company. Low-rated bonds then are better vehicles for speculation because of their greater volatility: purchase a low-rated bond when the company's prospects appear poor and then watch the value of the bond soar as its prospects improve. The volatility in low-rated bonds is similar to that in equity securities and, by facile timing of purchases, low-rated bonds could yield very high returns. Sobel (1993) cites a study by a New York investment advisory firm that indicated that low-rated bonds offered returns of around 30 percent per year in times of economic downturn when appreciation and interest payments are factored in:

> Owners of junk had to know more about the company than did those who held investment grade bonds . . . [whose value fluctuates] on news of interest and money rates, approaching maturities, and

changes in ratings. . . . Owners of AAA rated bonds don't have to pay much attention to earnings and dividends, except for unusually sharp degeneration in the former. Holders of junk bonds have to be concerned about such matters. If earnings increase sharply, the bond will bear less risk, and so its price might rise substantially. Poor earnings might not be reflected in major price declines, however, since the high yield already reflects the greater danger inherent in such paper. (P. 77)

So from a speculative standpoint, low-rated bonds are attractive vehicles first, because they already pay substantially higher rates of interest than high-rated bonds and, second, because there is the potential for dramatic price appreciation (or depreciation) with changes in the fortune of the firm and overall business conditions. A third reason why low-rated bonds make attractive speculative vehicles is that if the underlying corporation actually does go into bankruptcy, bondholders have "priority" over stockholders in any resulting reorganization. In bankruptcy reorganizations, stockholders of the bankrupt corporations frequently lose their investment whereas bondholders are often granted, if nothing else, the equity of the newly reorganized enterprise. In bankruptcy reorganization, "common stockholders probably would lose all, and the same might be true for the owners of preferred stocks. But bondholders could come out of the restructuring with new equity, which given the prices of the bonds, often would be worth substantially more than the investment" (Sobel 1993, p. 68). Hence, purchasers of the bonds of a company approaching bankruptcy are in essence purchasing an equity stake in the reorganized enterprise.

Milken even used his bond holdings and encouraged other bondholders to think of themselves as controllers of the enterprise rather than equity holders: "Milken also told investors that effective control of a company belonged to those who owned debt, and not to the stockholders." Milken once told a major stockholder in Rapid-American that Drexel's bondholders controlled the company. "How can that be when I own 40 percent of the stock?" asked Riklis. Milken replied, "We own $100 million of your bonds, and if you miss one payment, we'll take your company away" (Sobel 1993, p. 77).

So although most of the journalistic and academic interest in Milken has been in his ability to finance takeovers and leveraged buyouts, the bulk of his business was selling bonds to investors, especially institutional investors. Being able to articulate to them the high returns and relatively low risk that below-investment-grade bonds offered was essential. Milken toured in the early years of his Drexel operation, trying to raise the status of low-rated bonds (Sobel 1993, p. 77).

The interests of bondholders and stockholders diverged in takeovers and in the wake of takeovers. Bondholders' interest in creditworthiness directly conflicted with shareholders' interests in maximum profits:

> . . . if a firm had low debts and was paying a lot of corporate tax its managers were actually being incompetent: while proudly keeping their credit ratings high, they were handing their shareholder's [sic] money to the taxman. To do their shareholders a favor, they ought to borrow more. The value they were handing unnecessarily to the taxman offered a fine incentive to bidders to come along and do this for them. (Cited in Sobel 1993, p. 69)

In the wake of a takeover, stockholders might see the value of their shares increase greatly (especially shareholders of acquired firms), and they also benefited from special dividend distributions that were common during this period. But, longstanding bondholders saw the value of their bonds fall as firms leveraged themselves either to avoid takeover or respond to a takeover. The creditworthiness of firms eroded during this period, enriching shareholders but lowering the value of bonds.

One factor driving the 1980s takeovers was tax advantages to corporate raiders who engaged in highly leveraged purchases of firms. Two mechanisms were at work here. First, after purchasing a firm, the raiders are given the opportunity to write up corporate assets to fair market value (for tax purposes only, not for financial reporting purposes). This had the effect of radically increasing depreciation deductions on corporate tax returns, thus lowering taxes significantly. Second, the high debt load generated high interest payments that, unlike dividend payments to shareholders, are fully tax deductible. Hence, tax advantages to raiders were sufficient motivation for takeovers.

The 1980s corporate takeovers are profitably viewed as a transformation of earlier forms of corporate reorganization. Corporate raiders in the 1980s operated using similar tactics as conglomerateurs in the 1960s. Similarly, the 1960s conglomerateurs were using techniques to manage stock market values that had been developed in the 1920s bull market. New financial technologies, new views of "aggressively good management," and new "financial regimes of speculation" developed thereby enabling the financial sector of the economy to boom with consequences sometimes extraordinarily far-reaching for U.S. industrial production.

Many of the 1980s raiders had been 1960s conglomerateurs. Warren Buffett's comments on this matter are revealing:

> Wall Street never voluntarily abandons a highly profitable field. Years ago, there was a story about the fellow down on Wall Street who was standing on a soapbox at noon, and giving lectures like they do. He was talking about the evils of drugs. And he ranted on for 15 or 20 minutes to a small crowd, and then finally he finished, and he said, "Do you have any questions?" And one very bright investment banking type said to him, "Yeah, who makes the needles?" Well, the needles of the acquisitions game are now junk bonds, just as they were phony equity securities in the late sixties, and Wall Street makes the needles. (Coffee, Lowenstein, and Rose-Ackerman 1988, p. 18)

SHAREHOLDER INTERESTS AND STOCKHOLDER POWER IN TRANSACTIONAL FINANCE

Mid-twentieth-century investors were largely passive holders of securities. Berle and Means (1932) hit on this theme: share ownership had become sufficiently decentralized that the capacity for small investors to monitor firms and exercise control of firms was diminished. From Berle and Means's viewpoint, managers essentially had the control of mid-twentieth-century firms to themselves.

By the end of the twentieth century, however, shareholder activism intensified. The concentration of stock ownership in the hands of the managers of mutual funds, pension funds, insurance funds, all of which grew throughout the second half of the twentieth century, led to the advocacy of the shareholder rights movement. The consolidation of share ownership created real opportunities for collusive shareholder action to influence corporate affairs.

At its extreme, shareholder activism resulted in the dismantling of corporations. In the 1970s, sustained price inflation coupled with a tenacious bear stock market created a situation ripe for exploitation by activist owners. Low security prices and inflated underlying assets meant that the market value of the stock for some firms was less than the value of underlying assets. This created opportunity for activist investors to arrange financing, take firms private through leveraged buyouts, and profit from the piecemeal resale of corporate divisions.

Shareholder activism was an important component of the climate promoting restructuring in the late twentieth century:

> In those companies which were not the target of a stockholder revolt or takeover attempt, boards nevertheless became aware of the general mood of shareholder dissatisfaction and rising militancy. . . . [Boards became] significantly more sensitive and responsive to the perceived priorities of the shareholder constituency. (Donaldson 1994, p. 190–91)

A conspicuous rhetorical war was ongoing between managers and owners in the 1980s. The rhetoric of the most aggressive shareholders during the 1980s was distinctly antimanagement while several top managers sought government protection from the actions of aggressive shareholders. One outcome of this war then was the increased salience of shareholder concerns among the priorities of corporate managers.

Fligstein (2001) notes that managerial discourse in the 1980s emphasized shareholder value and argues that this represented a new "conception of control" of U.S. corporations. Shareholder value was certainly invoked with great frequency as a justification for takeovers and restructuring in the 1980s. One contemporary analyst lists the following reasons for the interest in shareholder value:

- the threat of corporate takeovers by those seeking undervalued, undermanaged assets;

- impressive endorsements by corporate leaders who have adopted the approach;

- the growing recognition that traditional accounting measures such as earnings per share (EPS) and return on investment (ROI) are not reliably linked to increasing the value of the company's shares;

- reporting of returns to shareholders along with other measures of performance in the business press such as *Fortune*'s annual ranking of the 500 leading industrial firms; and

- a growing recognition that executives' long-term compensation needs to be more closely tied to returns to shareholders. (Rappaport 1986, p. 3)

The rhetorical framing of the actions shareholder activists advocated is captured in two books: George P. Schwartz's (1995) *Shareholder Rebellion: How Investors Are Changing the Way America's Companies Are Run*, and Robert A. G. Monks and Nell Minow's (1996) *Watching the Watchers: Corporate Governance for the 21st Century*. Schwartz gives Robert Monks credit for leading the shareholder rights movement in the United States.

> . . . Bob Monks' . . . speech, "The Institutional Investor as a Corporate Citizen" . . . set institutional investment on its ear. It set a Labor Department policy that said that pension fund managers should be doing more than buying promising stocks and selling bad ones. It said that they should be exercising collective strength to rouse mediocre companies to perform to potential. It was not what corporate managers wanted to hear. (Pp. 5–6)

Monks later founded Institutional Shareholder Services (ISS), which analyzed corporate proxy statements surrounding takeovers. Monks's organization essentially articulated to shareholders the benefits of allowing takeover proxies to go through. He also was instrumental in blocking executive defenses to takeovers. Hence from the beginning, the shareholder rights movement was linked with takeovers, but outlasted this form of corporate change. Monks and other institutional shareholders learned that pushing managers to enact voluntary restructuring activities could generate large price breaks, moves that would maximize shareholder value. Monks was involved in a campaign against Sears Roebuck and Co. that wished to see the company spin off its financial services units: Dean Witter Reynolds, Caldwell Banker, and Allstate Insurance. The spin-offs boosted shareholder value by an immediate $1 billion.

One researcher studied 12 major corporations' financial management processes in the 1970s and found that discounted cash-flow analysis was not routinely performed and was not instrumental for decision-making at many companies. Discounted cash-flow analysis essentially compares various decision options for effects on shareholder wealth. During the 1970s management often thought other objectives, such as long-term survival of the firm, were more salient than maximizing shareholder wealth. Institutional investors apparently pushed for the use of discounted cash-flow analysis (Blair 1993, p. 95).

> What benefited shareholders, at times, seriously disadvantaged bondholders. Bondholders who through the 1960s and 1970s had enjoyed predicable returns at minimal risk suddenly found their risk raised and their priority downgraded as the junk bond invasion hit the balance sheets of many previously respectable corporations. Changes in the sources and quality of earnings could and did occur overnight, and some lenders faced substantial loss of value of their securities. (Donaldson 1994, p. 166)

Sometimes lenders were the losers. Donaldson (1994) cites Burlington Northern, whose bonds were downgraded from AA in 1988 to BBB+, causing a loss in value of existing bonds. The winners in the "capital-market induced restructuring" of the 1980s were shareholders, who "cashed in on the run-up of market values of their securities after restructuring initiatives" (p. 166).

THE INCREASED IMPORTANCE OF SHAREHOLDER RELATIONS IN TRANSACTIONAL FINANCE

The relationship between managers and investors in the mid-twentieth century was notoriously lax. Many corporate managers simply ignored shareholders. Financial markets themselves were unimportant to managers because most firms were capable of generating sufficient capital for improvements and operations from their retained earnings or bond offerings. Therefore midcentury managers did not particularly need the equity markets. Shareholders were to be quiet and passive, and vote by proxy for the slate of candidates that management had hand-picked to serve as directors. Joseph A. Livingston describes mid-twentieth-century shareholder relations in his book *The American Stockholder* as a contemporary plea for improved shareholder relations in U.S. firms. His book describes the slovenly manner of managers toward absentee owners, who were weak in the face of managerial power. The 1930's security regulations required that corporations hold annual meetings of shareholders. Managers who wished to avoid confrontations with share-holders would schedule the annual meeting in out-of-the-way locations at inconvenient times to minimize the number of shareholders who would attend. Firms whose operations were in New York City or other large financial centers would travel to a courthouse in Delaware or New Jersey for their annual meeting, ensuring that busy Wall Street analysts and investors would not attend the meetings. If the company were in-corporated in New Jersey or Delaware, that would be the location of the meeting. The main goal was to prevent shareholders from attending the meetings. The meetings themselves were orchestrated to minimize the opportunity for shareholder dissent.

An extreme example was a major railroad that held its annual meeting at a whistle stop in rural Kentucky, hundreds of miles from any financial center or indeed from the railroad's operational headquarters. Again, the primary purpose was to minimize the likelihood of share-holders attending the meeting:

> Once upon a recent time, Southern Pacific held its meetings at Spring Station, Kentucky, a town known only to Wall Street for that reason. But Kentucky imposed a tax, and Southern Pacific fled to Wilming-ton, much to the annoyance of Gilbert [a shareholder], who argues that Los Angeles or San Francisco would be more sensible. On the West Coast, company officials would be able to court thousands of shareholders and shippers. That is the area it serves. (Livingston 1958, p. 75)

Complaints about the inaccessibility of corporate managers to shareholders was a common complaint in the mid-twentieth century, and shareholder meetings of the time were usually calm affairs if for no other reason than that few shareholders attended. An early version of the shareholder rights movement, the 1950's corporate democracy move-ment, emphasized the right of shareholders to convenient meetings:

> Wilma Soss has periodically asked the United States Steel Corpora-tion to change its annual meeting place from Hoboken, New Jersey, to New York City. Why make shareholders take a ferry ride? She rightly asks. Yet, U.S. Steel, year after year, has refused to grant a request which seems entirely reasonable. The effect on shareholders who are sufficiently interested to attend meetings is imaginable. . . . Doesn't

the management want to meet as many shareholders as possible? Isn't it anxious to have shareholders attend meetings? . . . If managements have sales and executive offices in financial centers, such as New York, Philadelphia, Chicago, or San Francisco, cities which are handy to officers and customers, why should they force shareholders to go to small, out of the way localities such as Flemington, New Jersey (Republic Steel, American Tobacco); Watertown, New York (Woolworth); Wilmington, Delaware (Cities Service, General Dynamics); Hoboken, New Jersey (U.S. Steel)? (Livingston 1958, pp. 75–76)

In comparison, by the late twentieth century most firms had created shareholder or investor relations departments. Many have separate corporate offices that handle the informational requests of institutional and small investors. The officer who specializes in relations with institutional investors generally provides a superior level of service, information, and access than the officer charged with small investor relations. More detailed information, access to senior managers, special large owner meetings, and other enhanced opportunities are routinely offered to institutional investors in America's largest firms. Contact with large shareholders is a significant part of the top manager's job in the late twentieth century, consuming a great deal of time. Consider the following summary of shareholder interaction from the Sears Roebuck and Co. 1987 annual report:

Financial Analyst Meetings: To ensure the flow of information about the company to investors, Sears strives to meet with representatives of the financial community on a timely basis, both domestically and overseas. In 1987, company officers met with groups of analysts representing more than 750 financial institutions in Chicago, Edinburgh, London, Zurich, Frankfurt and Tokyo. In addition, company representatives met with analysts at more than 300 financial institutions in major U.S. cities during the year, and hosted over 50 meetings at Sears Tower for individuals representing financial institutions from seven foreign countries and the United States. (P. 21)

As described herein later, 1992 changes in proxy laws allowed collusive interaction among large investors and between large investors and senior managers. This elevates the importance of shareholder concerns and interests in the management of the firm.

TRANSACTIONAL FINANCE GENERATES AN INCREASE IN STOCK OWNERSHIP

One cause of the power of transactional finance in the late twentieth century is the sheer increase in size of the financial sector. Although the market for corporate securities during the 1920's bull market has sometimes been characterized as a mass market, after the 1929 crash and for the subsequent three decades, retail investors avoided corporate security ownership and the percentage of the American population participating in financial markets contracted. Retail participation in financial markets in the United States remained minimal until the 1950s when public participation in financial markets began to expand, growing steadily before peaking at the end of the 1960s. During the long bear stock market of the 1970s, American retail investing again retracted. By the early 1980s, only 8 percent of U.S. private assets were represented by stock market accounts (direct and indirect combined). The last two decades of the twentieth century, however, witnessed both a phenomenally strong bull stock market (approximately a tenfold increase in major stock market indices during the last two decades of the twentieth century) and a radical expansion of mass participation in financial markets. By the end of the 1990s, financial commentators commonly noted that "the majority of Americans own stock" and the stock market represented more than a quarter of total private wealth in the United States (see Figures 2.1 through 2.6).

Macroeconomic policies supported and encouraged this astounding increase in the breadth of financial marketing participation. The creation of individual retirement accounts (IRAs), changes in pension laws (401[K]), low capital gains tax rates, banking deregulation, and a sustained emphasis on the fiscal crisis of social security helped channel Americans into the securities market. The policies of U.S. business—corporate restructuring, downsizing, and defaults on defined benefit plans—also funneled Americans into the security market to fund their retirements on their own accounts.

Significant security holdings are no longer confined to a thin stratum of capitalists at the top of the class structure, but are spread through a broad spectrum of households. This has led to a fundamental shift in the financial sophistication and awareness. Americans are more aware of and worried about finance because their well-being is intimately tied to the market. Whether and where their children will attend college, at what age they can comfortably retire—these and other major life decisions are dependent on the value of corporate securities

FIGURE 2.1

Median Net Worth of U.S. Households during the Era of Restructuring, 1989–1998 (in thousands of 1998 dollars)

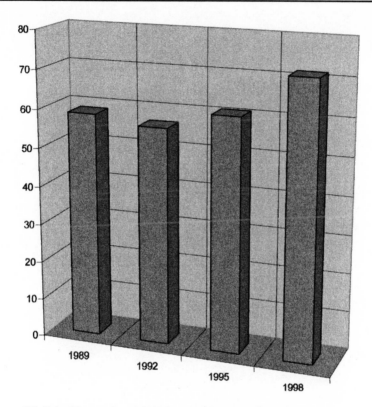

Source: U.S. Federal Reserve Board, 1998 Survey of Consumer Finance.

on secondary financial markets. The part of the lifeworld devoted to finance has increased—conversation about the stock market's daily gyrations, frequent tracking of one's portfolio, the pondering of investment decisions—has increased. The public's desire for financial news and advice has increased as well evidenced by the explosion of financial news networks, periodicals, and Web sites.

Expanded participation in financial markets has increased the share of U.S. wealth floating on the securities market and elevated the awareness of financial news and financial matters in American culture.[9]

FIGURE 2.2
Stock Holdings as a Share of U.S. Households' Financial Assets during
the Era of Restructuring, 1989–1998

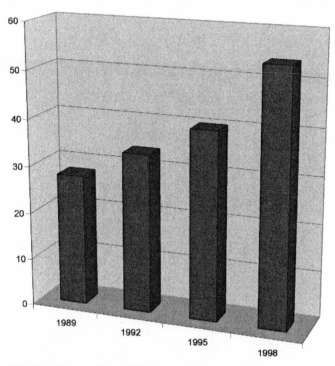

Source: U.S. Federal Reserve Board, 1998 Survey of Consumer Finance.

The Federal Reserve Board, which tracks Americans' participation in securities markets, reported both the vast expansion of market participation and the growth of interest in the market in its 1999 report:

> The value of U.S. household's stock portfolio's rose 20 percent to $10.77 trillion last year and now represents 25 percent of total household assets, higher than at any time in the post–World War II era, according to new Federal Reserve Board data. Equities represented a growing portion of U.S. household wealth in the 1950s and 1960s,

FIGURE 2.3
Percentage of U.S. Households with Direct and Indirect Holding of Stock during the Era of Restructuring, 1989–1998

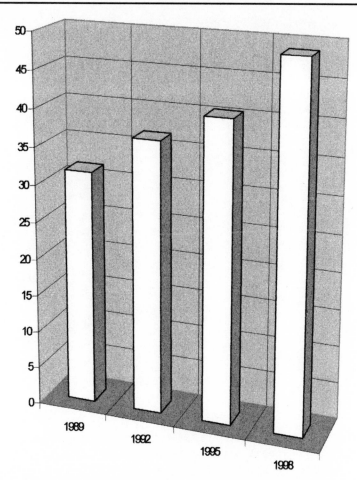

Source: U.S. Federal Reserve Board, 1998 Survey of Consumer Finances.

reaching a peak of 23.7 percent in 1968. But that trend reversed during the bear market years of the 1970s, both because of the declining value of American's portfolios and because many people lost interest in the market. In 1984, only 8 percent of American's wealth was in stocks. . . . But the soaring stock market of the 1990s and the expan-

FIGURE 2.4
Financial Assets of U.S. Households as a Percentage of their Total Assets
during the Era of Restructuring, 1989–1998

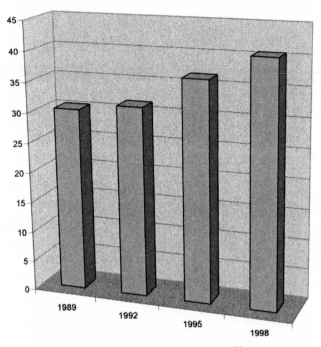

Source: U.S. Federal Reserve Board, 1998 Survey of Consumer Finances.

sion of retirement plans that allow workers to direct investments in to
the market has changed the trend again. Just 10 years ago, only 10.4
percent of Americans' wealth was in the market. The percentage has
grown steadily since then . . . the value of their stocks has increased
381 percent [whereas] consumer prices rose by 38 percent over the
decade. . . . The collective net worth of U.S. households continued to
climb last year, reaching $36.79 trillion at year end, up 10.2 percent
over 1997. (Wessel 1999, p. A6)

The expansion of financial market participation should not be interpreted as a democratization of capitalism. Even in the late 1990s,

FIGURE 2.5
Median Value of Stock Holdings among U.S. Households with Stock,
1989–1998 (in thousands of 1998 dollars)

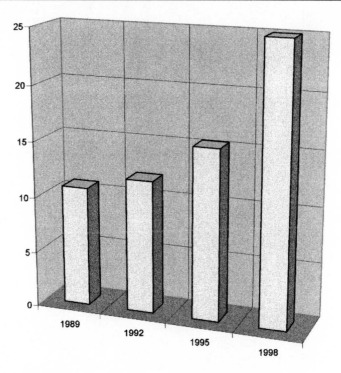

Source: U.S. Federal Reserve Board, 1998 Survey of Consumer Finances.

approximately half of U.S. households held no equity securities. Although the percentage of Americans who own shares of stock has been rapidly increasing, stock ownership remains extraordinarily unequal. The same Federal Reserve Board report cited previously indicated that the bulk of capital gains accrue to the wealthiest individuals in the United States:

A 1995 Fed survey, now being updated, found that 68 percent of the stock-market wealth owned by households was held by the richest 5 percent of the population. "If patterns of equity ownership have not changed much since 1995, the steep rise in stock prices over the past

FIGURE 2.6
Market Value and Number of Shares Traded on New York Stock Exchange during the Era of Restructuring, 1980–1997

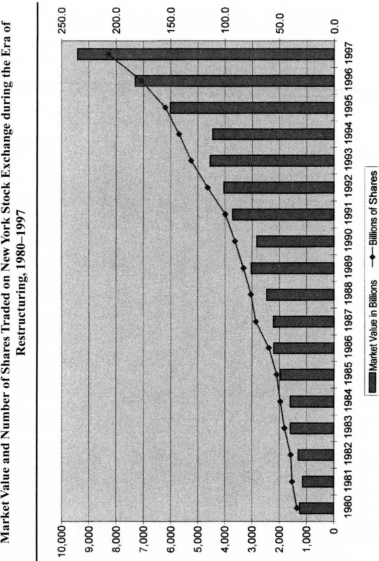

Source: New York Stock Exchange Fact Book 1998.

several years would suggest a further increase in the concentration of net worth," [said] Fed Chairman Alan Greenspan. . . . Extrapolations by economist Edward Wolff, done by the Economic Policy Institute, a liberal Washington think tank, suggest that more than 40 percent of the gains created by the bull market of the 1990s have been claimed by the wealthiest 1 percent of the population and that more than 85 percent of the gains have gone to the top 10 percent. (Wessel 1999, p. A6)

The fastest growing type of share ownership during the 1990s was indirect ownership of stock through mutual funds. However, the value of equity securities individuals hold directly ($6.28 trillion) is four times the value of equity securities in mutual funds ($1.73 trillion) in 1998 (Wessel 1999, p. A6). The expansion of equity ownership in the last two decades of the twentieth century has not democratized capital or corporate decision-making, but has rather concentrated financial power in the hands of wealthy individuals and institutional investors.[10] The extension of mass participation in U.S. financial markets has also increased the "public" for finance in the United States and expanded the liquidity, volatility, and volume of the U.S. market for equity securities. The relative size of the financial sector grew (as a percentage of gross domestic product, or GDP) and increased the ability of actors in the financial system to control industrial production. The relative decline of financiers' power that occurred during the Fordist period was reversed.

THE EXPANDED PRESENCE OF FINANCIAL MARKET INTERESTS INSIDE CORPORATIONS

The rise of transactional finance in the late twentieth century is based, in part, on the expanded participation of a broad spectrum of Americans in the securities market. It is also based, in part, on the development and institutionalization of financial deal-making through mergers and takeovers. Transactional finance has also helped to expand the presence of financiers and financial market interests inside industrial firms. This is the mechanism through which speculative financial market orientations are injected into corporate management. Conglomerateurs and other stock-swap deal-makers have an absolute dependence on high market valuations of their securities. If the value of stock falls, they cannot profitably complete stock-swap deals, and if they cannot do deals, the valuation of their securities falls permanently because the basis of the high valuation (price-earnings ratio) was the market's expectation that the firm would be doing deals. The situation of a conglomerateur can be likened to that of a shark, which drowns if it ever stops swimming. A conglomerate's security sinks if it ever stops growing and doing deals—share price permanently plummets. The financial imperative of conglomerateurs was intense: they were forced to take into account the perspectives and orientations of financiers. Close contact between conglomerateur and mutual fund manager heightened awareness of what will sell on Wall Street. Transactional finance injects a financial imperative into the firm.

This financial imperative is especially visible in the takeovers of the 1980s. Once hostile takeovers became routine, managers of every firm in the United States had to be on the lookout for an unsolicited hostile bid. Most of the managerial defenses to takeovers were preemptive. The idea was to take away the incentive for a predator to seize the firm by preemptively breaking up and restructuring the firm. Because one of the normal posttakeover moves is to saddle the firm with large debt payments, increasing the financial leverage or debt-to-equity ratio was an important takeover defense. A large pool of cash makes a firm an attractive target because these funds can be deployed immediately to help a takeover artist finance the deal. The preemptive strategy is to distribute this cash to shareholders or use it to purchase another firm. Get rid of cash and any other easily disposable assets. If divisions of the firm can be easily disposed, do so. If the firm has not cut costs in a restructuring, do so. If there is a large research and development (R&D) budget and a large R&D staff, downsize them. Because takeover targets were firms in good financial condition relative to a low stock price, management either had to weaken the financial condition, raise the trading price of stock, or both. The same actions accomplished either end.

By spurring on these preemptive strategies, the hostile takeover movement injected financial market interests and orientations into the management of the firm. Managers who successfully fended off hostile takeovers did so by learning to think like the market, or even to think like a hostile takeover artist. Raising the market valuation of security was essential to preventing a takeover, so managers had to think like the market to understand how to increase the valuation. Successful speculative management required an awareness of prevailing market conceptions of good management practice and strategic alignment of corporate actions with those conceptions.

Michael Milken, in a 1999 article, defends the use of junk bonds and his record, claiming that the reason U.S. capitalism prospered during the 1990s was because of the junk bonds and restructuring of the 1980s:

> Back in the 1960s, a small number of money-center banks and large insurance companies pretty much determined who got access to U.S. financial capital. Their customers were large, established corporations. . . . Tens of thousands of smaller enterprises—companies with prospects—scrambled for crumbs at the tables of the capital club. . . . Over the last third of the twentieth century, control of capital in America has shifted away from private institutions and toward public markets, making the process of financing growth more forward-looking and democratic. (P. A22)

The high volume of trade in secondary financial markets has been a characteristic feature of American (or Anglo-American) finance and is one dimension that separates the U.S. economy from its Asian and European counterparts. Stabilized, bank-meditated, high finance centered on primary securities markets are more characteristic of continental Europe, whereas disruptive, low finance centered on secondary markets has become a characteristic trait of the United States. This is especially true in the late twentieth century after financial deregulation in the post-managerialist era has eliminated the distinction between high and low finance. Finance in late-twentieth-century America is uniquely speculative and transactional. The bulk of the revenue U.S. finance generates no longer comes from investment banking in the traditional sense of offering securities for the primary market for a commission, but rather comes from trading, from "deal-making."

CONCLUSIONS: TRANSACTIONAL FINANCE IN THE LATE TWENTIETH CENTURY

This chapter reviewed the emergence of transactional finance. Compared to the mid-twentieth century, finance in the late twentieth century occupies a more central position in the U.S. economy. The mid-twentieth century is sometimes aptly characterized as a period of *managerial capitalism*, a time when essentially sovereign executives of America's largest industrial corporations made decisions that determined the conditions of life for Americans and the U.S. economy as a whole. Decisions GM, AT&T, and IBM made determined the life chances of millions of people and set the tone for the entire economic system. This chapter outlined the decline of managerial sovereignty over U.S. capitalism in the late twentieth century. Changes in the structure of financial markets and corporate organization that resulted increased the importance of speculative secondary financial markets over corporate affairs. The power of the financial markets in the late twentieth century conditioned executive decisions and actions. In recent times, finance overshadows U.S. corporations.

The late twentieth century marked a turn toward a form of *speculative capitalism*—an economy based on profit from the trade of fluctuating property values. The rise of transactional finance makes understanding the relationship between what Veblen (1904) called "business and industry"—between financial markets and product markets—critical. This book does not assume that financial markets efficiently represent value corporations produced in product markets, that stock price increases represent real improvements in long-run profitability. As a partly autonomous institutionalized order situated actors with bounded rationality staffed, the stock market relies on imperfect representations of value and enables the generation and capture of profits that are not based in production. In fact, a central argument of this book is that actors in stock markets can profit from the destruction of productive value. As U.S. corporations became more powerfully embedded in speculative finance, the speculative logic of the stock market conditioned corporate actions. This book views the restructuring of U.S. corporations in the late twentieth century, the full range of mergers, acquisitions, takeovers, subsidarization, and internal restructuring, as pecuniary reorganizations—corporate actions intended to generate and capture increased stock market prices (reorganizer's profit).

An apt historical account might view the mid-twentieth century as a time of rare autonomy of the industrial sector from the financial sector in the United States, brought about in large part by government control of the financial domain by legislation in the wake of the 1929 stock market crash.[11] The history of the twentieth century U.S. economy, at least through the 1960s, is one of the extension of public policy into the realm of finance, taking some of the profit, control, and autonomy out of this domain, while shifting its allegiance to assisting industrial production.

Transactional finance shaped late-twentieth-century economic life in the United States. The power of finance to reorder industry, to disrupt and reorganize, was merely latent during the stable financial world of the 1940s and 1950s. This power was made manifest in conglomeration in the 1960s and especially in the takeovers of the 1980s, when junk bond financing and the enabling legal structure of the multilayered subsidiary form made nearly every company a potential takeover target. Takeovers forced executives to be constantly attuned to and aware of the actions of financiers or risk dismissal. Management had to take financial markets into account daily, not only at select moments of deal-making.

Corporate restructuring arose in an environment conditioned by transactional finance. The managerialist scenario of U.S. capitalism, where corporate managers rule empires unchallenged by shareholder interests, seems ill-suited to comprehend corporate affairs in recent times. Whereas mid-twentieth-century managerialist firms were largely self-financed through retained earnings, the financial crises and reorganizations of late-twentieth-century corporations forced managers into a new relation with financial markets. Corporate restructuring, like many late-twentieth-century corporate events, was oriented to secondary security markets.

The next chapter begins with a consideration of market power in economic life and an examination of the mechanisms through which the stock market shaped corporate restructuring in the late twentieth century.

Chapter 3

SOCIAL INTERMEDIARIES AND THE WAVE OF INTERNAL CORPORATE RESTRUCTURING IN THE LATE TWENTIETH CENTURY

How is stock market power generated, exercised, responded to, and turned by corporate actors to their own advantage? What were the consequences of this power for corporate restructuring in the late twentieth century? Academic analysts of economic life have long theorized the embedding of corporations in markets, especially product markets. The rise of transactional finance prompts a fresh look at the embedding of corporations in speculative financial markets. In this chapter, the power of secondary financial markets in corporate restructuring leads to a consideration of *social intermediaries*—connective structures linking secondary financial markets and corporations. Three important social intermediaries—financial accounting, business news media, and corporate governance—contributed to the rise, reign, and decline of internal corporate restructuring among the largest U.S. corporations.

MARKETS, SOCIAL INTERMEDIARIES, AND CORPORATE RESTRUCTURING

In the late twentieth century, opinion in circles as varied as sociology, economics, management theory, and the popular media converged on the idea that markets caused corporate restructuring. Michel Aglietta (1979) and others loosely affiliated with the regulation school of political economy developed one of the most sophisticated market-centered theories of corporate restructuring.

Deeply inspired by Marx's writings and employing Marxian language and imagery, Aglietta (1979) explained late-twentieth-century corporate restructuring as part of a larger transformation in capitalism's "regime of accumulation," which includes state regulation, labor–management agreements, production forms, and consumption patterns. The stabilization of a regime of accumulation into a sustainable, self-reproducing industrial–capital complex greatly facilitates capital accumulation. Beginning immediately after World War II and ending sometime after 1970, a long wave of economic growth was structured and sustained in the United States (and to a lesser extent most European industrial economies) by a regime of accumulation termed *Fordism*, typified by mass production, mass consumption, and intensive labor. Due to a saturation of product markets and a productivity crisis in labor markets, the Fordist system broke down in the late 1960s and conceptualizing the regime of accumulation that is replacing the Fordist system, usually called *neo-Fordism* or *post-Fordism*, has occupied regulation school writers and their critics. Corporate restructuring has tremendous significance to these writers because the twenty-first-century regime of accumulation is being forged and, once stabilized, will structure another wave of capitalist accumulation.[1]

The Fordist regime of accumulation reached its internal limits by the end of the 1960s and was no longer a viable arrangement for the profitable expansion of capitalism. Overproduction and saturation of global product markets limited continued growth. A crisis of productivity in labor markets[2] and a crisis of profitability in financial markets were related, but secondary limits. The late-twentieth-century macrolevel transformation of the United States and other Western capitalist economies, of which corporate restructuring was a part, reconfigured the regime of accumulation and ruptured the social order associated with Fordism. A new capitalist order is being created through restructuring, a reconfiguration of capitalist product, labor, and financial markets. In these writings, corporate change resulted from and responded to alterations in global markets, especially product markets.

Regulation school accounts of corporate change tend to be deterministic, arguing that changes in macrolevel product markets necessitated changes in the productive organization of firms. This study aims to conceptualize less deterministic conditions for restructuring that leave room for flexibility, opportunism, and strategic action. Restructuring, to a significant degree, resulted from the active agency of speculative teams searching for innovations that would enrich them by increasing the trading price of corporate stock. This study seeks to conceptualize how institutional structures of markets, firms, and the links among them enabled as well as constrained the agency of economic actors who produced corporate restructuring.

Other academic and journalistic writings emphasized product markets as both the primary cause and the primary target of corporate restructuring activity. Moving beyond an appreciation of the causal role global product markets played, this study aims to understand how restructuring resulted from and responded to speculative secondary financial markets. Because different markets—product, labor, real estate, primary financial, and secondary financial—have distinct structures and procedures, they are worthy of separate description and conceptualization. This study suggests that understanding corporate restructuring in late twentieth century requires a close analysis of relationships of firms with secondary financial markets, markets that cannot be viewed with sufficient clarity from production-oriented perspectives.

Financial economics produced the most technically elegant conceptions of financial markets and constructed a sophisticated justification for corporate restructuring (Baskin and Miranti 1997). A weakness, from the standpoint of this study, is that financial economists tend to conceptualize financial markets deductively, treating them as "efficient mechanisms" for the transmission of production efficiencies and profitability. In this respect, secondary financial markets are remarkably underconceptualized, more often taken as a starting assumption than as an object of study. As frictionless transmitters of economic efficiency, markets are theoretically important but not the subject of empirical investigation or thorough conceptualization. A deductive theory of "markets" along the lines of neoclassical economics is insufficient to help us to understand ways that markets may have driven late-twentieth-century capitalism.

Inductive conceptualizations of the institutional structure of specific markets are useful to understand how specific markets differ from generalizing classical ideas about product markets. Sociologists have begun to study markets inductively, treating them as social institutions (Abolafia 1996; Adler and Adler 1984; Baker 1984, 1990; Fligstein 1996). However, this work most clearly theorizes markets as organizations rather drawing conceptual attention to intermediating structures between markets and (corporate) organizations.[3]

This study aims to understand not only markets as institutions but also particular pathways and mechanisms through which markets affect firms. How are changes in markets and market structures transmitted to firms? Rather than deducing the disciplining influence of markets on firms, by studying social intermediaries this study seeks to investigate the mutual influence of secondary financial markets and corporate organizations.

Since Adam Smith popularized the imagery of the "invisible hand" of the market in 1776, the idea that markets control firms has been a cornerstone of socioeconomic thought. Unregulated, free competitive markets transform (or select) the firms that operate within them, rewarding those that are productively efficient and punishing those that are not. The invisible hand of the market coordinates economic action so that the aggregate effect of individual economic actions disciplines firms who are not optimally productive. Sociological investigations of capitalism must empirically identify market control of firms. In fact, market magic may only occur under select conditions, conditions that should be theorized. Under what conditions is the pursuit of wealth transformed into the accomplishment of maximum production efficiency? One can imagine markets structured in a way that the pursuit of gain and maximum profit is not effectively channeled into productive outlets, and hence does not lead to maximum production efficiency. Classical economists stress that a free market structure disciplines market actors so that they can only achieve maximum profit through the pursuit and accomplishment of production efficiency. The present study suggests that the structure of secondary financial markets allows for the pursuit of profit through means other than efficient production. *Speculation*, trading in the fluctuating value of property, is a particularly widespread nonproductive pursuit of profit. The secondary market for corporate securities in the United States is a market decisively driven by a logic, and institutionalized processes, of speculation. In this market, currents of profit finding are not channeled into the long circuit of commodity production, but into the short circuit of speculation.

Like Alfred Chandler (1978), we ought to identify visible hands in modern capitalism—not the hands of managers who constructed modern production organizations, however, but the visible hands that link firms to secondary markets for corporate securities. This requires specification and conceptualization of how firms and secondary financial markets interact. As causes of organizational change, examining market processes, procedures, practices, and structures that contribute to and shape that change is essential.

We turn, then, to the central concerns of the current study: the rise of secondary financial market power in the late twentieth century, the speculative management that it encouraged, and the corporate restructuring that resulted. *Social intermediaries* are the institutional structures that link corporations to secondary financial security markets. Three of these structures directed the timing, extent, and character of internal reorganization in the largest U.S. firms: corporate governance structures that teamed big owners and top managers, financial accounting rules and procedures, and conceptions of aggressively good management practice the business news media disseminates. These intermediaries were the channels corporations and financial market participants used to assess and influence each other, the transmittal path of stock market power to firms.

INVESTIGATING THE WAVE OF CORPORATE RESTRUCTURING

In the last two decades of the twentieth century, large U.S. corporations engaged in an impressive series of reorganizations. These were of two types: *external transactions* through merger, acquisition, and divestiture, and *internal reorganizations* through downsizing, rationalization, and reengineering (Table 3.1). The remainder of this chapter reports the findings of an examination of approximately 500 *internal* restructuring initiatives recorded in the regulatory filings and annual reports of 167 very large U.S. firms between 1984 and 1997. The role of three social intermediaries linking corporations to secondary financial markets—accounting, business news media, and corporate governance structures—were critical for determining the timing and extent of restructuring activity in the late twentieth century.

Empirical materials for this analysis were collected from several sources. Corporate investor relations departments were contacted directly to request printed copies of corporate reports. Printed copies of the annual report to shareholders and SEC filings (primarily forms 10–Q, thequarterly unaudited financial statements, and 10–K, the annual audited financial statements) were examined for all companies in the study for 1991 to 1993, the period when internal reorganizing was at its peak. The physical reports were supplemented with elec-

TABLE 3.1
Comparison of External and Internal Corporate Reorganization

	External Reorganization	Internal Reorganization
Mechanism of reorganization	transactions	accrual
Typical actions	mergers, acquisitions, divestitures, spin-offs	reengineering, downsizing, rationalization, streamlining, restructuring
Locus of action	primary financial markets	secondary financial markets
Intermediating structures	financial intermediaries such as investment banks, commercial banks	social intermediaries: governance structures, financial accounting, business news media

tronic reports downloaded from corporate Web sites and the Lexis-Nexis database.

Because the goal of the study was to understand corporate restructuring activities in America's leading firms, the companies chosen for the study were taken from the 1993 *Fortune* 500 rankings. Because restructuring in the 1990s has so often been analyzed as an industrial phenomenon, the bulk of the companies included in this study were chosen from the largest 100 corporations (in terms of revenues) on *Fortune's* Industrial 500 list. Sixty-seven additional corporations were chosen from *Fortune's* Service 500 list (Tables 3.2 and 3.3).[4] Including nonindustrial firms allowed the comparison of corporate restructuring across a wider range of very large companies in diverse economic sectors. As the figures in the chapter reveal, corporate restructuring occurred with greater frequency among industrial firms, which can be read as support for a production-centered interpretation of restructuring such as post-Fordism. However, corporate restructuring importantly also occurred in the other economic sectors, which indicates the usefulness of a finance-centered understanding. Restructuring occurred simultaneously at firms in very different product markets and with very different production processes. Shared

TABLE 3.2
Industrial Firms Selected from *Fortune* 500, 1993

Abbott Laboratories	Du Pont	Mobil
Alcoa	Eastman Kodak	Monsanto
Allied Signal	Eli Lilly	Motorola
Amerada Hess	Emerson Electric	Occidental Petroleum
American Brands	Exxon	PepsiCo
American Cyanamid	Ford Motor	Pfizer
American Home	General Electric	Philip Morris
Products	General Mills	Phillips Petroleum
Amoco	General Motors	PPG Industries
Anheuser-Busch	Georgia-Pacific	Procter & Gamble
Apple Computer	Gillette	Quaker Oats
Archer Daniels Midland	Goodyear Tire	Ralston Purina
Ashland Oil	Hanson Industries	Raytheon
Atlantic Richfield	Hewlett-Packard	RJR Nabisco
Baxter	H. J. Heinz	Rockwell International
Bergen	Hoechst-Celanese	Sara Lee
Boeing	Honeywell	Shell
Borden	IBM	Sun
Bristol-Myers Squibb	IBP	Tenneco
Campbell Soup	Intel	Texaco
Caterpillar	International Paper	Texas Instruments
Chevron	Johnson & Johnson	Textron
Chrysler	Johnson Controls	TRW
CITGO	Kellogg	Unisys
Coastal	Kimberly-Clark	United Technologies
Coca-Cola	Levi Strauss	Unocal
Colgate-Palmolive	Litton Industries	USX
Compaq	Lockheed	W.R. Grace
Conagra	Martin Marietta	Warner-Lambert
Cooper Industries	McDonnell Douglas	Westinghouse Electric
CPC International	Merck	Weyerhaeuser
Dana	Miles Laboratories	Whirlpool
Deere	Minnesota Mining &	Xerox
Digital Equipment	Manufacturing	
Dow Chemical		

financial markets, not product markets, were common to restructuring firms. The study used *Fortune*'s categorization of corporations into industry groupings for comparison among industrial, financial, diversified service, transportation, and utility firms. The Lexis-Nexis

TABLE 3.3
Nonindustrial Firms Selected from *Fortune* 500, 1993

Financial	Fleming	Kmart
Aetna Life	Fluor	Kroger
American International	Halliburton	May Department Stores
Banc One	Manpower	Melville
California Federal	Marriott	Price
Chase Manhattan	MCI	Sears Roebuck & Co.
Chemical	McKesson	Wal-Mart Stores
Citicorp	ServiceMaster	Winn-Dixie
Fed. Natl. Mortgage	Sprint	Woolworth
Glendale Federal	Supervalu	
Great Western Financial	Sysco	*Transportation and*
H. F. Ahmanson	Time Warner	*Utilities*
Merrill Lynch	Walt Disney	Ameritech
Morgan Stanley	WMX	AMR
NationsBank		Bellsouth
New York Life	*Retail*	Burlington Northern
Travelers	Albertsons	CSX
	American Stores	Delta Air Lines
Diversified Service	Costco Wholesale	Federal Express
Alco	Dayton Hudson	GTE
ARA group	Food Lion	Norfolk Southern
AT&T	Gap	Pacific Gas and Electric
Beverly Enter	Great Atlantic & Pacific	Southern
Capital Cities/ABC	Home Depot	UAL
Carnival Cruise	J.C. Penney	USAir Group
Columbia Health		

database provided annual reports and SEC filings back to 1984 and forward to the year 1997, the period covered by the study reported in this chapter.

These materials were examined for evidence of corporate restructuring and any instance of external or internal reorganization was noted. The examination of materials proceeded in several ways. First, physical materials were read, searching for evidence of and references to restructuring activities in the management letter to shareholders, the financial statements, and the footnotes to the financial statements. This was not a straightforward process. Restructuring was held in such high regard during the early 1990s that many companies that did not have formal restructuring plans and had not incurred a restructuring charge still talked about their "restructuring" activities. Sorting the companies that were "simulating" restructuring from those that were actually changing their organizations was difficult (although, as indicated following, the business news media was of some value here). The covert nature of restructuring actions at some firms (especially engineering-driven firms), where layoffs and major organizational changes were ignored or hidden in shareholder communications further increased the difficulties. The electronic media was somewhat easier to search, especially in the latter phases of the study after devising complex search algorithms comprising terms that companies typically used for their restructuring activity. The general search procedure was to download an annual report or SEC filing and use the "Find in Page" function to search for an array of restructuring terms. If none were found, the document was skimmed to search for reorganizing activity described in unusual terms.

To ensure further that reorganizing activity was not missed, the Lexis-Nexis business news media files were searched for articles describing restructuring announcements or activities at each firm. This was helpful because the business news media did employ a common language to describe restructuring activities even when corporate management did not. For example, one company engaged in stealth restructuring had their cover neatly blown by a business news article critical of massive layoffs at the firm (TRW). Similarly, a company that conspicuously affirms its commitment to cost cutting and restructuring in its annual reports is probably *simulating* restructuring if business news articles on the firm highlight the way a failing management is trying to boost share prices by adopting the latest corporate fads (W. R. Grace and Co.).[5]

External reorganizations include mergers, acquisitions, disposals, spin-offs, and divestitures and are, in essence, business reorganizations occasioned by purchase or sale of corporate assets (see Table 3.1). Internal reorganizations include actions described as *restructuring, rationalization, streamlining, downsizing, workforce reduction*, and *realignment*. Internal reorganizations are not associated with a transaction, but are discretionary management actions. Internal reorganizations are otherwise referred to in the academic literature and business news media as *organizational restructuring*, or *corporate restructuring*, terms that I occasionally employ.

Internal reorganization was at the very center of the overall transformation of late-twentieth-century U.S. capitalism. As described in chapter 2, financial restructuring involved minimizing accounting costs and boosting market value by increasing leverage. Asset restructuring dealt primarily with exiting lines of business, entering other lines, or both. But internal reorganization (corporate restructuring) altered production processes and rationalized operations, changing the way work was done to boost profits. This aspect of corporate restructuring captured the imagination of financial markets in the very late 1980s and early 1990s. Reorganizing work for heightened profit resonated not only with finance market participants, but also corresponded closely with academic theorists of postmodernity.[6]

The primary materials reviewed were financial statement accruals that represented costs associated with internal reorganizations, referred to here and in the business news media as *restructuring charges*. The following criteria were followed to identify instances of restructuring. A restructuring was included in the study's data if it was conspicuously identified by the corporation or the business news media as significant intraorganizational change and if these changes resulted in an unusual or nonrecurring charge against earnings. *Simulated restructuring* (an announcement of restructuring, but no implementing action) did not generate a charge against earnings and was not recorded in the study's data.

The corporate reporting of external reorganizations is more straightforward and constrained by regulatory and financial accounting rules than reporting of internal reorganizations. Because external reorganizations change the form of the business, they must be fully disclosed and discussed in the company's SEC filings. Furthermore, these changes in business form result from an economic transaction and by default, and by regulation, are amounts represented in the financial accounts of the firm. The price of the transaction, gain or loss on disposition, "goodwill" (excess of price paid over identifiable assets acquired) generated, and other costs associated with a transaction must be fully recorded in the financial accounts of the firm. Because external reorganizations are arm's-length transactions that are externally verifiable, the amount recorded in the firm's books for the transaction is fixed and easy to establish. Internal reorganizations, on the other hand, are not generated by transactions and hence the "reporting" of these alterations in the business of the firm is much more flexible and subject to management discretion.

Two basic types of bookkeeping entries occur in the financial accounts of a firm: transactions and accruals. *Transactions* generally involve exchanges for cash, and the amount of cash used in the transaction determines the amount of the financial statement entry. Because financial statements are periodic summaries of business activity, the financial accounts of the firm are adjusted with *accruals* to provide an accurate picture of the business activity and financial condition of the firm at a particular date. For example, depreciation accruals are made to reflect the loss of utility of machinery and buildings during the course of a year (even though no actual costs arose). Restructuring charges are accruals that represent management's estimate of the full cost of completing a restructuring plan. They are recorded on the books of the firm at the time of the announcement of the plan even though the actual expenses may not come due for several years. Because of their large size and discretionary nature, restructuring charges can be used to manage the bottom line earnings of firms.

Although several important efforts were made (chapter 4) to constrain accounting manipulation of restructuring costs, regulators allowed significant managerial discretion in both regulatory reporting and financial-accounting recognition of corporate restructuring through 1994. This discretion extended to the timing of the recognition of reorganization incidents and the size of the accrual for expenses related to the restructuring initiative. Hence, the decision to report organizational restructuring was laden with strategic opportunities to signal management's intentions to shift ordinary expenses into the restructuring charge, thereby enhancing short-term profits. These signals were particularly alluring to financial markets actors. Their responses to these announcements accomplished the speculative purposes of internal restructuring, namely, the rise in stock prices from which top managers and large equity holders extracted value. Used strategically, a large restructuring charge actually raised the short-term future ordinary earnings of a firm and triggered an upward reevaluation of corporate value on secondary security markets (Table 3.4).

TABLE 3.4
Demonstration of the Effect of a Restructuring Charge on Current and Future Corporate Earnings

Strategically used, restructuring charges can function to boost both current and future *operating* income by shifting normal operating expenses into the one-time charge.

Without Restructuring Charge (Dollars in Millions):

	Current Year	*Next 5 Years*
Operating revenues	$100	$500
(Operating expenses)	(95)	(475)
Operating profit/(loss):	5	25
Net profit/(loss):	$ 5	$ 25

With Restructuring Charge:

	Current Year	*Next 5 Years*
Operating revenues	$100	$500
(Operating expenses)	(85)	(375)
Operating earnings:	15	125
Restructuring charge:	(110)	(0)
Net profit/(loss):	$(95)	$125

Financial analysts typically focus on a corporation's operating earnings in their valuation models. Losses or reduced income due to nonrecurring charges have no effect on analysts' computation of market value. Because they boost operating earnings, large restructuring charges often increase analysts' calculations of expected future profit, raising the firm's market valuation.

THE EXTENT OF RESTRUCTURING

In the 14-year period between 1984 and 1997, 497 instances of internal reorganization that resulted in a recorded restructuring charge against earnings were found among the more than 2,000 reports of the 167 companies studied. Industrial firms more often used corporate restructuring of all types than did nonindustrial firms (Figure 3.1). In the sample of firms examined, internal organizational restructurings—identified by a restructuring charge that was not linked to a coincident external transaction such as a merger—were especially concentrated among the industrials (Figure 3.2). The 100 industrial firms generated 370 instances of internal reorganization (an average of 3.7 per company), whereas the 67 nonindustrial firms generated 127 instances of internal reorganization (an average of 1.8 per company). Only 13 industrial firms avoided any internal reorganization during the study period. Most industrial firms recorded multiple incidents of restructuring, with 2 companies recording 11 separate restructuring incidents (Figure 3.3).[7]

The trend of internal organizational restructuring among the largest firms in the United States exhibits a clear wavelike pattern (Figures 3.4 and 3.5). The number and magnitude of reorganizing initiatives grew rapidly in the late 1980s, reached peak activity in the early 1990s, and then declined. The number of restructuring incidents among the 167 firms increased steadily from less than 10 per year in 1984 to more than 20 in 1989, and then jumped sharply to 60 in 1991 before peaking at 70 in 1993. In 1994, the number of restructuring incidents fell by more than half and remained well below peak levels for the remainder of the study period. The dollar value of restructuring charges taken in each year follows a similar, wavelike pattern.

Internal reorganization was already well established among these very large firms in 1984 (the earliest year for which annual reports and SEC filings were available from Lexis-Nexis). However, internal reorganization during this period was a mere adjunct to the external reorganization process. In the very late 1970s and early 1980s, external restructuring of U.S. corporations through takeovers and buyouts yielded incredible speculative gains for raiders, arbitrageurs, and other owners of U.S. equity securities. The dramatic bull stock market of the 1980s was driven in large part by external (transactional) restructuring. The "big movers" on the market—the stocks that had the largest increase or decrease in value on any given day—in the 1980s were often

FIGURE 3.1
Aggregate Yearly Reorganization Charges Taken by Large Firms, 1984–1997
(by industrial classification)

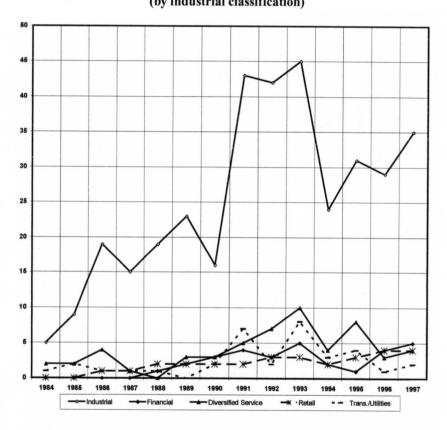

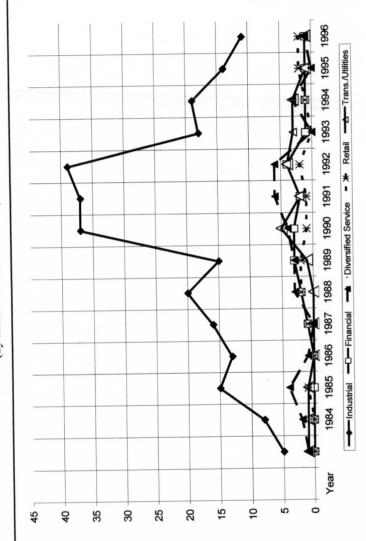

FIGURE 3.2
Intraorganizational Restructuring Charges, 1984–1997
(by industrial classification)

FIGURE 3.3
Accumulative Incidence of Restructuring among Industrial Firms,
1984–1997 (number of firms taking specific number of charges)

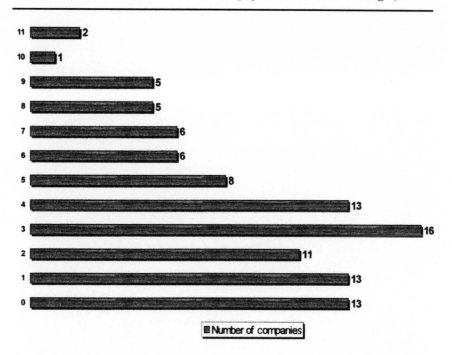

firms rumored to be involved in these takeover deals. External reorganization, by the mid-1980s, was widely recognized as a powerful practice of speculative management. Large increases in equity (stock) valuations were possible through transactions and deal-making.

THE RISE AND REIGN OF INTERNAL RESTRUCTURING

The practice of internal corporate restructuring initiated collaterally with earlier waves of corporate mergers and acquisitions. From comparative data corporate managers presented in their 1984 annual reports, internal reorganization, sometimes even called *restructuring*, clearly

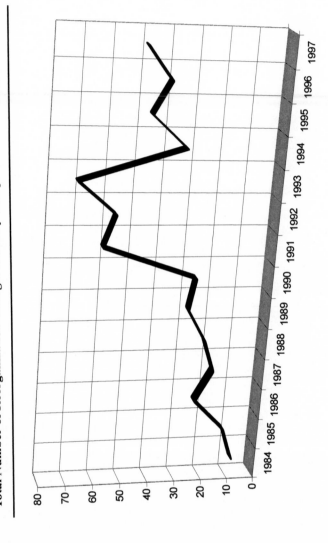

FIGURE 3.4
Total Number of Reorganization Charges Taken by Companies in the Study, 1984–1997

FIGURE 3.5

Total Value of Corporate Restructuring Charges Taken by Companies in the Study, 1984–1997

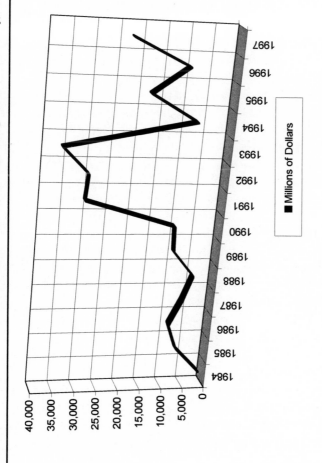

appeared in the financial statements of some firms, although attention was not drawn to restructuring activities in the narrative of the reports during this early period. From 1984 through 1988, internal organizational restructuring activities grew in frequency and began to occupy a more central position in managers' communications with shareholders. However, analysis of the narratives of the corporate reports from this period indicates that most internal corporate restructuring firms recorded during this period were explicitly linked to a prior incident of external reorganization. Internal organizational restructuring arose in conjunction with external restructuring (corporate takeovers, mergers, and acquisitions) in the early 1980s and became a familiar speculative management practice by the end of the decade.

When external reorganizations slowed in 1990, managers pursued internal organizational restructuring as a stand-alone strategy for improving corporate profits and stock prices. The years 1991 through 1993 mark the peak years for internal reorganizations at very large firms (Figure 3.4 and 3.5). Corporate restructuring activity spiked sharply in 1991, increasing from fewer than 30 restructuring initiatives among the 167 companies in 1990 to 60 in 1991. The increase in internal restructuring was related to a decline in the economic conditions that had supported record external reorganization activity in the 1980s. Mergers and takeovers plummeted in 1990 due to several factors, including an impending recession, regulatory actions constraining takeovers, and negative coverage by the business news media of the meltdown of the junk-bond market (see Figure 3.6). In 1990 corporate restructuring ceased to be a synonym for *takeovers* and instead became associated with internal reorganization and downsizing. During the peak period of the early 1990s, internal corporate restructuring was decoupled from external reorganization.

Restructuring charges were of sufficient size to affect profits significantly and, by extension, were important enough to be a strategy of speculative management. One keen British observer of U.S. restructuring describes the use of restructuring to manipulate earnings:

> Substantial restructuring charges have been taken by many big U.S. companies in recent months. They reflect a clearing of the corporate decks, as companies position themselves for a new period of growth. Such charges, often running into billions of dollars, also serve a use-

FIGURE 3.6

Transactional and Internal Reorganization Compared: Dollar Volume of U.S. Mergers, Acquisitions, and Divestitures and Total Number of Internal Restructuring Charges, 1984–1997

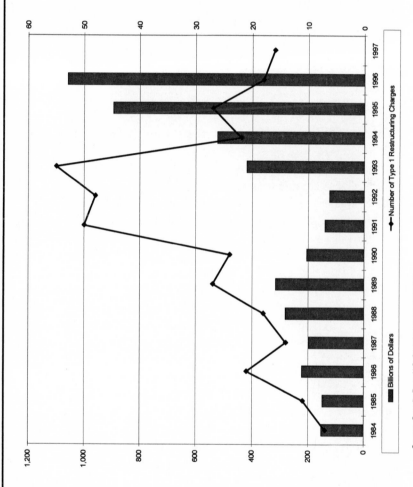

Source: Security Data, U.S. Statistical Abstracts Online

ful accounting purpose. By reporting the charges now, in some cases wiping out current period earnings altogether, companies are able to bring forward costs which they may not actually incur for several years to come. The effect: to produce a more flattering profit trend in future. . . . The SEC clearly feels the whole process is open to abuse. "It looks as if some companies are including in the restructuring charges the costs of ordinary operations—for example advertising, legal settlements and the like," says Mr. Walter Schuetze, the agency's chief accountant. "It may be some of these are ordinary, on-going, necessary, day-to-day costs." (Waters 1994a, p. 12)

Figure 3.7 depicts the average ratio of restructuring charge to total revenue of companies taking restructuring charges in each year of the study. Figure 3.8 depicts the average ratio of restructuring charges to total profit of companies taking restructuring charges in each year of the study. These figures indicate that although the magnitude of restructuring charges seems relatively small compared to the total sales, they are often quite large when compared to profits. Restructuring charges during the peak years of restructuring activity averaged more than 100 percent of corporate profits. In a secondary securities market that values corporations as capitalized earnings, restructuring charges (until 1994) had the capacity to alter radically the assessed valuation of a firm because routine costs could be shifted from future years and included in the restructuring charge. Managers rightly came to view restructuring charges as a powerful mechanism to alter the bottom line and trading price of the firm. *Speculative management* refers to practices managers used to attempt to influence secondary financial markets' valuation of corporate securities. Corporate restructuring emerged as an important speculative management practice.

All three social intermediaries contributed to the rise of internal corporate restructuring as speculative management (Table 3.5). The "takeover" era of external restructuring had strengthened relationships between top managers and big owners of corporate shares and was instrumental in creating big-owner–top-management teams unified by the very strong common interest in stock prices that typifies late-twentieth-century U.S. capitalism. The financial accounting profession ruled in 1986 that restructuring charges could be treated as a legitimate line item in corporate annual reports and allowed managers almost unlimited

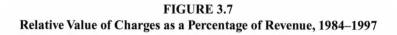

FIGURE 3.7
Relative Value of Charges as a Percentage of Revenue, 1984–1997

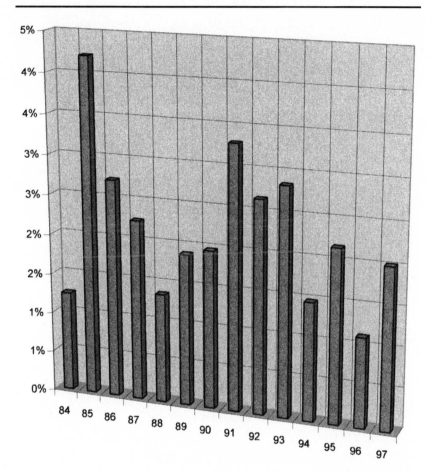

flexibility in the timing and components of these charges. This allowed firms to use restructuring initiatives strategically to manage profits and influence share prices (Table 3.4). The business news media helped to legitimate internal restructuring. In the early 1980s, internal reorganization had been a necessary adjunct to external reorganization as managers sought to restructure production operations in the wake of takeovers. In the late 1980s leading analysts in the business news media

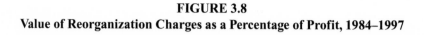

FIGURE 3.8
Value of Reorganization Charges as a Percentage of Profit, 1984–1997

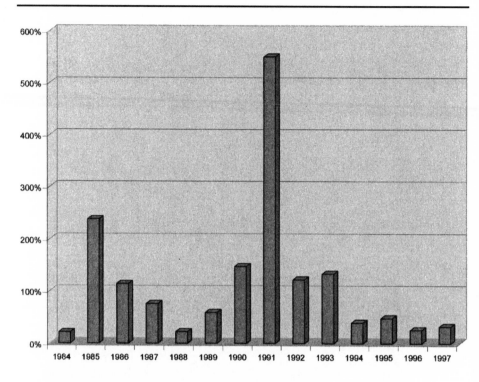

articulated the contribution that internal reorganization had made to the enhancement of corporate profits and share prices. Managers, shareholders, and the business news media all began to view internal reorganization as a distinct, useful, speculative management practice.

The three social intermediaries identified in this chapter also heavily influenced the peak of corporate restructuring (1991 to 1993). Owners and managers controlling U.S. firms, unable to use external reorganization as a speculative management practice, vigorously embraced internal reorganization. During 1992 the SEC approved changes in corporate proxy rules, which govern the relationship between firms and owners to allow groups of owners to meet with each other and with senior management without informing or including the full contingent

TABLE 3.5
The Role of Social Intermediaries in Channeling Restructuring Activity,
1984–1997

	Social Intermediary		
	Accounting Rules	*Big Owner/Top Manager Control Configuration*	*Business News Media*
Period of Emergence 1984–1990 Transaction-based reorganization: leveraged buyouts and hostile takeovers, active "market for corporate control"	• 1986 FASB ruling enables restructuring movement by allowing accounting flexibility for restructuring charges.	• Rise of configuration of financiers in corporate boardroom with the onset of takeover, leveraged buyouts.	• Reported successful gains of business reorganizers. • Carried legitimating rhetoric for pecuniary gains. • Specified logic of restructuring and tracked successes.
High Point of Restructuring 1990–1993 Nontransaction-based reorganization: internal organizational restructuring, downsizing, reengineering	• Accounting authorities withhold further regulation, allowing for continued flexibility and innovation.	• 1992 Proxy rules change formalizes the informal relationship between big owners/top managers. • Allows for legal collusion to boost returns.	• Restructuring portrayed as aggressively good corporate management. • Socially costly, but powerfully profitable for shareholders.
Period of Decline 1994–1997 Reemergence of transaction-based reorganization through stock swap mergers, continued economic growth lessens appeal of downsizing	• EITF issues new disclosure requirements in the fall of 1994, which disallows simulated restructuring, places time restrictions on expenses.	• Pressure to maintain stock prices encourages further innovation and aggressive pursuit of reorganization through mergers/acquisitions/spin-offs.	• Increased scrutiny of downsizing failures, serial restructuring, and the missed opportunities for growth. • Articulated the logic and reported the successes of merger related reorganization strategy.

of shareholders. This formalized the kind of command structure that had been dominant among these very large firms for a decade: small groups of big owners meeting with stock-optioned top officials to direct corporate affairs for the benefit of the inside group. The change in proxy rules was supported by an expansion of stock-option compensation plans among senior executives in U.S. firms and an acceleration of the shareholder rights movement in U.S. capitalism, both of which strengthened the interests binding big owners and top managers. Financial accounting also supported the peak period of restructuring by refraining from constricting the use of restructuring charges. Although some accounting regulators wished to restrict restructuring charges, notably the SEC's chief accountant Walter Schuetze, accounting regulators remained inactive and allowed speculative managers to use restructuring charges strategically (until 1994). A generally uncritical business news media, were willing to pass on management's claims regarding productivity gains that would result from restructuring, also supported the peak of the wave. During this period financial markets commonly increased the valuation of corporate stock dramatically in response to announcements of downsizing and other corporate internal restructuring activities. The analytic business news media reported this relationship and articulated management's rationale for these actions.

THE DECLINE AND DELEGITIMATION OF INTERNAL RESTRUCTURING

The number of internal reorganizations among firms in the study plummeted from 70 in 1993 to slightly more than 30 in 1994 (Figure 3.4 and 3.5). This sharp decline was linked to changes in two of the social intermediaries: a 1994 change in accounting rules governing restructuring charges and an analytic business news media increasingly skeptical about the benefits of restructuring (Table 3.5).

During the 1980s and early 1990s, speculative managers exploited the lax accounting rules for restructuring activities by using these events as opportunities to manipulate their financial results. Future operating costs could be shifted into the restructuring charge, reducing future expenses, improving future profits, and—as this became recognized in financial markets—stimulating stock prices. In the fall of 1994, the EITF, the FASB subcommittee expressly designed to address accounting issues in financial innovations, issued a ruling that constrained the timing

.

and content of restructuring charges. This ruling required full footnote disclosure of specific components of restructuring charges and the timing of the ultimate discharge of these expenses. The ruling further limited the range of items that could be included in restructuring charges and required that severance pay expenses and other costs be actually expensed within a short period of time. Most charges were still allowed, but had to be reported and related to restructuring in far more transparent ways. Charges had to be linked to real expenditures incurred in a reorganization, limiting the utility of restructuring for the management of earnings. This ruling had the effect of drastically reducing corporate restructuring announcements because they no longer led to enhanced market valuations.

Before the new ruling went into effect, the EITF sent a warning letter to 300 very large corporations in the summer of 1994, indicating a pending crackdown on abuses of restructuring charges. These actions effectively blocked the year-end flurry of restructuring initiatives and corresponding charges that had been announced in the three preceding years. The 1994 EITF ruling constrained this flexibility, effectively choking off the wave of business reorganization.

Also significant is that after 1994, the business news media increasingly criticized downsizing, reengineering, and internal corporate restructuring, not only on humanitarian grounds, but also on strictly financial grounds. Many analysts found that the long-term positive benefits of restructuring were nonexistent, whereas the short-term costs of restructuring were considerable. Important opinion leaders in the business news media, such as Morgan Stanley chief economist Stephen Roach and SEC chief Arthur Levitt, conspicuously criticized internal restructuring and downsizing as business practices.

Contributing to the decline in internal reorganization was the improvement in the macroeconomic conditions for external reorganization after 1993. Mergers and acquisitions (and divestitures and spin-offs) set new records every year beginning in 1994 for the remainder of the decade. The attractiveness of external reorganization directed speculative management activity away from internal reorganization. Figure 3.6 graphically depicts the inverse relationship between external reorganization and internal reorganization. Note that the peak of internal restructuring activity corresponds with the trough of mergers and acquisitions.

After the peak downsizing and restructuring years of the early 1990s, internal organizational restructuring declined dramatically when accounting regulators tightened the standards for reporting restructuring activity. Additionally, the business and financial news media increasingly criticized internal reorganization in the form of downsizing and restructuring in the late 1990s, and most large firms no longer considered it a legitimate practice of speculative management by 1997. The reinvigoration of external reorganization in the late 1990s also influenced the decline in the preponderance of internal reorganization. Although the peak of internal reorganization corresponded with the trough of external reorganization during the early 1990s, internal reorganization began to fall in importance as the market for mergers, acquisitions, and divestitures recovered. Managers seeking enhanced equity valuations in the late 1990s increasingly turned to mergers and spin-offs to increase value rather than downsizing.

CONCLUSIONS

Speculative management strongly influenced the rise, reign, and decline of internal reorganization in very large U.S. firms in the late twentieth century. The practice of internal reorganization grew in conjunction with the financially motivated external reorganizations of the 1980s, matured as a stand-alone speculative management practice in the early 1990s, and declined in the late 1990s as social intermediaries altered the effectiveness of restructuring as a speculative management technique. This study supports a broader interpretation of business reorganization in U.S. capitalism that seeks to explain changes in industrial organization in relation to the institutional structures of finance. The social intermediaries linking firms to secondary financial markets are important channeling mechanisms of managerial action and financial market interests.

By the end of the 1990s, firms engaging in internal reorganization often avoided using *downsizing* and *corporate restructuring* as labels for their activities. Many firms explicitly denied in their announcements of internal reorganization initiatives that their plans were to be thought of as downsizing. Rather they were presented as strategic realignments to achieve growth. Many reorganizing firms at the end of the 1990s explicitly linked internal reorganization to a prior external transaction as had happened in the 1980s. Figure 3.9 depicts the decline in the legitimacy of corporate restructuring labels for business reorganization in the late 1990s. This figure breaks down the restructuring initiatives at the

FIGURE 3.9

Reorganization Charges among 100 Industrial Firms, 1984–1997 (by Type)

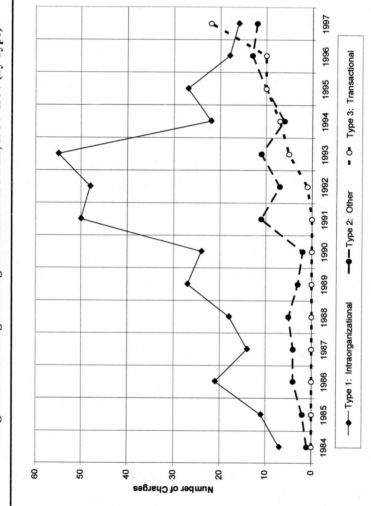

industrial firms in this study into three categories: Type 1 restructuring, which is rhetorically presented in corporate reports as a largely discrete business activity that is described in terms such as *downsizing, restructuring,* and *reengineering*; Type 3 restructuring, which is rhetorically linked to a transaction and described as *merger-related charge,* and *postmerger rationalization*; and Type 2, a default category for other types of initiatives. Figure 3.8 demonstrates that organizational restructuring of the downsizing variety declines steadily throughout the late years of the 1990s, whereas transaction-linked reorganization grows (note that this figure is only applicable for activity after 1990).

Corporate restructuring (internal reorganization) occurred in a wave that began in the 1980s, peaked in the early 1990s, and then declined. A decisive outcome and alleged purpose of corporate restructuring was the promotion of speculative interests. Stock market power was transmitted to firms through the social intermediation of accounting, the media, and governance structures. The chapters that follow explore the role of these social intermediaries in the speculative management of corporate value and interpret the rise, reign, and decline of corporate restructuring as a management practice.

Chapter 4

FINANCIAL ACCOUNTING AS A SOCIAL INTERMEDIARY

Increasingly, I have become concerned that the motivation to meet Wall Street earnings expectations may be overriding common sense business practices. Too many corporate managers, auditors and analysts are participants in a game of nods and winks. . . . I fear that we are witnessing an erosion in the quality of earnings. . . .
  —Arthur Levitt, chairman, Securities and Exchange Commission, in September 1998, commenting on major techniques of accounting "hocus-pocus."[1]

There's probably more pressure to achieve results than at any time that I've seen. Not only do bonuses and stock options depend upon earnings growth, so does a company's ability to do mergers, raise money and survive as an independent entity.
  —J. Terry Strange, head of auditing, KPMG Peat Marwick.[2]

How auditors report these charges in financial statements doesn't change the value of these companies. But the disclosure and transparency of these charges should certainly be improved so investors and analysts can properly assess the value of these companies.
  —Pat McConnell, accounting and tax analyst, Bear, Stearns & Co.[3]

. . . when management in effect reports on itself, the report would not be worth much without some restrictions on their freedom to write A+ report cards. We need rules, in this case, the celebrated GAAP [generally accepted accounting principle], if the accountants are to have some objective standard on which to base their opinions. But GAAP is essential, too, as a fence around management's discretion, which otherwise would know no limits.
  —Louis Lowenstein, author of *Sense and Nonsense in Corporate Finance*, on the tension between accounting and management.[4]

Extra-ordinary or non-recurring additions to income, as well as extraordinary or non-recurring charges to income, the proverbial big bath, tend to be harbingers of ill tidings if they occur with some frequency. The really good news is almost always ordinary news. There is nothing wrong with selling lands or factories at a profit, but too often these transactions were conceived or timed to produce a reportable profit

and to paper over what would otherwise have been a decline in earn-
ings or some other piece of bad news.
—Louis Lowenstein on discretionary expenses and unusual items.[5]

Chapter 3 demonstrated the significance of social intermediaries—
connective structures between corporations and secondary financial
markets—to the rise, reign, and decline of internal corporate restructuring. This chapter and the next develop the conceptualization of social intermediaries and their broad significance in modern capitalism and
corporate affairs. Three social intermediaries are particularly important
for understanding how the speculative logic of modern U.S. secondary
financial markets is transmitted to and exploited by corporations: the financial accounting profession, the business news media—mass and specialized communications media reporting business news, and corporate
governance structures, incorporating certain large owners and top executives.[6] These structures serve as channels that enable actors in financial
markets and corporations mutually to monitor and influence each other
and are critical to U.S. capitalism in recent times.

The widely used term *financial intermediaries*, which designates
institutions between corporations (as users of capital) and primary financial markets (as suppliers of capital), inspired the conception of social intermediaries. Financial intermediaries include investment banks,
commercial banks, and the institutions that support them. Financial intermediaries supply corporations with capital and investors with investments. Corporations relate to primary financial markets through these
institutions to obtain loans or float new equity or debenture securities.
Through bank deposits and security purchases, investors supply funds to
corporations through these institutions. The process of financial intermediation has received extensive attention in academic writing, and indeed the entire field of financial economics was traditionally aimed at
understanding primary markets and the issuance of securities. But this
literature is of limited use for this study because secondary markets have
supplanted primary security markets as the most consequential environment of corporations. This study seeks to develop a conceptualization of
institutional ties between corporations and the increasingly critical secondary market for already-issued corporate securities.

Chapter 2 described the rise of transactional finance in the late
twentieth century that made secondary security markets a permanent

environment toward which corporations and investors continuously orient their actions. Although primary markets and the financial intermediaries that link firms to them are fleetingly critical to corporate management, secondary markets are a chronic aspect of the daily command and control structure of U.S. corporations and were of prime importance for explaining corporate restructuring. In recent times, even primary security markets cannot be fully comprehended without an understanding of secondary market dynamics and the structure and function of social intermediation because boundaries between primary and secondary financial markets are blending. To a considerable degree, successful primary market actions—successful flotation of new securities—depend on secondary market skills such as shrewd trading and speculative management of value. Conceptualizing the way firms are connected to secondary markets is one of the most critical tasks facing twenty-first-century economic sociology.

This chapter focuses on the financial accounting profession, which provides consequential data to financial markets about corporate activities and is arguably the most important link between firms and securities markets. Modern American corporations and financial markets are inconceivable without the modern financial accounting that both guides and monitors financial reporting. Financial accounting data are the most important sources of information used to assess and weigh corporate performance and to assess corporate securities values. Those who seek to understand corporate activity and to interpret, assess, and monitor corporate management turn to financial accounting statements. Corporate managers who wish to convince financial markets that a higher valuation for their firms' securities is warranted attempt to use financial accounting data the firm released as a means to send appropriate signals to the market.

Chapter 5 focuses on the other two intermediaries that were crucial to corporate restructuring: business news media and corporate governance structures. Anglo-American financial markets are impossible to envision without modern business news media. In modern markets the financial news media is a primary mechanism of communication between markets and firms, covering corporate events and developments that affect corporate valuation. Modern business reporting is reflexive and analytical, advancing and critiquing conceptions of aggressively good management, organizing opinion in the financial community. An impressive expansion of financial news on television and an expansion of financial pages in daily newspapers occurred along with the massive growth of participation in the financial stock market of the 1990s. Financial news was disseminated continuously and instantaneously, rather than occasionally with the delivery of the morning newspaper. The growth of electronic media, the Internet, and day trading, which used both of these technologies, made financial markets incredibly responsive to changes in corporate news. Not surprising, then, the financial news media were important for the spread and legitimation of corporate reorganization as a conception of aggressively good business practice.

Chapter 5 also examines a third social intermediary—corporate governance structures that coordinate big owners with top managers. The findings of this study suggest that during the restructuring wave, corporate governance underwent a transformation, creating a community of speculative interests the elite strata of owners and managers shared. The unified interests of elite owners and managers were teamed within corporate governance structures to control corporate responses to and orientations toward secondary financial markets.

These ties between firms and markets—financial accounting, the business news media, and corporate governance structures—are the pathways through which speculative management operates. Corporate actors who wish to attract outside buyers to their stock and otherwise influence markets use these pathways to align corporate events and activities with market conceptions of good management practice. Alternatively, participants in financial markets use these three intermediaries to control and manage corporate activity. Modern equity markets, based on collective assessments of future profits and corporate value, require intermediating structures to operate. Speculative managers must use them to affect the trading price of the firm. These three social intermediaries then are essential structures linking firms to secondary markets, enabling, constraining, and channeling business actions for speculative gain.

Financial accounting is essential to this assessment process. In this chapter, the role that this social intermediary plays in linking firms to secondary markets is described with special emphasis on the determination of corporate value. We begin by examining the use of accounting manipulation or "earnings management" for speculative gain. The chapter then highlights gaps in generally accepted accounting principles (GAAP) that financial innovations create and how such innovations are strategically important to speculative managers who exploit the lack of clear accounting standards to manage income and boost stock prices. Attention turns to the accounting standard-setting process, especially the procedures the accounting profession's EITF used to develop accounting rules for financial innovations such as internal restructuring. The mobilization of business interests, especially speculative interests, and their influence on the standards-setting process, is also discussed. Controversies over new accounting standards reveal the players, the practices, and the interests that contribute to speculative management in the late twentieth century.

FINANCIAL ACCOUNTING AND SPECULATIVE MANAGEMENT

When assessing the value of corporate stock, analysts can chose among several valuation models. They can assess the value of stock in terms of the value of the property that it owns (the asset-backed model), the value of its routine dividend payments (the dividend-payout model) or in terms of its expected future earnings (the capitalized-earnings model). The last model of equity valuation, capitalized earnings, has dominated U.S. secondary markets in recent times. In this model, an assessment is made of the aggregate earnings per share that the corporation will generate in the future. This aggregate is then "discounted" or reduced by an appropriate rate of interest, yielding a final value that is often expressed in terms of the firm's current earnings per share (price-to-earnings ratio). The price-to-earnings ratio of *Fortune* 500 in the late twentieth century ranged from 8 to 25, depending on market estimates of future earnings. Stock analysts make calculations of discounted expected future earnings, a calculation based primarily on the corporation's current earnings per share, which corporations release four times each year. Estimates are adjusted for interest-rate expectations, changes in general economic climate, competitive pressures, product life cycles, political events, and a host of other factors. In a broad way, the consistent appreciation of corporate stock in the 1980s and 1990s was due to analysts' expectations for higher future earnings. Apart from firm-specific factors, the faith in increased earnings was due to the weakness of the labor movement, the end of socialism, the triumph of conservatism, the small and ever-decreasing tax bite on capital earnings, and continual release of a flood of money into secondary markets by retail investors in mutual funds. Social and political factors are involved in the determination of corporate value, but the most important information determining the value of any company is its current earnings.

Corporate managers wishing to convince financial markets that a higher valuation for their firms' securities is warranted look first to the financial accounting data the firm released as a means to send appropriate signals to the market. Because modern financial markets value securities as capitalized earnings, the most important information for the imputation of market value is the accounting data presented in the firm's financial statements. These include a statement of income; a statement of total assets, liabilities, and equity (called a balance sheet); a statement of changes in financial position that occurred during the accounting period; and a host of supporting footnotes to these statements. Members of the accounting profession who are trained in accepted techniques of translating business activity into financial statements prepare and review these data. The rules and procedures of the financial accounting profession constrain and enable the speculative manipulation of financial data in corporate restructuring. Public accountants in the United States apply two lawlike systems of rules in their work. The GAAP are the precedents and statutes that determine the financial-statement impact of corporate activity, including corporate restructuring. Generally accepted auditing standards (GAAS) are the rules governing the independent audit that is required of the financial statements of all publicly traded corporations. Together, GAAP and GAAS determine the manner in which business activity, including restructuring, is translated into financial statements and communicated to stockholders and other audiences of the firm.

Financial accounting data are the basis of market valuation, and changes in accounting rules can have important financial consequences for the corporation and its owners. During the 1990s, for example, many corporations declared large losses attributable to the adoption of new accounting rules required by the FASB. Organized corporate groups contest rule changes. Adopting new rules requires financial-statement recognition, and although financial statements may naïvely present the effect of these changes, they may also be exploited as an opportunity to improve financial results. These rules determine performance on key financial indicators, such as net income, earning before taxes, and cash generated. To affect stock prices, improvements in production efficiency must be filtered through the rules of evidence and procedures of financial accounting. If financial profits unexpectedly fall, investors are most likely to reassess the value of a company. Speculative management is particularly useful at these moments of reassessment. Management often attempts to forestall the "earnings surprise" by announcing to analysts who follow the stock that profits will be down well in advance of the formal release date of the figures. This allows management to "package" the disappointing earnings figures with legitimating rhetoric with a story aimed at shoring up demand for the firm's stock.[7] If management thinks earnings for a particular quarter will fall below street estimates, then it seeks to cushion the impact of the earnings surprise by releasing its own "earnings estimate" with a covering rationale.

An example is the preemptive, carefully packaged earnings release that prompted a 13 percent drop in the value of the shares of Campbell Soup in February 1999:

> Yesterday, the Camden, NJ, food company startled investors with a morning disclosure that it expects profit to fall short of expectations. . . . Campbell blamed unusually warm weather for slower sales of condensed soup, its principal business. . . . But analysts are skeptical that warm weather in November and December was the primary culprit. Rather, Wall Street believes consumers are shunning condensed soup for other, less transitory reasons. . . . "To blame the majority of this issue on warm weather is a little too optimistic," said John McMillin of Prudential Securities, Inc. "The fact is that condensed soup is used primarily for cooking, and Campbell is discovering that, no matter how much it spends on marketing, it can't get people to cook more." (O'Connell 1999, p. A7)

Management preannounced the shortfall in profits and included a covering story that sought to prevent analysts from lowering their expectations for future profits for the firm. Analysts however did reassess and lower the value of the firm, and the shares dropped 13 percent. Speculative management exploits and manipulates the intimate relationship among stock prices, accounting data, and the market processing of information.

In recent times, corporate managers often attempt to deliver profit and revenue numbers that conform to (or exceed) market expectations security analysts set. Several information agencies, including First Call, aggregate, organize, and publicize analyst opinions. Indeed, Internet access has made the proprietary earnings expectations of security analysts widely available. These analysts, unlike average shareholders, have direct access to and are actively courted by speculative managers who aggressively seek favorable recommendations from the analysts who cover their firm (Dunlap 1996, for example). This study brings into view the way inside members of corporate speculative management teams rely on these estimates to determine targets for speculative management. Business news media judgments of corporate performance are often based on a comparison of analyst estimates with reported corporate performance. Beating the street estimate was an effective means of increasing security values in the late twentieth century.

The imperative for managers to match street estimates, the consensus or average opinion of analysts for the firm's earnings, is illustrated in the following case of accounting manipulation at W. R. Grace and Co. In this example, the firm actually reduced its earnings in years when it exceeded analysts' estimates and held them in a sort of reserve account, where they could be used to shore up earnings in a year when the company fell below analysts' estimates:

> The Securities and Exchange Commission, in the latest crackdown on alleged accounting fraud, accused W. R. Grace & Co. and former senior executives of manipulating the chemical maker's earnings over five years. The Civil Complaint, filed yesterday in federal court in Miami, alleges that from 1991 through 1995, Grace inappropriately used reserves to report inaccurate results for the company. . . . "Extra earnings were put into a reserve to save for a rainy day so they could use it when they wanted to goose up the numbers," said Richard Walker, SEC enforcement director. . . . The alleged violations occurred when Grace owned National Medical Care Inc., which made medical products and provided kidney-dialysis and home-health services. The Waltham, Mass., unit, which Grace sold in 1995, produced an unexpectedly large part of Grace's earnings. To avoid showing profit that exceeded Wall Street estimates, the company allegedly set aside National Medical's earnings in an "excess reserve" fund. The reserve was drawn down to bring Grace's reported earnings and per-share earnings in line with financial targets, the SEC said. . . . (Schroeder 1998, p. A22)

W. R. Grace's managers learned firsthand of hazards that follow from failing to meet analyst estimates or of failing to frame such failure in a manner financial markets accept as legitimate when their corporate stock declined 10 percent on the day of the preceding announcement. The relationship between accounting techniques, financial statements, financial news media, and stock prices is further illustrated in the following case:

In early October 1997 a Connecticut-based food service company called Fine Host Corp. was flying high. Going public in 1996 at $12, it was at $42 barely a year later. A half-dozen analysts followed the company. . . . All were rhapsodic over its future. Two months later Fine Host warned investors that its accounting in recent years was "aggressive." That day the stock hit $10, culminating a long decline that wiped out more than 75 percent of its all-time-high price. Just how aggressive the accounting was became clear in mid-February. Even before going public, Fine Host had failed to book expenses properly and recorded profits on food-service contracts earlier than was proper. Sorry, a new management said, we'll restate earnings. Restate is putting it mildly. For the 3 ¾ preceding years Fine Host had reported total earnings of $13 million. Oops! Make that a loss of nearly $18 million. NASDAQ delisted the shares for almost three months. They began trading again March 3, fetching $3.63 each. . . . (Condon 1998, p. 124)

In this case, accounting rules apparently were not a sufficient constraint on overly aggressive inflation of corporate profits, lying close to the line separating speculative management from corporate crime. After the corporate scandals involving Enron, Arthur Andersen, WorldCom, and other firms that made headlines throughout 2001 and 2002, business news media and political attention heavily covered the scandals in terms of corporate crime. This study wishes to avoid shifting undo attention onto cases in which accounting rules were clearly and criminally broken. Attention is instead focused on the more significant and numerous cases in which the flexibility of rules was pushed up to, but not past, the breaking point. This study draws attention to noncriminal, routine corporate orientation to speculative management through strategic navigation of the institutionalized order of financial accounting—the surprisingly sophisticated bending of accounting rules for speculative purposes rather than the crude breaking of them.

Among the most widely discussed accounting scandals of the late 1990s was Waste Management, which had aggressively booked earnings throughout the period. In February 1998 the company was forced to restate its financial statements from 1992 through 1996, essentially erasing 40 percent of the profits it had booked during this period (a total of $3.5 billion) with a devastating effect on its stock price (Condon 1998, p. 125). The practices at Waste Management did not greatly differ from what was rewarded as aggressively good management and was widely practiced at other firms.

The accounting function at most corporations occurs under the supervision and oversight of an audit committee, a subcommittee of the board of directors. The audit committee is responsible for reviewing and scrutinizing financial statements, the operation of financial controls within the firm, and the annual independent audit of the firm's operations. As argued in the next chapter, the members of the governance structure in late-twentieth-century U.S. firms, senior executives, big owners, and outsider notables, share an interest in the value of corporate securities. When members of the audit committee were compensated with stock and stock options, as they increasingly were during the 1990s, they had an interest in the appreciation of security values and the approval of aggressive accounting techniques to achieve it, compromising their oversight. Equity compensation of corporate directors encouraged, rather than restrains, aggressive accounting treatment.

In 1998 numerous highly publicized accounting fiascoes led to dramatic declines in market valuations; Sunbeam, Cendant, and Waste Management are the three firms that received most extensive business news media coverage. In each of these firms, aggressive accounting practices that overstated earnings were reversed, causing a meltdown of the firms' stock prices. Sunbeam and Cendant both lost more than half of their market value shortly after the reversal of overstated earnings. As described in chapter 1, Sunbeam shares eventually lost all of their value. (The Waste Management case is discussed later herein.) In the wake of these accounting fiascoes, the SEC began an inquiry into the role of the board of directors in overseeing the financial statements of management on behalf of the shareholders. The SEC inquiry is concerned that audit "committees are failing to do their jobs properly because their members are either unqualified or are too close to company management." A study conducted by Directorship, a research firm in Greenwich, Conn., found that 125 of 860 publicly held companies reviewed had "current or former insiders on their audit panels" in 1998 (Lublin and MacDonald 1999). Furthermore, some of the companies had immediate relatives of CEOs on the audit committee. Criticisms of the composition and independence of corporate directors escalated after 2000 in the wake of the corporate scandals at Enron and other firms.

ACCOUNTING RULES AND THE MANAGEMENT OF ACCOUNTING PROFITS

Analysts of comparative economic systems have noted the relative "transparency" of Anglo-American capitalism. The business news media and the financial accounting profession provide a far more comprehensive view into the workings of Anglo-American firms than their counterparts in other economic systems. In a relative sense this comparison with continental capitalist firms is valid. My research (and experience as an auditor), however, has encouraged me to explore how this apparent transparency is actually opaque in practice. How do the rules and practices designed to make firms visible to outsiders simultaneously provide opportunities for strategic representation of the firm in a light favorable to the interests of those who own and control it? Regulations in the United States do require firms to publicize quarterly financial information and comprehensive annual, audited financial reports; financial market participants do rely heavily on these reports when assessing value. But precisely because corporations know that market participants are watching, U.S. firms have an incentive to conceal the bad and exaggerate the good, turning the intended constraint of regulatory filings into an opportunity to boost market value. Regulated, audited financial statements do not provide candid snapshots of firms, but carefully posed and idealized portraits.

A financial statement as something other than a naïve reflection of corporate business activity is demonstrated in the following example, which also shows how accounting information affects stock prices. In April 1999 McKesson, a large company, announced in a news release that "accounting improprieties" had been discovered in the books of its recently acquired HBO and Co., a health-care information business. The accounting adjustment required the firm to restate 1999 earnings, lowering them by $42 million, on which the trading price of the firm's securities dropped 48 percent, shaving $9.7 billion from the firm's market value. In the aftermath of the scandal, McKesson's board of directors fired the CEO and five other top executives for the accounting scandal that "allegedly involved 'intentional deception.'" HBO had grown rapidly during the 1990s by engaging in a series of stock-swap mergers, made possible by HBO's high stock price. HBO had attained a high market value by delivering unfaltering, growing earnings "as promised quarter after quarter [, which] . . . delighted analysts." Apparently, these results were at least partially manufactured. Insiders at HBO had booked sales that were not final, backdated sales contracts to inflate quarterly revenues and profits, and booked as sold software that merely had been shipped to offsite locations. The rapid decline in share price in the wake of the discovery of accounting manipulation demonstrates the financial markets' dependence on the financial information contained in accountants' reports (King 1999, p. A3).

Speculative managers have an incentive to manipulate their firms' financial reports to boost stock values. The academic literature on "earnings management" reveals that certain corporate events frequently increase the incentives for firms to manage earnings. Stock options and other forms of equity compensation, threats of takeovers, and rapid market reactions for lower-than-expected earnings all promote earnings management. Analysts therefore focus almost entirely on "earnings per share and the associated price-earnings ratio" (Samuels, Brayshaw, and Craner 1995, p. 41). Several researchers have found that companies often engage in earnings management prior to issuing additional equity shares on public markets. The capital "seasoned offerings" (as opposed to IPOs) raise is affected by the current trading price of existing shares, which are, in turn, affected by the earnings of the firm.

Managers use a variety of accounting practices to manipulate or manage earnings, including *discretionary accruals*,[8] which are adjustments to financial statements that are not linked to transactions that require judgment to determine the proper amount to be recorded and are therefore sources of significant accounting flexibility. Accruals and other accounting manipulations to boost earnings prior to a seasoned offering, therefore, increase the amount of capital brought into the firm (Srinivasan 1998; Teoh, Welch, and Wong 1998). Pourciau (1993) demonstrates that incoming management teams will often take discretionary accruals to decrease earnings for the year that they come on board, thus increasing earnings for future years (by cost shifting). Similarly, when new management comes in after a proxy battle, the new management will most likely take a large "big bath" accounting charge to improve future performance (Collins and DeAngelo 1990). One researcher found that when analysts reach a consensus in their earnings forecasts, "managers have an incentive to manage earnings through discretionary accruals to achieve market expectations" (Robb 1998, p. 315). In a sample of banks, Robb found that if analysts reach a consensus on expected earnings, managers manipulate a discretionary accrual, the loan loss provision, to bring earnings in line with analyst expectations.

Two business school professors at the University of California, Irvine, Carla Hayn and Dan Givoly, studied financial statements of hundreds of firms for a period beginning in the 1950s and continuing through 1996. They note that:

> Companies have over time taken ever-larger write-offs and taken them sooner, something that has substantially depressed book value. For example, for their sample they found that between 1973 and 1996, the average ratio of a company's stock price to its book value per share doubled to 3.4 from 1.7, consistent with the widespread view that stocks are at record valuations. But when the academics added back to book value all the "discretionary accruals," primarily write-offs that the companies took over that time the ratio began and ended the period unchanged at 1.6, well below its level typical of the 1960s. (Ip 1998c, p. C1)

These two researchers attribute the growth of accounting write-offs to an increase in accounting "conservatism" (that is, modesty in future-earnings claims) by corporate managers. "In aggregate, we feel the quality [of reported earnings] has improved" (Ip 1998d, p. C1). Such an interpretation neglects speculative management. Another explanation, consistent with the findings and viewpoint of this study, is that write-offs have increased in size and frequency because they are potent tools to manage financial statements and to affect the price of corporate securities. Write-offs are an effective speculative management technique for various reasons. Companies use write-offs to smooth income, to inflate income in future years, and to increase the current year's income by shifting costs into a big bath charge. In all of these cases, write-offs and other discretionary accruals allow management to deliver earnings to meet or exceed market expectations. By the late 1990s, the magnitude and prevalence of discretionary accruals were scrutinized in the business news media:

> Write-offs indeed have become part of the landscape. Last year, for example, reported S&P 500 profits rose just 2.6 percent. But Goldman

Sachs estimates that after adding back write-offs, which nearly doubled last year, profits were up 10 percent. (Ip 1998d, p. C1)

Employing large, discretionary write-offs has often been used to enable managers to practice income smoothing. Income smoothing is the practice of discreetly, but actively, removing quarterly fluctuations in earnings to create a smooth and predictably increasing trend line that financial markets reward with higher valuations. Of two companies with identical total earnings over say a five-year period, one with consistent or smooth earnings will have a higher market value than one with sporadic earnings. Financial markets award premium value to predictability, and corporate managers routinely engage in earnings management to smooth income (see, for example, Burgstahler and Dichev 1998, Chaney and Lewis 1995). Effective income smoothing neatly combines financial accounting with conformity to a prominent conception of aggressively good management. General Electric, which Jack Welch headed during the late twentieth century, had for many years the highest market value of any corporation (although not the highest revenues, employees, or earnings per share). The source of the high value was GE's famously unbroken string of progressively increasing quarterly earnings for 20 years. Managers typically use "discretionary accruals" to manage financial results and smooth their earnings (Chaney and Lewis 1998), understating earnings in particularly good years in anticipation of future bad years and overstating in bad years. This enables a firm to meet analysts' expectations consistently, a key to high valuation (Defond and Park 1997).

An important study of income smoothing, *Smoothing Income Numbers: Objectives, Means, and Implications* (Ronen and Sadan 1981), demonstrates that income smoothing is a long-rooted and pervasive distortion of financial statements. Income smoothing was recognized as a managerial objective in the accounting literature in the 1950s, when it became clear to some analysts that "maximizing profit" in any given year resulted in lower equity valuations than reporting smooth but increasing earnings over a period of years. Although Ronen and Sadan do not emphasized this, the rise of income smoothing as a managerial objective coincides with the rise of conglomerate firms (which required stock-swap mergers and, therefore, high valuations).

The income that managers most often smooth is ordinary income or income from operations. This is the bottom line figure of prime interest to security analysts, who essentially ignore nonrecurring revenues and expenses—such as nonoperating income and unusual or extraordinary items—when assessing corporate value. The rationale is that recurring, or ordinary, income enables analysts to best assess the profitability of the firm as a viable business:

> Presumably the object of smoothing is selected by management according to its perception regarding what accounting information is utilized by those users that influence its compensation. Management is not indifferent to what particular measure is selected by users, and it may indeed attempt, through its signaling activity, to affect their choice. (Ronen and Sadan 1981, p. 59)

Ronen and Sadan (1981) found that corporate managers engaged in significant amounts of income smoothing.[9] Their primary motive was speculative: they wished to affect the stock market price. There were other self-interested, opportunistic reasons for income smoothing. Managers could enhance their own wealth in special circumstances by manipulating corporate income. Certain performance-sensitive pay plans established a ceiling or a floor to the amount of income subject to bonus payment, and managers smoothed earnings to them consistently within those parameters. Ronen and Sadan do not specifically address the effect of mostly stock compensation on management smoothing action. But their work confirms that managers smooth income using extraordinary items such as restructuring charges when it was in their interest to do so. This study emphasizes that executive stock options and influential large stockholders directed corporate interest toward speculative management and provided a clear rationale for income smoothing and other financial statement engineering.

Earnings may also be "managed" by altering the assumptions used to calculate discretionary accruals, such as depreciation expenses. The following is a description of how such accruals, which even in the best circumstances are subjective, judgment-based estimates open to strategic manipulation, were used to manage income:

> In 1987 General Motors decided to increase the estimated useful lives of its plant and equipment, thus reducing that year's depreciation and amortization charges—and increasing pretax earnings—by over $1.2

billion. The change accounted for $1.28 of the company's $5.03 of net earnings per share that year. (Lowenstein 1991, p. 99)

General Motors reported an increase in earnings between 1985 and 1989 even though its sales of vehicles declined from 9.3 million units to fewer than 8 million during this period. A close examination of GM's financial statements reveals that they took advantage of an array of flexible accounting rules to shore up their financial results. First, it decreased its depreciation expenses during this period by assuming a longer useful life for its auto plants and equipment (1987 and subsequent years). Second, it decreased the pension expense and actually booked a pension gain by changing assumptions of its pension plan—assumed a shorter life expectancy of workers and a higher rate of return on pension assets (1986 and subsequent years). These two changes alone accounted for more than $1 billion of 1989 after-tax earnings and accounted for all of the increase in earnings between 1985 and 1989. Importantly, GM accomplished this "earnings management" without breaking any GAAPs, but merely by following rules that allowed for flexibility (Lowenstein 1991, p. 103).

Firms can also manage their earnings by engaging in sham transactions that allow them to record gains:

> In 1981, when American Express's earnings growth was lagging, its Fireman's Fund subsidiary traded essentially identical pension liabilities with another insurance company. The trade, technically a reinsurance treaty, did not significantly affect the two companies' respective risks. For both insurance companies, however, the accounting effect was to accelerate to 1981 and 1982 income that would otherwise not have been realized, and under GAAP could not be booked, for a number of years. A senior officer at Fireman's Fund conceded that the purpose of the transaction, which was not disclosed to the American Express board of directors until the story broke in the press, was to circumvent the rule against recognizing unrealized income. The eventual disclosure made a shambles of Fireman's Fund's boast of record earnings. For its parent, American Express, the liability swap accounted for 45 percent of the "increase" in profits for 1982. (Lowenstein 1991, p. 102)

Investigations into the Enron scandal revealed that Enron (and Dynnergy, CMS Energy, Reliant, and other firms) heavily exploited

TABLE 4.1
Areas of Financial Accounting Subject to Manipulation for Earnings Management

1. Write-down of preacquisition costs or potential future costs
2. Profits on disposal of a business
3. Deferred purchase consideration
4. Extraordinary and exceptional items of income and expenditure
5. Off-balance-sheet finance
6. Contingent liabilities
7. Capitalization of costs
8. Brand accounting (classifying goodwill as brand value, which does not have to be expensed)
9. Changes in depreciation policy
10. Convertible securities
11. Pension fund accounting
12. Treatment of foreign currency items

Source: Samuels, Brayshaw, and Craner 1995, p. 38.

similar, largely fictitious swaps between legally related entities to generate revenue and profit in the late 1990s and 2000.

Firms seeking to manipulate their financial results used numerous additional techniques in the late twentieth century. Table 4.1 shows one authority's compilation of areas of financial accounting that are subject to discretionary manipulation within GAAP. In other words, management can manipulate these areas without necessarily violating accounting rules.[10]

ACCOUNTING FLEXIBILITY SURROUNDING FINANCIAL INNOVATION

Accounting rules are sufficiently flexible to allow for strategic manipulation of income by corporate controllers with an interest in boosting stock prices. However, some areas of financial accounting allow for greater flexibility and managerial discretion than others and these were of high strategic value for speculative management in the late twentieth century. One such important area of accounting flexibility surrounds financial innovations. The GAAP, the lawlike system of rules that guide financial accounting, are developed in a manner not unlike the common law.

Innovations generate a variety of accounting treatments as practitioners stretch existing precedents to translate the innovative activity into the financial statements of the firm. Statutelike rules emerge, if at all, only after a pattern of practice has been established and a kind of consensus has emerged as to the best accounting representation. Financial innovations, then, generate a gap in GAAP, a period of accounting flexibility during which accounting practitioners and governing boards deliberate about the best way to recognize the innovation on financial statements. Novel financial innovations provide an opportunity for managers to manipulate corporate results and market valuation strategically. As discussed following, a portion of the regulatory structure of the accounting profession, the EITF of the FASB, creates standards for financial innovations.

Aggressive accounting around financial innovations can yield significant increases in corporate equity values. The business news media may decry these aggressive tactics, but often only after lowered stock values discredits them. The following selection from a *Wall Street Journal* editorial, "Flaky Accounting on the March?" reviews the dramatic drop in share prices after aggressive accounting was discredited in several large corporations (including Sunbeam, Cendant, Waste Management, WorldCom, and W. R. Grace). The editorial highlights the nature of accounting as an important area of aggressively good management, and it defends corporate managers for pushing the line of acceptability in accounting treatment of transactions in trying to use accounting treatments that will boost shareholder value:

> Surely when uncertainty exists over what constitutes permissible accounting, some of the competition between companies will be transferred into the accounting area. If it becomes the norm when doing technology mergers to take a big write-off for research and development efforts (one of the SEC's *bêtes noires*) a company would be almost irresponsible not to take a write-off if its peers are taking one. By such means does the inherent and necessary flexibility in GAAP give rise to informal traditions that make for comparability. Moreover, except by selling out his stake and fleeing to the Bahamas in the rosy glow of a doctored earnings report, it's hard to see how a CEO could be anything but the victim of his own doctoring. . . . Arguably, the SEC should exercise some leadership to keep companies from chasing each other to the edge of absurdity when the rules are inescapably arbitrary to begin with. ("Flaky Accounting" 1999, p. A14)

Therefore managers are largely excused for knowing manipulations of accounting, as long as these have the potential to be acceptable. But the SEC sees things differently, and the editorial notes that the SEC's position indicates that the curtailment of aggressive accounting to boost income (and stock prices) is a major obligation of public accounting. As the preceding quotation makes plain, members of the accounting profession are often brought on board as adjunct members of the speculative management team. Rather than constraining the manipulation of earnings to boost equity values, they are the experts that assist speculative management in subtly stretching accounting rules:

> Mr. Levitt has been hell on the auditing profession, which he charges has been reluctant to challenge "aggressive" accounting because the Big Five get half their revenue from consulting work for many of the same companies whose books they flyspeck. True, surveys by Business Week and CFO magazines separately reported that half of financial executives claim to have been pressured by their bosses to tweak the books in a flattering direction. ("Flaky Accounting" 1999, p. A14)

From the viewpoint of this study, the exploitation of financial innovations for their accounting flexibility is an effective technique of speculative management. Speculative management teams have a clear incentive to deliver accounting reports that will enhance the value of equity shares. The financial accounting profession serves both to restrain efforts to manipulate income and to channel them in particular directions. Financial accounting does not constitute an iron set of regulations. Managers are held bound, but loosely, so that sufficient play remains within accounting rules and practices to allow for the strategic manipulation of indicators of value in financial markets. Understanding how financial accounting contributed to the rise, reign, and decline of corporate restructuring in the late twentieth century requires us to view accounting not only as a constraining structure, but also as an institutionalized order that allows for managerial agency. The constraint of accounting practices surrounding financial innovations is particularly loose and the most important innovation of the late 1980s and early 1990s, exploited heavily for its accounting flexibility, was corporate restructuring.

The legal restructuring of corporate divisions as subsidiaries facilitated the exploitation of accounting flexibility for speculative management (Prechel 1997, 2000; Prechel and Boies 1998). Anglo-American accounting and auditing rules evolved as workable representations of corporations organized in divisions, enabling financial market monitoring of corporate activity. The labyrinthine complexity of the MLSF is not readily translated into corporate financial statements. The thicker the layering of subsidiaries and divisions, the more difficult becomes the accounting and auditing problem and the greater the scope for speculative management. In the most complex MLSF corporations, such as General Electric, financial statements provide a view so murky that only the bottom line is clear. Analysts' singular focus on operating earnings is made necessary by their literal inability to focus on anything else.

SETTING ACCOUNTING STANDARDS: THE ROLE OF THE EMERGING ISSUES TASK FORCE

The 15-member EITF was created in 1984 as a "response by FASB to identify and to address problems with the implementation of accounting standards and other emerging accounting issues on a timely basis. In other words, when the accounting standards process is too slow, or existing standards fail to address practice, then EITF comes to the rescue" (*American Banker–Bond Buyer* 1994a, p. 5). Between 1984 and 1994, the committee addressed more than 250 accounting issues. The EITF members are mostly practitioners of public accounting, but also include corporate accountants and representatives of accounting trade associations. The SEC's chief accountant, during this period Walter Schuetze, was a participant in discussions but not a formal EITF member. The EITF would arrive at a consensus on an issue and deliver a "consensus letter" to the FASB. The SEC chief accountant has the authority to override any consensus the EITF reaches, but this is rarely exercised.

> The EITF mandate is to deal with transactions that are not contemplated by the accounting literature, perceived abuses or inappropriate answers to accounting, or issues where a diversity of practice has arisen and no guidance seems to apply. In essence, the task force plugs the holes where accounting standardization and regulations fail. (*American Banker–Bond Buyer* 1994a, p. 5)

Significantly, the EITF opens up the process of accounting standards setting to the lobbying power of organized business interests. Prior to the mid-1980s, the FASB and other accounting standard setting bodies were not particularly open to pressure groups outside the accounting profession. The regulatory bodies comprised members of the public accounting profession, leaders in the auditing field.[11] Standards were determined on technical criteria to be consistent with the somewhat arcane GAAP that govern the profession. As with other accounting standards-setting bodies today, the EITF is less sealed off from the business world at large and is more susceptible to outside influence. Rather than accounting standards being set by technicians whose primary concerns are accounting principles, the EITF balances the technical requirements of accurate accounting against the wishes of corporate interests. In composition, the EITF includes members from corporate finance and accounting departments, who use their positions to block the passage of standards that would be detrimental to their corporations. Today the standards-setting procedure is much like the legislative procedure—it attracts intensive lobbying efforts by organized interests who seek to veto any attempt to limit a favorable or flexible accounting practice. In the 1990s, the issues attracting the most intensive business-interest lobbying efforts were all related to speculative management: recognition of restructuring charges, accounting for stock options, derivatives, and merger accounting.

Business mobilization was also evident in issues surrounding merger accounting. In May 1996 the FASB proposed to limit the ability of merging corporations to employ favorable pooling of interest accounting procedures. Corporations favor the pooling of interest method because it avoids the financial statement recognition of goodwill, an amount equal to the purchase price of an acquired firm that cannot be attached to specific assets. Goodwill is a strange accounting entity known as an abstract asset, and it is slowly removed from the firm's books by recognizing periodic goodwill amortization expense. Goodwill is bad speculative management because it reduces the accounting profits of the firm and does so for many years. Good speculative managers, then, sought to avoid it by manipulating their acquisition procedures to qualify for pooling of interest accounting. This required the retirement of existing shares of stock in both of the merged firms and the issuance of new, pooled shares (in a predetermined formula) to replace them.

In the 1990s some corporations almost immediately repurchased shares on the open market equal to the value of the acquired enterprise. Because these acquisitions were in effect a purchase, the swapping of stock being a mere pretext to obtain favorable accounting treatment, FASB proposed to disallow the use of pooling of interest accounting if a corporation issued stock to consummate a pooling merger, but then repurchased the newly issued stock. FASB recognized that many companies were simply using stock as an intermediate currency to carry out mergers that were really purchases to avoid the recognition of goodwill:

> Michael Sutton, the SEC's chief accountant, says the new rule isn't intended to affect the economics of any transaction but to make sure the accounting used is correct. "We didn't write the rule to cause companies to buy back or not buy back their stock." But accountants say that the SEC generally is wary of pooling transactions because companies tend to orchestrate their acquisitions to avoid goodwill. (Burton 1996, p. A3)

Because goodwill reduces earnings, avoiding it raises earnings and, hence, market value. Because transactional reorganization was such a large component of speculative management practice in the late twentieth century, merger accounting rules remained an open and contested accounting issue throughout the period. For example, in 1998 the FASB proposed a change in the rules for merger accounting that would force corporations to accelerate the amortization of goodwill. Prevailing standards held that the goodwill generated by a merger or acquisition must be amortized or expensed against earnings over the lesser of the useful life of the assets acquired or 40 years. Given this choice, most firms chose to spread goodwill amortization over the maximum 40-year period to minimize the yearly drag on earnings. The new proposal sought to force corporations to identify specifically the useful life of the assets acquired in a merger, and to expense the goodwill over this typically short period. Rather than simply implementing the rule change, the FASB published its proposal in February and gave business executives a period of several months in which to comment on the proposal before it would be formally considered for adoption in the fall (MacDonald 1998a, p. A2).

THE EMERGING ISSUES TASK FORCE AND THE 1994 CONTROVERSY OVER EXECUTIVE STOCK OPTIONS

Stock options were the tool that welded big owners and top managers into speculative management teams with an interest in high stock prices. The magnitude of executive stock compensation doubled between 1987 and 1993 and most likely doubled again before the end of the decade. Stock options became a primary form of executive compensation, rather than a fringe benefit around the edge of large salaries, and were critical to the accumulation of executive wealth.

Looking back on the major accounting issues of the 1990s, the accounting dispute generating the most organized opposition was not the alteration of restructuring write-offs, but rather the proposed alteration of accounting rules for executive stock options. Not coincidentally, efforts to tighten restructuring accounting and efforts to tighten stock option accounting appeared on the agenda of accounting standards setting boards at the same time because both of them were intimately connected to the rise of speculative management in the late twentieth century.

In 1994 the EITF announced plans to change accounting procedures for recognizing executive and director stock options in financial statements. Unlike salaries and other forms of compensation, stock options do not generate transactions for the firm and are not recognized in the financial statements. One reason corporate managers like stock options is that they allow the full costs of executive compensation to remain largely hidden from investors who review the financial statements of the firm. Strictly speaking, the corporation does not pay the executives the stock options, but merely grants them. If executives seek to turn these options into cash, they must first exercise the options by buying the shares of stock from the company at the strike price and then reselling the shares on the open market, pocketing the difference as capital gains income. Strictly speaking then, it is not the corporation but other investors purchasing the shares of stock from the executives who pay the executive the compensation embedded within the stock option.[12] Hence, this is a very attractive form of compensation—it can be extremely large without being recognized in the financial statements of the firm.

When the EITF tried to force corporations to recognize the cost of executive stock options, the *Wall Street Journal* reported that this proposal met the most focused, organized attack against the EITF and

FASB of any previous proposal. This proposal was being considered during the very period that the EITF was considering the changed rules on restructuring charges. Furthermore, the SEC's chief accountant, Walter Schuetze, resigned immediately after this period.

> Corporate stock options can turn well-paid executives into extremely well-paid executives—and into Washington lobbyists. MCI Communications Corp.'s chief executive officer, Douglas Maine, is working the Senate. Citicorp's chief executive, John Reed, recently bent the ear of Arthur Levitt Jr., chairman of the Securities and Exchange Commission. Raychem Corp.'s chief executive, Robert Saldich, cornered Commerce Secretary Ron Brown in California, then snagged a few minutes with Deputy Treasury Secretary Roger Altman. . . . The executives' cause: stopping the Financial Accounting Standards Board from requiring companies to calculate the value of certain employee stock options and charge that amount against earnings for the first time. The complaints about the obscure accounting-rules body have even reached President Clinton. "I've never seen the amount of corporate anxiety that this issue has raised," Mr. Levitt says. . . . Seventy witnesses plan to address FASB . . . in five days of public hearings that begin today in Stamford, Conn., near the board's Norwalk headquarters. (Harlan 1994, p. A1)

The proposal to force corporations to recognize stock options in their financial statements was initially considered in 1984, and the *Wall Street Journal* reported that the resurrection of this proposal came about after President Clinton's election, when he promised to raise taxes on the wealthy. Clinton's election triggered an avalanche of executives cashing in their stock options before Clinton took office. For example, in the winter of 1992, Walt Disney's Chairman Michael Eisner and other executives exercised stock options to buy 6.6 million shares of Disney; 5.1 million shares were immediately resold for a $187 million profit.

Pearl Meyer and Associates, a compensation consulting firm, estimates that nearly 30 percent of top manager compensation was in the form of stock options in 1993, up from an estimated 17 percent in 1987. The ratio is much higher for some firms, especially high-tech firms such as the Internet stocks and for "turnaround" firms such as Scott Paper and Sunbeam. Both granted Al Dunlap the bulk of his compensation in the form of stock options. Michigan Democratic Senator Carl Levin supported the FASB's efforts to force reporting of stock options.

A high stock options grant is "misleading to potential investors, dilutes the value of the stock held by current shareholders, short-changes the company by foregoing capital and jeopardizes employee morale. . . . It also encourages compensation excess because options can be given without reporting any cost to the corporation" (Harlan 1994, p. A1).

The executives in the *Wall Street Journal* article used the same shareholder value logic to argue against the FASB ruling that they use to justify their stock options in the first place. Raychem's CEO Robert Saldich, who received more than half of his more than $2 million compensation in the form of stock options in 1993, said that when he first learned of the FASB's proposal, "The first stage I went through was total rage. . . . [The plan would hurt more than] just fat-cat business guys like me" (Harlan 1994, A1).

> If companies had to take a charge, executives warn, earnings would drop, depressing stock prices. Raychem, which extends stock options to 800 of its 11,000 employees, estimates that the proposal would slash its annual earnings as much as 30 percent. MCI, which gives options to about 4,500 employees, says that if the FASB rule had been in effect in 1992, its profit would have been reduced 12 percent. ShareData Corp. of California estimates that Cypress Semiconductor Corp.'s 1993 earnings would have been wiped out. (Harlan 1994, p. A1)

Had this ruling been passed, it would most likely have curtailed the granting of stock options. Facing the potential loss of such lucrative compensation, corporate executives lobbied hard to defeat the proposal. The major accounting firms also opposed the proposed change, possibly to ingratiate themselves with corporate managers and preserve their auditing and consulting contracts. Stock option accounting reemerged as a major issue after the 2001 corporate scandals, and although business regulators considered requiring the expensing of executive stock options, several firms, including Warren Buffett–influenced Coca-Cola, conspicuously began expensing the options voluntarily.

The 1994 mobilization against the expensing of stock options was well funded, well organized, and effective:

> High-tech companies, a crucial constituency for the Clinton administration, are at the forefront of the lobbying drive. The American Electronics Association is spending $150,000 on such lobbying, including

an airlift of 100 executives this Thursday to call on officials in Washington. Other technology companies are working with a Washington lobbyist, Ken Hagerty, who formed the Coalition for American Equity Expansion to fight the FASB proposal. Among the 34 companies that signed up are Apple Computer Inc., International Business Machines Corp., and MCI . . . the Nasdaq . . . the Business Roundtable, made up of top executives of many corporate giants; and the National Association of Manufacturers . . . the Council of Institutional Investors. . . . They are treating this as a life-or-death struggle. A news release last October from the Coalition for American Equity Expansion dubbed the FASB proposal "a potent and poisonous job killer that would hinder the formation of new companies." The American Electronics Association trumpeted its "major effort to kill FASB options proposal." (Harlan 1994, p. A1)

In 1995 the FASB ruled that the cost of stock options did not have to be deducted from earnings on a firm's financial statements, but need only be disclosed in a footnote to them. Had the FASB required income-statement recognition of stock-option costs, the earnings of many firms would have declined precipitously and, with earnings, the price of stock. The footnoting compromise prevents a loss of shareholder value that would have resulted from the forced expensing of huge options to executives and other insiders. Interestingly, shareholder value was *increased* by the actual grant of huge stock options but would most likely *decrease* by the accounting recognition of them. For all of the glorifying of the U.S. capitalist system as "transparent," in this case opaqueness leads to higher shareholder value. Transparency can be a threat to shareholder interest.

The cost of stock options was quite large during the late twentieth century. Estimates stated that the earnings of large corporations would be reduced by 4 percent and the earnings of high-tech firms would be reduced "anywhere from 10 percent to 100 percent" (MacDonald and McGough 1999, p. C1). The legitimating rhetoric surrounding the battle over executive stock options aimed to convince shareholders that large grants benefit them while proposed accounting rules to recognize the cost of these options would hurt them. A more straightforward illustration of financial accounting as an intermediary of corporate value would be hard to find. The political mobilization as described in the contemporary press was impressive:

Treasury Secretary Lloyd Bentsen weighed in . . . with a letter to FASB Chairman Dennis Beresford urging the board to give "careful consideration" to "an alternative approach which would emphasize full disclosure but retain current stock-option accounting standards," in other words, no charge to earnings. [This is the version of the rule change that ultimately prevailed.] Commerce Secretary Brown, after Mr. Saldich and other Silicon Valley executives cornered him for 40 minutes at a conference in San Francisco, ordered a study of the plan's effect on the U.S. economy. . . . The lobbyists even reached the White House. . . . Mr. Clinton warned that "it would be unfortunate if FASB's proposal inadvertently undermined the competitiveness of some of America's most promising high-tech companies." . . . "I think everybody in this building is being lobbied, from the people who guard the front door to the chairman," says Walter Schuetze. . . . SEC Chairman Levitt [commented], "When I have dinner with business executives, I tell them we'll talk about stock options for 30 minutes, no more. Then we talk about something more interesting." (Harlan 1994, p. A1)

BUSINESS MOBILIZATION AND THE ACCOUNTING STANDARDS PROCESS

In January 1993 nine companies—including IBM, Apple, Compaq, and Oracle—formed the Coalition for American Equity Expansion (CAEE) to fight accounting and tax-related threats to stock options. The CAEE had the assistance of 12 California congressional representatives who wrote to President Clinton that the changes in the accounting rules for stock options were a hazard to the new high-tech, high-growth economy. All of the major accounting firms, the FASB's primary constituents, joined in the criticism of proposed rule changes, arguing for fuller footnote disclosure of stock options rather than expensing them on the income statement (Schatz 1993, p. 26). In the end, this is the proposal—greater disclosure but no income-statement effect—the FASB approved.

Proponents of executive stock options routinely refer to them as employee stock options and argue that they are very widely distributed in the corporation, never revealing that the bulk of options go to a very small number of people. The people who really benefit from options at most firms are very senior managers and directors who receive the majority of their compensation in this form. The CAEE formation was clearly part of the business mobilization counteroffensive in the wake of the outcomes of the 1992 elections, as Harlan's *Wall Street Journal* article suggested.

The CAEE began a campaign of news releases and advertising directed at shoring up support for stock options and eliminating any proposal to force companies to expense them against earnings. Here is the text of one of the earliest CAEE news releases, which quotes heavily from a statement George Sollman, president and CEO of Centigram Communications Corp. and co-chair of the CAEE, made and released on the same day that the FASB announced its proposed changes to the accounting rules. This was released in an effort to have the business response become a part of news stories written about the FASB proposal:

> "The entrepreneurial culture of America's vital high technology industries would be severely damaged if a regulatory decision announced today be the Financial Accounting Standards Board (FASB) is ultimately implemented. . . . One of the foundations of our industries' culture is the large percentage of employees who now participate in stock option plans. The FASB rule announced today would force a highly speculative estimate of the value of these options to be charged against a company's reportable earnings. This could make it prohibitively expensive for companies like mine to continue granting options to our entire workforce," said Sollman. . . . "We're surprised and disappointed that the Board chose to ignore the strong recommendations of industry, the accounting profession, the institutional investor community and even the Clinton Administration in deciding to require companies to charge stock options against their earnings," concluded Sollman. ("FASB's Stock Option Rule" 1993, para. 2–3)

Computerworld was one publication that carried the CAEE argument against the FASB proposal in its short news article announcing the FASB proposal:

> In a blow to small high-tech firms, the Financial Accounting Standards Board said last week that by 1997 it would require companies to deduct from earnings the estimated value of stock options granted to employees. The options are the only major form of compensation that does not hit the P & L [profit and loss] statement. The Coalition for American Equity Expansion, a group of computer hardware and software firms, said the proposed ruling would inhibit hiring in an indus-

try that has used stock options as a way of attracting and motivating people in high-risk ventures. ("Stock Option Reporting Rules Tightened" 1993, para. 1)

The following week, *Computerworld* reported that CAEE was gearing up for an intensive lobbying effort to block the FASB stock-option proposal. The thrust of its media attack on the FASB ruling is that stock options are granted to a broad base of employees at high-tech firms and are essential to these industries. Eliminating options would inhibit "the firms' ability to attract and retain the best talent in risky ventures." CAEE's media campaign tried to discredit the notion that stock options are granted primarily to wealthy executives and are instead given to employees at all levels. For example, Apple Computer grants some stock options to 75 percent of its employees. But this is like saying that Apple gives cash to all of its employees—there are no efforts made to demonstrate the inequality of the distribution of these options, which are heavily concentrated at the top of the organization. Indeed, by summer of 1993, CAEE members consistently referred to "broad based employee stock options" as the target of the FASB rule changes (Anthes 1993, p. 123).

In June 1993 CAEE had found congressional and senatorial sponsors for its bill. Connecticut Democrat Joseph Lieberman introduced the bill into the U.S. Senate. The bill called for the elimination of taxation on employee stock-option grants, and the reduction of the tax by 50 percent when the employee exercised a grant. The bill primarily called for the blocking of any accounting changes that would require income-statement recognition of employee stock options. In a most obvious statement, Cheryl Breetwor, president of ShareData, Inc., and a member of CAEE, noted in a news release: "[This bill] will enhance America's global competitiveness because companies that make extensive use of equity compensation programs like stock options consistently outperform those who don't" ("New Lieberman" 1993). In part, one could argue, they outperformed other firms because the bulk of their executive compensation went unrecorded on the profit and loss statement, overstating earnings by 50 percent or more. They operated on a different set of accounting rules than firms not using options for compensation. Furthermore, they outperformed other firms, at least in short-range accounting terms, because the executives who received these options have a large incentive to engage in aggressive speculative management to keep the financial statements attractive and the share prices high.

One of the companies who formed the CAEE, ShareData, Inc., released a survey of "920 companies that offer stock options from a broad range of industries." The survey documents the widespread use of companywide plans. Nine out of 10 of the smallest companies (fewer than 100 employees) offer options to every single employee. Two-thirds of the companies with up to 500 employees also give options to everyone, according to the ShareData survey. "Much of the political pressure on FASB to make this change is based on the mistaken belief that stock options are only for 'fat cats,'" said George Sollman, CEO of Centigram Communications Corp. and co-chair of CAEE. "This survey solidly refutes that fallacy." The CAEE distributed this news release, titled "FASB Stock Option Proposal Blasted in Senate Testimony; FASB's Plan a 'Potent and Poisonous Job Killer,'" on the day its representatives read these survey results to a Senate Banking Committee subcommittee (*Business Wire* 1993).

Although CAEE tried to demonstrate how broadly U.S. corporations use stock options, stock options remained largely a "form of stealth compensation for very top executives," in the words of Michigan Democratic Senator Carl Levin, who introduced legislation to force companies to expense stock options. Levin cited a "survey of 6,000 American companies indicating that 97 percent of the stock options in 1992 went to 15 or fewer people in each company" (Mathews 1994, p. B17). In the cases of Scott Paper and Sunbeam, very few people indeed received stock options. The reality is that both facts are probably true: like equity ownership in mutual funds, the breadth of equity ownership has increased greatly over the past 10 years, but the distribution of the value owned has not broadened. Ownership of equity shares remains extraordinarily concentrated in the hands of a very few.

In the end, the FASB proposal to require an earnings hit for stock options was dropped the same week that the new restructuring guidelines were released. Both plans shifted away from requiring income-statement recognition of costs and instead focused primarily on increased "disclosure" of the value of stock options and the makeup of restructuring charges in the footnotes to the financial statements.

The media coverage of the FASB decision to require mere disclosure of stock options rather than cost recognition focused on the business opposition to the proposal as the primary cause of its failure.[13]

In what passes for high drama in the quiet world of financial numbers, the accounting industry's standards board today bowed to feverish business opposition and dropped its plan to deduct the cost of stock options from profit and loss statements. . . . Corporate representatives praised the board's turnabout, and predicted it would lead to further blossoming of stock option plans as congressional Republicans move toward reducing taxes on the capital gains that can come from such plans. . . . During nearly two years of debate over the board's proposed rule change, its members were flooded with angry letters and met by angry demonstrations. . . . Several members of Congress threatened action if the new rule went through. . . . Levin, in a statement released today, blamed the FASB decision on a "lobbying blizzard." . . . The heated reaction, particularly from small high-technology firms that use stock options to lure talented executives, slowed the board's move toward adoption of the rule. . . . Beresford said the degree of opposition "was so unprecedented" that he feared the board risked losing some of the respect it needs to keep the profession in order. "Our standard-setting process is a delicate one and requires that we have the confidence of the people who work with us on a regular basis," he said. (Mathews 1994, p. B17)

The 1995 FASB guidelines required mere disclosure (not financial-statement recognition) of employee stock options.

The footnotes were the result of heated battles between options-happy technology companies and accountants. In 1995, accounting regulators tried to force companies to expense employee stock options against profits. Companies hollered that it would be the end of Western civilization, in one regulator's phrase. The regulators retreated, only requiring companies to disclose the "pro forma" effect of options on earnings in a footnote. Since then, the use of options in several industries, particularly high-tech and pharmaceutical, has flourished, buoying bottom lines. (MacDonald and McGough 1999, p. C1)

Most of the major accounting issues of the 1990s were attempts to constrain the use of recently developed arrows in the quiver of speculative management.[14] Each issue involved accounting rule makers who sought to constrain the strategic manipulation of financial accounts by managers who sought to preserve maximum accounting flexibility. Because of effective business lobbying, the outcome of many of these disputes was to forgo clear recognition of items in financial statements in exchange for mere disclosure of them in financial statement footnotes. The 1990s were a period of extensive development of accounting footnotes, which complicates the interpretation of financial statements by those who assess corporate value. If financial markets were comprised only of investment virtuosos expert at deciphering financial statements, footnote disclosure would represent a significant constraint on management's ability to speculatively manage firms. However, in late-twentieth-century America, secondary equity markets became mass markets. The bottom line moves corporate stock prices more than detailed disclosures in accounting footnotes. Mass markets are thought to respond (and hence do respond) to bold headlines not small print. This is one point at which primary and secondary markets sharply diverge: primary markets (both the financial intermediaries and regulators) perform intensive due diligence before the flotation of securities. Secondary financial markets, even the most sophisticated outside players in this market, stock analysts, perform a much less rigorous review before responding to "corporate events" (such as restructuring) with a changed evaluation.

The biggest accounting dispute of the 1990s was the dispute over stock options. Stock options were politically targeted in the early 1990s because of the public policy issue of executive compensation. In the early 1990s, in an era when downsizing and restructuring peaked, when the recession was threatening middle income and suburban workers as well as blue-collar workers, the disparity between the fate of workers and that of executives was a powerful social issue. In 1992 Bush traveled to Japan for an economic summit on trade restrictions in Japan, but the focus of the debate was shifted to a comparison between U.S. and Japanese executive compensation. Executive compensation was a potent political issue in 1992, which motivated the introduction of legislation. The FASB also offered a similar proposal: forcing executive compensation through stock options into the open by forcing corporations to recognize the cost of these options in their earnings. This seemed especially important given the tremendous size of the options. Ultimately, in the argument of FASB, stock options have a cost: the difference between the option price and the market price of the securities. This difference is what constitutes the "gain" to the executives, and it also represents the expense to the company, which receives less in its "cash" reserves for the same issue of securities.

The stock-option controversy occurred at the height of corporate restructuring and at the same time as the parallel controversy over restructuring charges. Although the business news media's coverage of stock options was far more extensive (and one suspects that the controversy was more heated), the restructuring rule change proposal mobilized the same actors using many of the same arguments.

The CAEE did not disband after the successful campaign against stock option recognition. Instead it joined the American Council for Capital Formation, Citizens for a Sound Economy, and other groups in pressing for a capital gains tax cut, which both Republican-majority houses of Congress passed and President Clinton signed into law in 1996.

CONCLUSIONS

In the late twentieth century, the vast apparatus of retail investing poured vast amounts of money into secondary financial markets. This study draws out the importance of connective structures between firms and these crucial actors in secondary financial markets. Speculative management teams have a clear incentive to manage firms in ways that attract investors' attention and money, thereby elevating the trading price of corporate stock. Financial accounting is an important, perhaps the most important, pathway linking corporate management teams and the secondary market actors they are attempting to influence. Late twentieth century Anglo-American financial markets are impossible to envision without modern financial accounting. Secondary security markets rely on the accounting profession to make firms transparent: to make the value of firms visible.

The importance of the financial news media and corporate governance structures as social intermediaries is discussed in chapter 5. A primary concern will be how the business news media carried and shaped prevailing financial market views of the legitimacy of restructuring as a management strategy. The late-twentieth-century era of transactional finance has witnessed an acceleration in financial news delivery and elite and mass responses to it. The massive growth of the retail stock market in the 1990s has been accompanied by the creation of 24-hour financial news channels, the expansion of other financial reporting on television, and the growth of financial news and services on the Internet. Round the clock coverage of the news, the Internet's capacity to relay moment-to-moment reports, and the growth of day-trading that uses both of these technologies, have helped make financial markets incredibly responsive to changes in corporate news. This has raised the stakes for speculative managers, who have very little time to respond to events that affect their corporation's value. Because the financial news media covers corporate events 24 hours a day, 7 days a week, the speculative management of corporate value must be an unceasing corporate focus.

Chapter 5

SOCIAL INTERMEDIATION, CORPORATE GOVERNANCE, AND FINANCIAL MARKETS

. . . Many so-called 'investors' are nothing more than predators, opportunists, speculators, traders, arbitragers, scavengers, even blackmailers, whose focus is on nothing more than trying to capitalize on the short-term . . . profit to them, regardless of the consequences. . . .
—Thomas A. Murphy, former chairman, General Motors, on the rights of shareholders.[1]

CEOs should consider selling stock in themselves to permit investors to profit from their low-risk, high-pay way of life. 'Who cares about Coleman? You buy Levin.'"
—Graef Crystal, editor of the *Crystal Report*, on the failsafe wealth given to CEOs who engineer mergers of their firms.[2]

These managements need shaking up—they're horrendous . . . they take money from the peasants [the stockholders] and then hire mercenaries [lawyers] to protect their castle, mainly by browbeating the peasants. So we attack the castle.
—Carl Icahn, on the entrenched management entrenched management in U.S. corporations.[3]

You cannot overpay a good CEO and you can't underpay a bad one. The bargain CEO is one who is unbelievably well compensated because he's creating wealth for the shareholders. If his wealth is not tied to the shareholder's return, everyone is playing a fool's game . . . at $100 million, I was still the biggest bargain in corporate America.
—Albert J. Dunlap, CEO of Scott Paper and Sunbeam Corporation, justifying his $100 million dollar take from the Scott Paper sale.[4]

In corporate circles, the world's most abused minority is the shareholder. Barely tolerated, not respected. . . .
—Albert J. Dunlap, CEO of Scott Paper and Sunbeam Corporation, on shareholder rights.[5]

BUSINESS MEDIA AS A SOCIAL INTERMEDIARY

Chapter 4 described how financial accounting rules constrain the successful manipulation of securities values. Successful speculative management also requires a sophisticated manipulation of other kinds of information attended to and used by the financial public to impute a market value to corporate securities. This section shifts to the discussion of additional cognitive elements in the process of value assessment that are not reducible to the analysis of financial data and that are not fully comprehended by an understanding of financial accounting as a connective between firms and markets. The primary carriers of this information are various business news media. This chapter describes and analyzes the business news media and corporate governance structures as social intermediaries affecting corporate value.

This chapter begins by examining changes in the organization of the financial media in the late twentieth century. Not only has business news expanded, but also new media outlets have arisen, especially electronic media, that instantly transmit corporate news. With instant news, the financial markets' response to news is accelerated. The increased responsiveness of markets to corporate news has increased the pressure for unceasing speculative management. The business news media not only carries news, but interprets it as well. Opinion leaders in the financial news media shape prevailing views of legitimate management practice. Speculative managers must attune closely to opinion leader assessments of corporate actions to manage their share prices effectively. The chapter then considers issues related to the governance structure of late-twentieth-century firms.

The late-twentieth-century bull stock market drew millions of retail investors into the secondary market for corporate securities. It also created a mass market for financial news. As the participation of the masses in secondary financial markets grew, so too did the audience for financial news:

> Ratings for financial news have never been better. CNBC which has seen its operating income nearly double over the past two years, to an expected $120 million this year, said viewership on Monday was the highest in the eight-year history of the network. According to data from Nielsen Media Research, the numbers peaked at 3:30 Monday afternoon, when more than one million homes were watching CNBC's

business news—with its never-ending crawl of stock quotes at the bottom of the screen. CNBC's viewership averaged 417,000 homes, also a record, during the hours the market was open. . . . CNN reported that "Moneyline," the network's evening business show, generated its second-best ratings of the year. (Pope 1997, p. B1)

The end of the 1990s saw two well-established, national financial news networks (CNBC and CNNfn) devoted principally to finance. The prominence of financial reporting in general news outlets also grew: the business pages of newspapers and the financial coverage on broadcast news programs dramatically expanded. Mainstream networks have increased their financial reporting: *Nightly Business Report* on public broadcasting stations, the spread of financial magazines, the growth and continued prosperity of the *Wall Street Journal* were signs of the demand for financial information.[6]

Overstating the degree to which financial news penetrated everyday life is difficult. In the late 1990s wireless pagers were available that delivered a variety of financial information to mobile investors, who programmed the system to page them if a stock they were watching moved significantly. Most airlines featured in-flight real-time stock quotes. The Internet dramatically expanded the "setting" of financial news consumption and of investment decision-making. Workers tracked their portfolios at their office workstations and the rise of Internet stock brokers enabled rapid and low-cost stock transactions enabling the rise in day-trading. Television screens in public areas were tuned to business news and, especially on dramatic trading days, large segments of the population joined the audience following the market on business news media.

During the mid-twentieth-century era of regulated finance, the primary financial news media was the press: the *Wall Street Journal, Barrons*, the *New York Times* Business Section, *Forbes, Fortune, Business Week*, and several more specialized trade publications. Print media were long the primary carriers of financial information, adequate for all but the most active trader. But the rise of transactional finance in the late twentieth century, which infused the financial world with a breathless, round-the-clock intensity, meant that instantaneous, electronic information sources significantly supplanted the print news media. Television, wire services, and the Internet were better equipped to delivery timely, market-moving information to speculative teams and traders and displaced the print media for the coverage of breaking financial news. The print media came to function as a repository of financial information as well as a forum for the analytic discussion of corporate and financial events and remained the leading window on market conceptions of aggressively good management.[7] Security traders came to rely on time-sensitive, market-moving financial news that electronic media provide.

The Internet's instantaneous, comprehensive, and geographically decentered delivery of financial information increased the potential sophistication of the market trades of amateurs outside of central money-centers. Market tracking, research reports, news digests, and historical trend analyses became universally available on investment Web sites, and on news wires, such as Yahoofinance.com, Businesswire.com, and Bigcharts.com. The electronic business news media widely expanded the cognitive participation in speculative capitalism in recent times.

Information conveyed through business and financial media outlets radically affected the market valuation of corporate securities. The Internet accelerated these effects, making down-to-the-minute timing of corporate information releases a critical strategic component of shareholder communications. An example: during the winter of 1999, a Xerox Corp. news release was accidentally prereleased by First Call, a business news wire service at 5:24 P.M. on Monday, January 25, after the close of the trading day, rather than at 10:00 A.M. on Tuesday morning. This prompted an after-hours buying frenzy that temporarily disorganized the market for Xerox stock. The strong demand the premature announcement generated, which included the reports of quarterly earnings in excess of analyst expectations, a 2-for-1 stock split, and an increase in dividends, created such overnight demand for the stock that the market opening was delayed until a market-clearing price (up 10 percent) could be established (Ip and Narisetti 1999, p. C1).

To ensure that disbursed news outlets release company news simultaneously, corporations predistribute news releases to wire agencies in advance with a specific release time indicated:

> "If a company wants the button pressed at 7 A.M., we need some prep time," said Cathy Baron Tamraz, executive vice president of closely held Business Wire. . . . John Williams, senior vice president at PR newswire, a unit of Britain's United News & Media, agreed that (prereleases) happen, but rarely: "When someone gives us a story that's material and we're held in confidence by the customer, it makes us insiders. So that makes us real careful." (Ip and Narisetti 1999, p. C1)

Because markets respond so rapidly to corporate news, delivering the news at strategic times is critical for speculative management. Television financial news began to displace the financial newspaper as an important and market-moving source of information at least as early as the 1980s. Television speedily broadcast rumors and news of corporate takeovers. "The new Wall Street media stars were not plungers but, rather, journalists who ferreted out news of potential takeovers. The most prominent was Dan Dorfman, a reporter who became a much-watched personality on the Cable News Network's 'Nightly Business News.' Should Dorfman write or say that some raider was taking off after a company, its shares would rise sharply" (Sobel 1993, p. 122).

An essential element of the business news media is the analytic contingent that provides detailed corporate financial information and interpretation. Although "public" reporters, employed as journalists for business news media, usually disseminate security analyses, private analysts employed by the security industry often generate the content of their reports. Security analysts track corporations, maintaining in-depth contact with the firms and make investment recommendations in proprietary reports made available to their employer's clients. As private analysts, their primary objective is not to provide the public with accurate information regarding a corporation's strategies and results, but rather to provide profitable guidance for their clients. Their close contact with speculative teams creates the possibility that their reports provide superior advice to clients regarding buy, sell, and hold recommendations (especially before Regulation FD reduced their privileged access in 2000).

The influence and importance of these private analysts would be significantly reduced if their reports were merely proprietary, but their opinions and recommendations find their way into the public business news media through several channels. The financial media turn to analysts of a particular company to provide insights and commentary when financial news affects that company. When a company's stock moves in a big way or when a corporation releases earnings or information about corporate strategy, security analysts are important interpreters of these events to the news media and their opinions often reinforce or even generate changes in stock prices.

Analysts are a primary source of in-depth interpretation and opinion regarding a particular company's performance. Appearing as expert witnesses in business reports, these private analysts had a profound impact on public information about corporate life in the late twentieth century. Information agencies aggregated analyst opinions for various firms and consolidated them into "consensus estimates" that frame expectations for the broad securities market. This information is also reflexively transmitted back to the corporation, providing management with a clear target for financial-statement engineering. Through these means, the proprietary opinions of security analysts joined the smorgasbord of public information about corporate prospects, performance, and management. The business news media routinely taps other private analysts, such as economists and forecasters employed by investment banks and brokerages, for expert opinion. Analysts, and the business news media in general, became important social intermediaries in recent American corporate life.

Many interpreters of recent capitalism see managers playing before an audience of owners. But the interests of big owners and top managers are so tightly connected that they form a single performance team. Big owners are not management's audience but are rather half of the cast. Big owners and top managers play together as corporate insiders before an audience of outsiders. Sitting in capitalism's box seats, an array of analysts, most privately employed, critically direct collective sense making of their performances.

In their role as critics of corporate action and prospects, analysts enjoyed privileged access to the teams in control of the corporations they researched. The corporate scandals of 2001 and 2002 featured revelations of systematic bias on the part of analysts, who often publicized positive recommendations that differed from their private judgment. Although often assumed to be disinterested interpreters of corporate affairs, analysts were in fact deeply embedded, highly visible adjuncts of speculatively managed corporations. In the case of Scott Paper, several analysts covering the firm became integrated the inner circle, providing scripts for performances by CEO Al Dunlap that they believed would boost the price of the stock (Bryne 1999, Dunlap 1996). Analysts were not in a strong position to resist managerial overtures because they were dependent on management to provide them with the privileged access and (before the SEC rule instituted in August 2000 prohibited it) unpublished inside information, which allowed them to cover the firm. Pressure to conform to management wishes came from the analyst's employers as well, who wished to keep corporate management on the hook for additional fee-based services. Lest their opinions offend corporate managers who were current or potential clients of the firm, analysts downplayed negative recommendations. Analysts rarely recommended that shareholders sell the stocks of the firms they covered: the normal range of opinions was from "hold" to "strong buy." Rather than risk exclusion from the inner circle or anger one's own employer by alienating potential clients, analyst coverage of firms tended to foster, rather than constrain, speculative management.

Independent stock rating agencies, such as Standard and Poor's, recognized the lack of independence of analysts' opinions and adjusts for them in its aggregate stock reports:

> Analysts' Consensus Opinion: The consensus opinion reflects the average buy/hold/sell recommendation of Wall Street analysts. It is well known, however, that analysts tend to be overly bullish. To make the consensus opinion more meaningful, it has been adjusted to reduce this positive bias. . . . Only companies that score high relative to all other companies merit a consensus opinion of "buy." . . . A rising consensus opinion is a favorable indicator of near-term stock performance; a declining trend is a negative signal.[8]

Each day, a large number of business analysts and economic forecasters are interviewed and quoted in the business news media, but their influence varies. Some opinion leaders hold considerable power to keynote market movements (at least the willingness of the financial media to attribute keynoting to these leaders is considerable). Alan Greenspan, chairman of the Federal Reserve, held the most prominent formal position as opinion leader of finance. Omaha, Nebraska, investor Warren Buffett was probably the leading market guru of the mid-1990s, his letter to shareholders in Berkshire Hathaway's annual reports were widely quoted in business news media, and they were even collected and published in book form.

Other financial opinion leaders of the mid-1990s include Morgan Stanley's chief economist Stephen Roach, Prudential Securities' director of technical research Ralph Acampora, and Goldman Sach's stock strategist Abby Joseph Cohen. Roach famously championed downsizing and restructuring and was one of the chief articulators of the conception of restructuring as aggressively good management. Roach championed many of the largest and most socially devastating restructurings of the early 1990s, but began to argue against further restructuring in 1996.

Roach believed that a political movement—a worker backlash—was mounting that would derail further benefits from restructuring. Acampora had remarkable success in timing the 1990s bull market. The business news media occasionally traced the cause of financial market revaluations to statements Acampora made:

> On Tuesday [August 4, 1998], Mr. Acampora warned that the Dow Jones Industrial Average could fall 15 percent to 20 percent from its high, to as low as 7400. The apparent change of heart of someone who had been famously forecasting a 10000 average this year seemed to feed that day's 299.43 point plunge in the average to 8487.31. . . . If Mr. Acampora's exact stance can sometimes be hard to nail down, it doesn't appear to have hurt his reputation. He was rightly viewed for years as one of the bull market's boldest cheerleaders, calling in June 1995 for Dow 7000 when the average was around 4500. His shifts in stance, while remaining fundamentally bullish, have done little to diminish his popularity. . . . Mr. Acampora . . . maintains he has caught some important peaks and troughs. When the Dow industrials plunged 554 points last October, "at that bottom, I said buy 'em." (Ip 1998e, p. C1)

It is interesting to note that the August 4 announcement of Acampora's changed opinion of the market was first made on CNBC-TV, a 24-hour financial news channel (not in the *Wall Street Journal*). Again, technological media changes allow fast, broad dissemination of market cues.

The next day, Abby Joseph Cohen, the "longtime bard of the bull market," publicly declared her support for a continued increase in equity values:

> . . . [Cohen] stepped in to calm the market yesterday morning by standing by her bullish views after bearish comments by . . . Acampora helped fuel a 299.43 point slide on Tuesday. . . . Much of the day's gains clearly lay at the feet of Ms. Cohen, who early in the day dispatched a note to her firm's many, mostly institutional clients urging them to stay the course. "Stocks are trading at undervalued levels. . . . We believe that market action in recent weeks represents an overreaction to incremental information.". . . Unlike Mr. Acampora, Ms. Cohen didn't appear on TV. Instead, the Goldman analyst delivered her thoughts in a 7:30 A.M. call to Goldman Sachs's sales force.

> Written comments were then faxed to clients, and later to the media. (Ip 1998f, p. C1)

This double dissemination may be done as a double benefit to private clients. The clients with a head start can make initial moves that reinforce the analyst's forecast. Media dissemination to the public and the initial move bring in other buyers, protecting the value of the purchases the clients initially made.

Acampora and Cohen represent very different types of market analysis: Acampora practiced technical analysis; Cohen, fundamental analysis. A technical analyst primarily examines the prices of securities on financial markets and looks for patterns in these prices. A fundamental analyst looks at the "underlying" business conditions of the firms.

> Mr. Acampora said his turnabout was prompted by recent drops in the stock prices of various Dow companies, dramatizing that "Asia is not a one or two quarter problem for big blue chip companies." . . . [Cohen] professed to pay "very little attention to what others may be saying," explaining that she focuses on fundamentals instead of the charts and other statistical material that form the basis for work by technicians like Prudential's Mr. Acampora. (Ip 1998f, p. C1)

Diverging opinions of market analysts were common in the late twentieth century and most likely contributed to market volatility:

> It was the battle of the Internet analysts yesterday over Amazon.com's highflying stock. Merrill Lynch analyst Jonathan Cohen took a swipe at CIBC Oppenheimer analyst Henry Blodget, telling clients that the online retailer's shares should trade at about $50 each over the next 12 to 18 months. The comments were a challenge to Mr. Blodget, who had raised his 12-month price target to 400 from 150 Wednesday, sparking a 46¼, or 19 percent, rise to 289. Yesterday, Amazon fell 12 ¼, or 4.2 percent, to 276¾. (Tessler 1998, p. C2)

Knowing that secondary markets react very rapidly and violently to news in the business news media, speculative managers attempt to control market reactions to company news and results. When the news is bad, one way to lessen the impact is to release simultaneous good news. "Over the past week, both Mattel and Coca-Cola have announced acquisitions on the same day they also issued warnings about disappointing earnings" (Sherer 1998, p. C1). This is a trend many other firms follow. The earnings warnings are given on the same day as positive news rather than waiting for the "surprise" response in a worse context in the following quarter. Earnings warnings, because they are discretionary, allow managers to time them to advantage and allow managers to control as much of the impression as possible. Earnings warnings are in essence a mechanism for managers to control the media coverage of their financial results.

THE BUSINESS NEWS MEDIA AND SECURITY SPECULATION

Control of the business news media has often been a primary means to influence equity values. This control the financial media had was great in earlier periods of U.S. finance. Indeed, we have seen a tight coevolution of financial media and equity security speculation and trading. Stock speculators, traders who touted stocks for profit and used the financial media as a mechanism to generate profitable price breaks, developed the early financial media. By championing particular stocks or particular industries in financial news articles, stock speculators increased demand for a particular stock and boosted its price. Big stock operators sponsored the early U.S. financial media and have often relied on it as an essential tool in speculative operations. Washburn and De-Long (1932) provide an excellent sketch of George Graham Rice, who began his career in finance by writing "tipster" sheets at race track and ended by creating a financial newspaper that promoted small stocks that Rice had a position in to his benefit.[9]

> Rice was the original "tipster," the inventor of the "tipster sheet," or "tout sheet," as it is generally known around the tracks. Tipster sheets became innumerable after his successful launching of the first one. . . . He started by placing advertisements in various New York papers, promising to furnish reliable tips on the races for one dollar each. If his tip missed, he guaranteed to refund the dollar. . . . The returns were enormous. It was comparatively simple to pick the three or four "favorites" in each race. He divided his tips evenly among these horses. One, of course, won and the several hundred dollars he

received from tips on this horse were his. Those on losing horses he returned. . . . He operated under the firm name of Maxim and Gay, and his tout sheet was called "Daily America." (Pp. 18–19)

Later, after authorities closed down his race operations, Rice became interested in stock promotions. In the late teens he "established a weekly financial sheet, 'George Graham Rice's Industrial and Mining Age,' with two widely known editors on his staff and a man who had been a former Controller of the Currency under the Roosevelt Administration. His associates' names had prestige and the publication was used by Rice to influence the buying and selling of stocks as he chose to manipulate them" (Washburn and DeLong 1932, p. 23). In the 1920s, he formed another paper, the *Iconoclast*, a "daily financial journal which attained the largest circulation of any financial paper in America." Although its slogan was, "The Truth, No Matter Whom It Helps Or Hurts," according to Washburn and DeLong, the paper was used primarily to tout particular stocks in which Rice had an interest.

Rice covered his manipulative operations by maintaining a rhetoric of moral outrage at financial manipulation and by conspicuously exposing corrupt practices in finance:

> . . . He had discovered the art of concealing his own sins by a loud denunciation of the sins of others. He opened his campaign with a merciless and vitriolic attack upon all stock swindlers. He exposed their methods and demanded that they be punished. He declared war on those "white-collar bandits," tipsters, bucket-shop operators, and "blue-sky salesmen who were preying on the innocent unwary investor." (Washburn and DeLong 1932, pp. 26–27)

After building newspaper readership to several hundred thousand readers, he began to systematically tout stocks. His appeals were not subtle, as demonstrated in the following advice in an April 1926 issue of the *Iconoclast:* "Sell any stock you own and buy IDAHO COPPER, now on the Boston Curb. We know what this language means AND WE MEAN IT." Idaho Copper was an abandoned mine in which Rice had purchased 1,300,000 shares for $10,000, or approximately $.10 per share. The articles in the *Iconoclast* raised that price to more than $6.25 per share. "Idaho Copper goes to 6¼—skyrocketing move to $25 now forecast as result of ore disclosures," ran one article. "If there came a lull in the buying the *Iconoclast* came out with an announcement of the discovery of a rich new vein and the frenzy was renewed. Of course, no one was selling—except Rice—at six and a quarter when Idaho Copper was certain to reach twenty-five or even higher." Of course, the mine itself was largely worthless, the discoveries of new ore were fictitious, and the value of the shares was entirely dependent on the positive news in the *Iconoclast* (Washburn and DeLong 1932, pp. 29–30). Eventually, Rice was exposed when a farmer in South Dakota tried to sell some of his Idaho Copper stock back to Rice, who refused to purchase it. The price meanwhile plummeted on the Boston Curb exchange and the farmer contacted authorities, who investigated the Idaho mine and found that it had remained undisturbed and unworked for more than 25 years. Rice eventually served a four-year prison term (p. 37).

The importance of financial media for successful speculation extends to commodities markets as well. The following, quite dated but still accurate, description of the importance of news for moving markets suggests how successful market timing requires close attention to business news media:

> Since successful speculation depends on an accurate estimate of the future, everything that helps to make this estimate more reliable will be a step forward in the development of business in futures. During the last half-century, the machinery of prediction has developed with amazing rapidity along with the machinery of speculation. In a vast business like cotton, where speculation plays so great a part in almost every stage from the planter to the merchant, the machinery of prediction is a complicated and delicate affair. Every hour of the day crop reports come in from America, from Egypt, from India, by cable, wireless or telephone. Every event which might have any bearing upon the coming crop—rain or drought or civil war or a mischievous plague of insects or often some apparently trivial occurrence—is instantly reported and acted upon. (Hirst 1931, p. 133)

During times of increasing mass participation in financial markets, such as the 1920s, 1950s, and 1990s, mass media have the capacity to move markets by attracting buyers (or sellers) to a particular company's stock. During Louis Rukeyser's reign as the popular host of PBS's weekly financial news program, *Wall Street Week in Review*, the program was occasionally cited as the cause of Monday morning price changes in stocks that had been discussed on the program the previous Friday. In the 1954, Walter Winchell (and others) exploited Winchell's popular radio and television broadcasts to promote more than 40 stocks, the price of which "responded immediately and dramatically":

> Summing up his record in January 1955, Winchell reported that the person who had bought a few hundred shares of each would have scored a paper profit of about $250,000. . . . Winchell came back, breathless as ever, with this flash: "Here's that exciting piece of advance news. The stock market boom, which took a dive for two days this week, had to come. All the experts wondered what delayed it. I am told now the recovery Friday will continue, because the national payroll is up 400 percent and American production is up over 300 percent over 1929. Here is another piece of big advance news. Pantepec Oil, Pantepec Oil, P-a-n-t-e-p-e-c Oil, on the Small Board. Pantepec Oil has newly discovered substantial oil reserves in the El Roble field in Venezuela. Pantepec Oil will hold a meeting on January 13th to increase its common stock to be used for stock dividends. I'll be back in a flash." (Croupier in Brooks 1958, p. 177)

As John Brooks (1958) reported, the announcement brought a buying frenzy of some 357,500 shares of Pantepec on Monday morning, which when traded, represented the largest block of stock ever traded on any stock exchange. This story of how a single broadcast moved secondary markets so dramatically serves as an important cautionary tale to those who assume that financial markets are efficient and that the share price is merely a rational estimation of discounted future earnings.

In the late-twentieth-century era of transactional finance, most business news was covered from a financial rather an industrial angle. News of industrial production and consumption was slanted to bring the financial impact into view. How will changes in business inventories affect the stock market? How do increased housing starts impact the outlook for stock prices? The "horse race" aspects of modern speculative finance—the daily fluctuations in the Dow Jones Industrial Average and the NASDAQ Index—received heavy coverage. The rise of financial coverage came at a cost. The *Wall Street Journal*, for example, has boosted its coverage of merely technical market indicators and has shifted away from company-level analysis toward analysis of much broader units. This nicely parallels the shift in stockholding away from direct investment in corporate stock to indirect ownership in stock mutual funds. Also this coverage has become increasingly abstract and decontextualized. The coverage of changes in market indexes, averages, and technical market indicators, as well as abstract interpretation of the causes of them, overshadows discussion of concrete production facilities in identifiable communities. This increasing abstraction parallels the shift in share ownership from direct investment in particular corporate securities to indirect ownership through mutual funds. Following the business news media to learn in a general way of the fate of mutual fund accounts, small retail investors developed a novice conception of markets valued as abstract wholes, devoid of context, and caring little for the fate of any single company or of downsized workers.

CORPORATE GOVERNANCE STRUCTURES

A sustained academic debate has surrounded the question: "Who controls the corporation?" Neither managerialism's answer of *management* nor investor capitalism's *owner* is satisfactory to understand the internal restructuring wave. Each misses decisive features of late-twentieth-century corporate governance structures—features brought more clearly into view by the insight that big owners and top managers collaborated as speculative management teams to enhance stock values. As detailed in chapter 3, from 1990 to 1994, such teams captured value for themselves by exploiting internal organizational restructuring—the speculative stratagem of the time. A common interest in enhanced stock values united elite managers and big owners. Corporate governance structures enabled the speculative collaboration of these elites and, with financial accounting and business news media, are a third essential social intermediary. Secondary financial markets were linked to corporations through the participation of big stockowners in corporate governance and through the transformation of top executives into large stockowners in their own right. Through these mechanisms, the speculative interests and logic of the market were imported into the highest controlling echelons of corporate governance. This section presents a perspective on the interests behind the collaboration of big owners and top managers and contrasts it with managerialist and investor-capitalism perspectives on corporate control.[10]

Managerialism provides one of the dominant images of twentieth-century U.S. capitalism. From the critical assessment of Berle and Means's (1932) early work to the more positive, fully developed statement of Alfred Chandler (1978), this tradition has developed a multisided figure of management-dominated corporations and the consequences of them for U.S. capitalism.

Managerialism's image of the corporation was constructed to understand large U.S. firms during the early and mid-twentieth century, after the decline of investment-banker control. In the early twentieth century, access to capital for industrial expansion and consolidation was crucial to corporate success. Investment bankers were critical financial intermediaries that provided corporations with access to investment capital in primary securities markets. Investment bankers, as intermediaries between primary security markets (mostly bond markets) and corporations, were important carriers of the point of view of primary security markets into the management of industrial concerns. Investment bankers often demanded and obtained positions as directors of the corporations whose bonds they floated. They used these positions to control the operations of industrial firms to maximize the interest of bondholders. In practice, this meant investment bankers occupied a controlling position within many industrial enterprises. They were important intermediaries linking firms to markets and took advantage of this pivotal position to control the operation of industrial firms and, in essence, to control capitalism.

Raising sufficient funds for industrial expansion and the acquisition and merger of industrial enterprises required expertise of investment bankers. Business historian Ron Chernow in *The Death of the Banker* (1994) and in *The House of Morgan* (1990) supports Berle and Means's (1932) basic managerialism by detailing how the power of investment bankers over corporate affairs declined during the twentieth century, leaving corporate managers as relatively autonomous actors. The decline in banker power occurred primarily because firms became less dependent on investment banks to raise funds and because dispersed shareholding, what Roy (1997) calls "socialized capital," worked against effective shareholder oversight of corporate affairs. The increased financial independence of firms was due to their expanded capacity to generate sufficient earnings from their operations to self-finance expansion through retained earnings. Chernow (1994) also calls attention to the ability of corporations to bypass large investment banks to seek financing directly in money markets by floating securities on their own account. This direct market access to investment funds weakened the power of bankers. Rather than obtain loans or bond offerings from banks, industrial corporations began to float "commercial paper," relatively short-term loans sold directly in money markets. The globalization of finance in the 1960s through the Euro market also helped free corporations from dependence on financiers, and left managers with more discretion. Hence, the power and importance of investment banks declined leaving managers alone on the corporate throne.

With justice, managerialism became a major image of U.S. capitalism in the mid-twentieth century, a period of stable corporate growth and low investor activism. Managerialism was not merely an account of mid-twentieth-century capitalism, but remains a live interpretation of late-twentieth-century corporate activity. Roe (1994), for example, has described the late twentieth century in terms of the continuation of the U.S. pattern of "strong managers" and "weak owners." Fligstein's work (1990, 2001) emphasizes that managers are the primary actors shaping and structuring U.S. capitalism as they create and deploy various conceptions of corporate control.

Although the writings in the managerial tradition are diverse and cover many themes, two themes consistently reappear in managerialism's account of corporate control. First, managerialist writings maintain that twentieth-century U.S. capitalism consolidates control over corporations in the hands of managers. This is primarily due to the pattern of corporate ownership that has characterized U.S. capitalism since the "corporate revolution" of the late nineteenth century. The diffusion of stock ownership in public financial markets diminishes the power of owners and reduces their capacity to monitor and control corporate affairs effectively. The increasing complexity of industrial production further augments the power of managers. Power-driven, continuous-flow production technology and geographically dispersed, functionally diverse organizations favor professionally educated, technically competent managers. Managers became strong relative to diffuse ownership, and their functional necessity increased their power to pursue an agenda of corporate growth and centralization of control.[11] Roe (1994) sums up the managerialist firm as follows: "This combination of a huge enterprise, concentrated management, and dispersed diversified shareholders shifted corporate control from shareholders to managers. Dispersed shareholders and concentrated management became the quintessential characteristics of the large American firms" (p. 4).[12]

Second, managerialist analyses of corporate control emphasize the near complete divergence of the interests of managers and owners. Owners seek maximum profit and high returns on their investment; managers seek high salaries, benefits and perks, and a growing corporate empire. Because managers are in control of the firm, the pursuit of profit, which would benefit shareholders, is subordinated to the pursuit of corporate growth. Growth benefits management in several ways, including increased employment, more corporate divisions, a larger staff, and larger expense accounts. For much of the twentieth century managers have pursued corporate growth at the expense of shareholders' desires for maximum profits. Managerialism paints a portrait of U.S. capitalism with managers seated firmly at the controls of modern corporations.

From a standpoint sensitive to the effects of finance, the model of equity valuation shareholders use further enhanced management control of firms during the mid-twentieth century. Contributing to managers' freedom to pursue their own interests was shareholders' low expectation for corporate profits during an era when equity securities were valued in terms of their dividend yield. Under this valuation model, equity investors expected that their returns from stockholdings would parallel those of fixed-return bonds. Equity holders expected, and corporate managers delivered, routine and stable dividends. Profits need not be maximized, which was viewed as unnecessarily risky and a frank waste of corporate resources during an era of high tax rates, but need only be just sufficient to cover dividends. Hence, the absence of capital gains expectations of equity holders supported the management-dominated, nonprofit maximizing firms of midcentury.

The pursuit of capital gains so dominated late-twentieth-century stock investing that envisioning shareholding without it is difficult. But capital gains are an unusual and uniquely speculative mechanism of investment return. Favorable mid-century tax treatment and an expanding and appreciating stock market encouraged capital gains. Disappointing capital gains spurred corporate restructuring. Interpreters of corporate restructuring, such as Harrison and Bluestone (1988), who emphasize the importance of the 1970s corporate "profit squeeze" as the most important cause of restructuring downplay the equally important loss of wealth to owners from a plunging stock market. Investors did experience seriously lower returns during the 1970s, but this was more proximately caused by flat to negative capital gains for stocks during the period rather than by "squeezed" corporate profits. The lack of capital gains in a market that valued securities as capitalized earnings precipitated aggressive restructuring activity of all kinds, including takeovers and internal reorganization.

Although well suited to the interpretation of corporate activity of oligopolistic, very large firms during the mid-twentieth century (with the important exceptions of conglomerates, glamour, and growth-oriented firms, all of which pursued capital gains financial market strategies), several events of the 1980s and 1990s challenged the aptness of managerialism as an image of U.S. capitalism.[13] Corporate takeovers, the emergence of a shareholder rights movement with a sharp focus on corporate profits, the rapid turnover of senior executives, and corporate downsizing that reduced the ranks of corporate management are difficult to interpret from a perspective that begins with an assumption of managerial control. Socioeconomists returned to the issue of corporate control and developed alternative owner-dominant accounts in opposition to managerialism.

One prominent and typical example of this literature is Michael Useem's (1996) "investor capitalism" model. In Useem's work, the increase in institutional investing mobilized the latent power of owners who staged a "shareholder rebellion" that shifted the balance of power in the firm and forced corporations to emphasize financial performance and production efficiency:

> After half a century of unchallenged supremacy, senior management at many corporations faced a revolt from one of the least likely of sources, the shareholders. They were, after all, the owners. But their real ownership powers had long been lost in an atomization of holdings that had left them weak and divided. The disenfranchisement seemed so irreversible that the managerial revolution appeared to be one of those fixed and perhaps even eternal qualities of advanced capitalism. (P. 329)

The investor capitalism standpoint is sympathetic to the shareholder rebellion. It tends to lionize shareholders as the saviors of U.S. corporations.[14] Useem (1996) cites two other leading contributors to the investor capitalism standpoint, Michael Jensen and Peter Drucker, to make this point:

> The assessment of Michael Jensen, a leading advocate of change in top management of publicly traded corporations, illustrates the critique that became widespread during the late 1980s: the autonomy of professional management from ownership oversight, he concluded, had caused: "widespread waste and inefficiency of the public corporation and its inability to adapt to changing economic circumstances." Peter Drucker echoed the appraisal: "What made takeovers and buyouts inevitable . . . was the mediocre performance of enlightened-despot management, the management without clear definitions of performance and results and with no clear accountability to anybody." (P. 310)

Two themes are emphasized in this literature. First, whereas mid-twentieth-century corporate managers dominated their firms, late-twentieth-century managers have become (re)subordinated to investors, investors who have been empowered by the rise of institutional shareholding. Big institutional owners shifted the balance of corporate power so managers were forced to pursue corporate policies favorable to the profit-maximizing interests of investors. The new, powerful, active owners employed a variety of strategies including corporate takeovers and downsizing to ensure that corporations are run efficiently for maximum profit. From Useem's (1996) perspective, crusading institutional investors forced on management corporate restructuring and other major managerial initiatives of late-twentieth-century U.S. capitalism for the benefit of "owners" as a class. The expansion of mutual funds and 401(k) pension plans, and (although not developed by Useem) the organization of managers of these funds into associations that helped them develop strategies for pursuing "shareholder value" initiatives, increased the relative power of investors.[15] Useem emphasizes several mechanisms investors use to exercise their power. These include investor control of corporate boards, special direct access to senior management and the files of the firm, and special conference calls with senior management to process corporate events and reports. Useem concludes that investors are largely in control of U.S. firms. Managers who do not do investors bidding are fired and replaced with those who will.

Second, as with managerialism, "investor capitalism" (inappropriately for the late twentieth century) emphasizes the divergence of interests between owners as a class and managers as a class. The investor capitalism argument follows. Shareholders are asserted to have a long-term interest in the firm due to their large equity holdings and to favor corporate policies that will maximize earnings in the end. Managers, whose stake in the firm is short term, have an opportunistic interest in firm growth. Managers receive salary, benefits, and the prestige of employment in a leading firm. Managers' status is largely dependent on the firm for which they work. Managers bathe in the reflected prestige of the firms to which they are attached. As the firm moves up the hierarchy of corporations, the managers themselves move up also. Power and prestige is associated with a higher status company. To Useem, managers apparently want the firm to grow regardless of profits, whereas shareholders want the firm to be profitable regardless of growth. The interests of managers are short term and growth oriented, the interests of owners are long term and focused on profits. Useem's conclusion: the supposed divergent interests of managers and owners explain the lively corporate power struggles of the late twentieth century. Useem's prominent work, for example, explores both sides of the line drawn by this dichotomy: One of his major contributions, *Executive Defense* (1993), explored tactics managers use to maintain control of firms, such as replacing disgruntled or troublesome institutional owners with shareholders who are friendly to management. Another, *Investor Capitalism* (1996), described the mechanisms institutional shareholders use to secure corporate control from managers.

To summarize, one of the most active debates is who controls the corporation. Answers to this question have often been framed in terms of manager versus owner control. Rather than contribute to this debate in these terms, this study approaches the problem of power and profit in contemporary U.S. capitalism from the view that neither managers nor owners are solely in control of firms. Instead, corporate governance structures comprise elite members of each group.

COMMON INTERESTS AND COLLABORATIVE CONTROL

In outline form, the governance structure of modern U.S. corporations resembles a sort of formal, although twisted, democracy. Ultimate sovereignty in corporate affairs lies with shareholders who elect (one vote per share) representatives to the board of directors, the highest governing body of the corporation. The board of directors has oversight over the corporation and appoints an executive team (usually a CEO, sometimes also a president, a chief operating officer, or COO, and a chief financial officer, or CFO) who appoint the rest of the executive team. The board of directors meets regularly with somewhat heightened activity around the time of the annual audit and during times of business reorganization. The board of directors of most large corporations includes representatives of large investors, notables drawn from key parts of the corporation's environment, and members of senior management. Struggles for corporate control usually play out at the board level, and the composition and procedures of the board are quite important and can be hotly contested.

A view of corporate control, focusing on corporate governance structures as important social intermediaries between firms and markets, allows us to analyze several dimensions of "control" in late-twentieth-century capitalism differently than either managerialist or investor capitalist perspectives.

First, both managerialism and investor capitalism deduce the interests of management and owners as classes and then explain corporate actions as a result of the pursuit of the interests of the class presumed to be in control. Both of these viewpoints identify the interests of managers as short term and oriented toward growth of the firm (or opportunism) and the interests of owners as long term and oriented toward profit. This study makes a similar interest-based argument, but specifies a very different alignment of interests in that the elite strata of both owners and management are unified with each other and divided from the lesser ranks of each class. Insight into late-twentieth-century corporate life might be better addressed if the question, "Who controls the corporation?" is supplemented by the question, "Who benefits when a corporation acts in particular ways?" For example, who benefited from internal organizational restructuring? Elite executives and large owners profoundly benefited from restructuring actions to stimulate the stock values of the corporation they jointly governed, whereas lower level managers were among the most profoundly harmed by these actions. Outside investors who lacked intimate knowledge of the actions of the inner circle were disadvantaged, and many purchased their shares at inflated prices as insiders sold out. An elite stratum of owners and managers, welded together into a cohesive speculative management team, was a crucial social intermediary between financial markets and corporations in recent times.

Second, the investor capitalism perspective correctly identifies the influence of financial markets through the interest of owners in profits, but the importance of secondary security markets in corporate affairs is not exhausted by this general specification of "investor interests." This study moves toward an inductive investigation of coalitions of interest among elite executives and large owners and the mechanisms they employ to realize them. To understand corporate control in late-twentieth-century America, noticing the variety of means through which corporations can be used to capture value is essential. Capturing value and corporate control could be distinct issues because the group that controls a corporation need not be the same group that profits from corporate actions. Indeed, rampant insider trading accompanied and tainted many of the takeovers of the 1980s, an illustration of the use of inside knowledge about corporate actions to generate profit rather than corporate control. Risk arbitrageurs, for example, "bought on the rumor [of takeovers] and sold on the news." These market operatives, although sometimes linked in a collusive alliance with corporate raiders, usually sought only short-term profit from their shareholding rather than control. Many of the inside trading scandals involved similar opportunistic profit making divorced from corporate control. Often, however, as in the case of the value captured through corporate restructuring, those who are in control of corporations are also capturing value. Currently, the secondary financial market figures prominently in strategies for capturing value from appreciation of stock prices.

Third, both managerialism and investor capitalism overemphasized the conflict between so-called long-term, profit-oriented shareholders and short-term, growth-oriented managers. Both of these viewpoints depict unified blocks of managers warring with unified blocks of shareholders. The view necessary to understand the internal restructuring wave recognizes that both managers and owners are stratified groups. Elite strata of owners and executives comprise a single interest group. In the business culture of the 1980s and 1990s the dominant corporate governance structure was a team of managers and owners collaborating to manage a modern corporation speculatively. Such a team has both the knowledge and the power to make the corporate changes and present the associated symbolic performances that can, if all goes well, affect stock prices. The corporate governance structure that dominates in the late twentieth century is welded together by a mutual interest in the share price of the firm. Useem (1996) and many other writers have noted the rise of equity shareholding among managers and in Useem's view executive stock ownership is a mechanism to ensure investor capitalism, because it encourages managers to pursue shareholder's interest in the long-term profitability of the enterprise. The view in this study interprets executive shareholding differently: Equity-compensated executives share with owners a speculative interest in the short-term trend of stock prices.[16]

One excellent illustration of the stratification of shareholders and managers is the use of executive stock options. Granting very large stock options to senior executives obviously benefits the executives who receive them, putting them in a separate class from managers who are compensated with salaries. Such grants are usually interpreted as an event that benefits shareholders as an undifferentiated group because executives are now tied to shareholder interests.

Granting of stock options does cost shareholders, even though these options do not directly add to the expense of the company. Shareholders as a class pay for stock options because they dilute their stock. On the exercise of the options, the firm's earnings are spread across a larger number of shares of stock, lowering the earnings per share. Often, companies use stock buyback programs to repurchase stock, reducing some of the earnings dilution. The cost of options is actually quite large. "If the full cost of stock options were deducted from the earnings of large corporations, their earnings would fall on average 4 percent. At high tech firms, including the cost of employee stock options as expenses reduces their earnings 'anywhere from 10 percent to 100 percent'" (MacDonald and McGough 1999, p. C1). Stock options benefit elite executives who receive them and large shareholders who effectively turn senior executives into speculative managers. That they benefit salaried managers and actually damage the interests of average shareholders does not follow.[17]

The conception of social intermediaries, then, draws attention to corporate governance structures as an important area of recent corporate life and an important factor in corporate restructuring. This argument suggests that several major changes occurred in late-twentieth-century American capitalism to place U.S. corporations firmly in the control of a specific type of corporate governance structure: speculative management teams. Speculative management teams were composed of the elite strata of owners and managers. An interest in maintaining and increasing the value of equity securities on secondary financial markets united these top managers (president, CEO, COO, CFO, and others) and very large owners (pension fund managers, mutual fund managers, other institutional investors, and large private shareholders).

The major changes addressed in this chapter were the rise of institutional investors and the rise of stock options for top management. First, the rise of institutional investors led to a concentration of ownership stakes in the hands of relatively few professional managers who shared an interest in boosting equity prices. This concentration of ownership led to the possibility and realization of an activist stance on the part of investors toward management. Berle and Means's (19__) characterization of 1930s U.S. financial ownership claimed that shareholders did indeed have an interest in maximizing profitability of a firm but lacked the means to realize that interest. The decentralized ownership structure of U.S. corporations with thousands of geographically and socially dispersed shareholders prevented the effective exercise of shareholder power. The late-twentieth-century concentration of ownership by institutional investors allowed for more effective exercise of shareholder power in the pursuit of shareholder interests, as Useem (1996) argues:

> Managerial capitalism permitted executives to ignore their shareholders. Investor capitalism does not. Managerial capitalism tolerated a host of company objectives besides shareholder value. Investor capitalism does not. In changing the balance of power between executives and owners, investor capitalism has ended an era of unrestrained managerial dominance. Overseeing the country's great companies now requires management of not only the inside troops but also the outside investors. (P. 10)

A second change was the rise of stock options for top management. The percentage of total top management compensation represented by equity-based compensation greatly expanded during the last quarter of the twentieth century. The most celebrated stock-optioned executive during the 1990s was Michael Eisner, who earned as much as $400 million in a single year from his Disney compensation package. Eisner came to Disney as chairman and CEO after a failed takeover of Disney in 1984. Eisner's compensation package was heavily weighted toward equity securities. His initial package (in 1984 dollars) was $750,000 in salary, $1 million in performance bonus, $750,000 signing bonus, and options on 510,000 shares of Disney stock at $57 per share (Taylor 1987, p. 233).

As the rise of institutional investors made it possible for investors to act like managers, the rise of stock options meant that top managers took on the outlook and interests of investors and began to act like big investors. As the percentage of top management compensation represented by equities increased during the late twentieth century, managers' incentive to boost share prices increased. Their focus shifted toward financial speculation and away from production efficiency.

The size of stock options granted to senior executives was impressive in the late twentieth century. Executives at some large firms were granted stock options so large that they became one of the largest shareholders of the firms they managed. Sunbeam's Al Dunlap, for example, was the fourth largest shareholder, with nearly 2 percent of the firm's outstanding stock. With such large equity stakes, even moderate changes in share price could seriously impact the wealth of senior managers. Although senior executives received huge windfalls if the price increased, they could also lose wealth rapidly if the share price declined. Top managers had an imperative interest in avoiding market signals that would trigger a fall in share price. When the overall stock market declined nearly 20 percent for a brief period in the late summer of 1998, the effect on senior executive wealth was quite marked:[18]

> Ten of the 138 chief executive officers of major U.S. companies given megagrants of stock options last year have suffered paper losses ranging from $4.1 million to a whopping $24.4 million. . . . Megagrants are those with a face value at least three times the size of an executive's annual salary and bonus [138 of the 500 largest companies gave megagrants to their CEOs in 1997!]. . . . Among the corporate chiefs hardest hit: Eastman Kodak Co.'s George M. C. Fisher (paper losses of $23.8); Oracle Corp.'s Lawrence J. Ellison ($18.2 million); CSX Corp.'s John Snow ($15 million). . . . For shareholder activists who have long attacked option megagrants as excessive, their steep fall in value is poetic justice. "Clearly, there is going to be a huge wave of option repricing going on," says Patrick McGurn, director of corporate programs for Institutional Shareholder Services, a proxy-advisory firm in Bethesda, Md. (Lublin 1998, p. B1)

Academic research into insider stock sales indicates that the timing of share sales by top executives often coincides with corporate news indicating that top managers synchronize news announcements and their share sales to maximize their own interests. Members of the speculative management team had access to privileged information that outsiders lacked, allowing them to time their market trades more effectively to maximize their speculative gains. Outsiders to the firm were aware of this and insider stock sales and purchases were closely examined for signals of impending market-moving news.

The following item about insider sales of stock at Lycos, Inc., demonstrates both the superior speculative positions of members of corporate governance structures and the constraint on the realization of speculative profits market regulation imposed. In early February 1999, the value of Lycos shares fell 26 percent on the news that the firm would merge with USA Networks in a stock-swap merger. Lycos declined largely because USA Networks did not pay a "heftier price" (award Lycos shareholders the full market value of their shares) in the merger. Market participants had been bidding up the price of Lycos shares as rumors of the impending merger spread (the price skyrocketed from $50 per share in early January to $145 per share on January 11). As the price peaked, Lycos insiders began selling large blocks of their shares:

> Just as the company's shares were soaring on hopes of a takeover at a big premium . . . Mr. Davis and Mr. Philip may have sold their shares at even higher levels than those included in the filing. That's because the Securities and Exchange Commission form, called a Form 144, often is filed by company insiders after a sale of stock, even though it is technically an "intention" to sell. It includes an estimate of the price the seller expects to receive but the real price of the sale won't be disclosed by the company until one month after the filing. (Pulliam 1999, p. C1)

Because they comprise both managers and owners, speculative management teams were able to manipulate effectively corporate actions and results to generate gains in the market values of equities they held. An example was the manipulation of corporate results prior to a management buyout. In a management buyout (which from the standpoint of this study should be renamed *speculative management team buyout*), managers of the firm and select owners arranged financing to enable them to make a tender offer for the publicly traded shares of the firm. If the offer were accepted, the team purchased all of the outstanding shares of stock and the corporation ceased to be publicly traded: it was taken private. The buyout team then engaged in actions to realize immediate profits and to increase the future market value of the firm. They sold off chunks of the business, rearranged the financial statements, restructured the organization, and laid off workers and demanded wage concessions. After realizing immediate profits from asset sales and improving the apparent profitability of the remaining operations, the team then sold shares in the company again on public financial markets with an IPO, usually realizing significant reorganizer's profit in the process. Academic research on buyouts reveals that they were a very profitable maneuver in the 1980s. In a sample of 87 management buyout cases from 1980 to 1987, Wu (1997) found evidence that "managers" manipulated earnings of firms prior to making a management buyout offer (MBO), Wu finds that earnings moved sharply lower in the year before the MBO, much lower than other firms in the industry. The stock prices also moved sharply lower in the months before the MBO, in a pattern that tracks the eroding earnings. Wu found that earnings and stock prices declined prior to management buyouts but not prior to third party takeover bids. "The overall evidence favors the hypothesis that managers manipulated earnings downward prior to the MBO proposal" (p. 376). Wu estimated that earnings management lowered the buyout price an average of $50 million for the firms in his sample. The speculative management team was a much more effective speculator than outsiders.

By the 1980s these two changes had enabled the formation of an inner circle of corporate control within most very large firms. Unlike those claiming that management or institutional investors dominated U.S. corporations, this study finds that in the late twentieth century a new configuration of control dominated and governed. Very senior managers and very large owners, welded together by an interest in higher equity values, possessed the knowledge and the power to control both corporate events and corporate reporting to increase equity values.

Corporate charters for most publicly traded firms required that "outside directors" be appointed as part of the firm's governance structure to monitor and balance investor and management interests. Strong outside directors might challenge the unity of owners and managers and make speculative management difficult. This potential difficulty was minimized through two mechanisms. First, the existing board of directors, dominated by owners and executives, held the power to select outside directors. This allowed the selection of outside directors who were predisposed to cooperate with speculative management teams. Although this quote refers to 1970s corporate boards, it demonstrates the way members of the inner circle of control can exercise discretion in the selection of new board members:

> Most boards in the past were ineffective because the management controlled board members. Directors were usually chosen by the CEO with top management's influence. The CEO would typically select some of the directors from top-level management (insiders) and others from outside the organization who were normally friends. No one would dispute the CEO's decisions and whatever he had to say was the way it would be. Myles L. Mace's 1971 interviews with chief executives support this conclusion. For instance, he quotes one chief executive who said, "In selecting new outsider directors, I pick them very much like a trial jury." Another president said, "Don't be surprised or disappointed if you find that most outsider members are known to be no boat-rockers. . . . You certainly don't want anyone on your board who even slightly might be a challenge or question to your tenure." (Alkhafaji 1990, p. 87)

The potential disruption of outside directors was further contained by making them part of the speculative management team. Dunlap (1996) described how shareholder activists demanded and often received director compensation packages that eliminated salaries and replaced them with stock options. This ensured that every member of the corporate governance structure shared an interest in boosting equity values. The corporate scandals at Enron, WorldCom, and other firms in 2001 and 2002 led to extensive questioning of the wisdom this form of compensation.

An important but little noted 1992 change to the SEC rules governing shareholder and management interaction (known as proxy rules) effectively solidified and institutionalized speculative management teams in corporate America. The rule change permitted small groups of shareholders to meet to discuss corporate affairs without formally notifying all shareholders and offering their inclusion. It also allowed small groups of shareholders to meet with corporate executives, also without formally notifying all shareholders and offering to include them. This ruling cleared the regulatory path for the completed transformation of corporate governance structures into effective speculative management teams.

CONCLUSIONS: FROM INVESTOR CAPITALISM TO SPECULATIVE MANAGEMENT

Social intermediaries are connective structures that link firms to secondary financial markets and are the pathways of speculative management. Examining the issue of corporate control in the United States with a viewpoint sensitive to the importance of social intermediaries brings an important but underappreciated control arrangement into view. Corporate governance structures bring financial market participants and corporate management into direct relation with each other. The peculiar composition and equity-based solidarity of corporate governance structures at very large firms in the late twentieth century made them eager and very effective instruments for controlling the price of corporate stock and were aptly labeled *speculative management teams*. This view of late-twentieth-century corporate control cuts across the long-running debate in socioeconomics over manager control versus owner control. The viewpoint is clarified with a final comparison to the current leading contender in this debate, Useem's (1996) *Investor Capitalism*, which affirmed the idea that the interests of big shareholders are long term.

As noted earlier, the investor capitalism viewpoint argues that investors, especially big institutional investors, are beneficial for U.S. capitalism because of their long-term focus. Big investors have a long-term interest in the firms whose stock they hold because they are unable to sell their stock without taking market losses. This idea is contained in the mission statement of the Council for Institutional Investors, an association of more than 60 pension funds created in 1985 to push for public policies that furthered their collective interests and to force management to promote shareholder interests. Useem (1996) notes that the association was formed on the premise that "the enormity of pension fund holdings limits their ability to sell stock and move money into other companies," and thus "pension funds' interests are truly inseparable from those of the country's economy" (p. 318).

Equating the interests of big shareholders with the country and claiming that big shareholders are sanctimoniously and patriotically performing society's dirty work is an effective covering rhetoric. It is, however, misleading because it fails to acknowledge that the interest of large shareholders in U.S. firms is essentially short term and speculative. In the late twentieth century, most pension funds held less than 1 percent of a corporation's stock. In the course of some 200 trading days each year, a volume equal to the entire outstanding shares of stock the average company was exchanged. In a market where the average annual turnover of shares in a given stock is more than 100 percent, an amount of stock equal to the entire position of a pension fund is turned over in two days of normal trading. Pension fund managers and other large shareholders were not locked into their holdings. If anything, the large number of other institutional shareholders increased the liquidity of institutional stockholdings, making selling shares in large block trades easier for fund managers.

Fund managers have short-term interests in any given company and (possibly) long-term interests in the stock market as a whole. Fund managers must diversify their holdings and do not concentrate more than 5 percent of their funds in the securities of one company. The claim that fund managers hold such large blocks of stock that they cannot be sold without driving down the market price is not supported. Fund managers have an interest in the growth rate of the overall market more than the long-term prospects of any one company.

Useem (1996) and others argue that the rise of investor capitalism has been good for the United States because these large owners have a true long-term, stewardship interest in the firm. They own too much of the firm's stock to sell easily and therefore have the long-term interests of the productive enterprise at heart. This is highly questionable. The managers of institutional investment funds (pensions, mutual funds, and insurance) have been among the most active traders in the market. The managers of investment funds are compensated for their performance no less than corporate managers. If their fund values are not high, their own compensation falls. Furthermore, the status ranking of fund managers is dependent on the performance of their funds, measured in the total financial returns generated (including dividends and capital gains). Strong performance ensures that a fund manager is highly compensated and sought after by other funds, whereas poor performance might lead to dismissal. Fund managers have an imperative to find maximum profits through short-term trades. Herzel and Shepro (1999) offer two reasons for the trading activity of fund managers:

> First, securities markets are very liquid, allowing the possibility of large short-run profits for individual investors. Second, because of the

possibility of these profits, institutional investment managers come under great pressure to produce them by investing for the short run only. . . . Since 1935 the situation has worsened. Markets have become much more liquid. And pressure for short-run results has intensified because of the enormous growth in institutional investment. The short-run success of money managers is closely monitored and encouraged by their clients. . . . Although some fund managers invest for the long term, most turn over their stock holdings rapidly in an effort to maximize the current value of their investment portfolio, since this is the main criterion against which their own performance is judged. (P. 28)

Large shareholders are traders as well as (and even more than) long-term holders. Their holdings in a given stock fluctuate widely as fund managers attempt to speculatively profit from price breaks.

The view of U.S. capitalism advanced in this study sees that fund managers of pension and mutual funds can be *institutional speculators*. Although some claim that investor capitalism's large, long-term owners are saving U.S. corporations from the sloth and opportunistic behavior of entrenched management, they ignore the short-term trading, collusive activity, and opportunistic behavior of institutional speculators. Investor capitalist writers identify short-term performance criteria for managers, usually in the form of quarterly and annual financial results, as the reason for manager's short-term focus. These are precisely the same performance criteria that have been used to evaluate and reward the managers of pension and mutual funds. Hence, managers of funds have been focused no less on the short term than managers of companies. Viewed from the angle of this study, both have an incentive in the opportunistic, speculative management of U.S. corporations. Both of these groups participate in corporate governance structures and have the capacity to act in their common interest in controlling corporations to increase the (short-term) price of equity shares as members of speculative management teams.

Chapter 6

THE RISE OF CORPORATE RESTRUCTURING, 1984–1990

*A new focal point of interest has captured the imagination of manage-
ment during the past couple of years—restructuring. Hardly a day
passes without some company announcing a major restructuring of its
businesses or capital structure.[1]*

*There is of course, no better means of avoiding a takeover than in-
creasing the price of the stock. Thus, increasing share price has
become the fundamental purpose of corporate restructuring.[2]*

During the 1980s U.S. corporations were engaged in tremendous pecuniary reorganization through external transactions: mergers, acquisitions,
and hostile takeovers. Internal reorganization accompanied these transactions, sometimes under the designation *restructuring*. Among the firms
studied for this book, Monsanto recorded the earliest write-off for such activity in 1979. In annual reports for the early 1980s, corporations engaging
in pecuniary reorganization rarely called attention to internal reorganization. When discussing business reorganization, these reports focused on
mergers, acquisitions, and especially, takeovers. Corporate predators presented takeovers to shareholders as a great opportunity, as the leading edge
of aggressively good management practice. Corporate prey presented
takeovers as a threat to corporate autonomy and long-term value. As corporate takeovers accelerated during the 1980s, internal reorganization (restructuring) grew apace as successful predators sought to improve cash
flow to meet takeover-related debt payments and potential prey sought to
increase share prices to reduce takeover threats.

This chapter attempts to sort out just what *restructuring* meant
during this time. Corporate restructuring in the 1980s referred to a
wider range of activities than the term eventually came to signify in the
early 1990s. Corporate communications departments and business news

media drew attention to a variety of takeover-related activities under the restructuring rubric including asset restructuring (selling corporate assets to raise cash) and capital restructuring (usually increasing the leverage of the firm by issuing bonds and repurchasing stock). Opinion leaders in corporate finance developed an interpretive framework and a specialized argot to explain and justify the frankly pecuniary and often-draconian actions associated with takeovers. Socially and politically polarizing, takeovers, and related business practices nevertheless attained financial market legitimacy in the United States and by the mid-1980s, were a leading form of aggressively good management practice.

Not all important causal elements of takeovers and related restructuring were emphasized in the cognitive framing of financial opinion leaders. One stealthy although critical aspect of late-twentieth-century corporate restructuring, the transformation of corporations with multiple divisions into complex configurations of legally independent subsidiaries, which Prechel (1997, 2000) and Prechel and Boies (1998) designated as the MLSF, was quietly undertaken by most large corporations in the United States during this period. Although the significance of the transformation to the MLSF escaped the notice of opinion leaders in financial markets, possibly because speculative teams subsumed the legal restructuring of divisions as subsidiaries within the larger package their MLSF reorganization to financial markets as a stand-alone justification of value reassessment—and has indeed escaped the notice of many academic studies of restructuring, it was an important enabling legal structure for takeovers and related restructuring activities described herein.

Transactional reorganization in the late twentieth century was greatly facilitated by the transformation to the MLSF. Corporate divisions are wholly owned by the corporation, but subsidiaries only require majority ownership. By adopting a subsidiary structure, the parent corporation can complete acquisitions with roughly half the capital. By strategically layering subsidiaries into complex laminations—enabling subsidiaries to own subsidiaries—a parent corporation can leverage a small amount of capital into control of a vast herd of business units.

Internal reorganizations in the 1990s were conspicuously linked to a prior incident of external reorganization in corporate communications. As described in chapter 7, when macroeconomic conditions discouraged takeovers and other transactional reorganization, corporate restructuring ceased to designate external reorganization and instead became associated with internal reorganization (downsizing, streamlining, and reengineering). By the 1990s, the connection between internal and external reorganization was cut, and internal reorganization stepped out of the shadow of takeovers to reign as a leading practice of aggressively good management.

All three social intermediaries contributed to the rise of corporate restructuring and internal reorganization as practices of speculative management. The transformation of corporate governance structures into speculative management teams (or simply speculative teams) occurred during this period for many of the firms in the study. The transformation of governance structures into speculative teams coincided with the emergence of an active market for corporate control. Takeovers, the threat of takeovers, and defenses to takeovers were instrumental for strengthening relationships between top executives and big owners and closing the circle of interest between them. Reviewing accounts of takeovers in the contemporary business news media, determining if speculative teams caused takeovers or takeovers caused the formation and strengthening of speculative teams is difficult. Either way, speculative teams encouraged the pursuit of increased equity valuations through reorganizations.

Financial accounting contributed to the rise of restructuring by allowing the flexible and strategic use of restructuring charges to manage corporate profits. In 1986 the SEC issued Staff Accounting Bulletin no. 67, *Income Statement Presentation of Restructuring Charges* (SAB 67). The FASB, the primary standards-setting body of the financial accounting profession in 1987 that serves as the definitive guideline for accountants and auditors on the restructuring issue until 1994 acknowledged the statement.[3] The SAB 67 was intended to constrain the use of restructuring charges to manipulate corporate income. It had the effect, however, of sanctioning great flexibility in the timing and content of these charges, flexibility that managers learned to exploit strategically during the late 1980s and early 1990s.

Business news media played a supporting role in the rise of takeovers and the institutionalization of internal reorganization. The news media covered takeovers and restructuring extensively and helped to publicize the relationship between these activities and rising share prices. Indeed, the news media were an essential intermediary for the takeover game because leaks of pending takeovers were often important to strategies of both raiding and defending corporate teams. The analytic business news media, in particular, clarified and communicated the utility of reorganizations for increasing corporate value and the specific value of internal reorganization as an important contributor to high values. By the end of the 1980s, business news media helped to create a climate where stock market participants and corporate managers viewed internal reorganization as a distinct, useful (speculative) management practice.

EMERGENCE OF RESTRUCTURING IN THE CONTEXT OF TAKEOVERS

Corporate restructuring became widespread in U.S. corporations as a technique for cleaning up the operations and financial statements of firms after corporate takeovers. The term had been used occasionally prior to the 1980s as a synonym for extensive Chapter 11 bankruptcy reorganizations. Some analysts had also used the term to refer to macroindustrial reorganization prior to 1982.[4] Rappaport (1986) commented on the diversity of meaning of the term in the early to mid-1980s:

> Some executives have used the term "restructuring" to justify almost any strategy that departs from business as usual. *Business Week* humorously (I assume) defines restructuring as "writing down and leveraging up." (P. 242, fn.)

Not until the very late 1980s did corporate restructuring come to signify the intentional, voluntary kinds of internal reorganization that are the focus of this study. For most of the 1980s, corporate restructuring referred to a mix of diverse actions: the closing of plants, the shifting of corporate focus to different lines of business, reordering the organizational structure of the firm, creating new channels of communication, and flattening hierarchies of authority.[5] Along with other terms such as *greenmail, Pac-man defense,* and *leveraged buyout,* the term *corporate restructuring* became part of the vernacular of the business world in the context of takeovers and LBOs of the 1980s.

The 1980's flurry of corporate takeovers and the personalities who orchestrated them featured prominently in the news media. High-profile takeovers that corporate raiders such as T. Boone Pickens, Carl Icahn, Jerry Levin, and Charles Hurwitz arranged, and the emerging organizational structure that made their actions possible, especially Drexel Burnham Lambert's junk bond market, were the subject of extensive business news media and academic analysis. Although a significant portion of the business news coverage of takeovers emphasized their destructive aspects, academic writings on takeovers, especially those published in the *Harvard Business Review* in the late 1980s and early 1990s, often portrayed takeovers as beneficial for U.S. business. The article on corporate takeovers that is most often cited in the academic literature is Michael Jensen's (1989) "Eclipse of the Public Corporation."[6] Jensen characterizes the rise of takeovers in the United States during the 1980s as the creation of a "market for corporate control" by "activist investors" who disciplined U.S. management and created value for American shareholders and the United States at large:

> Takeovers and buyouts both create new value and unlock value destroyed by management through misguided policies. I estimate that transactions associated with the market for corporate control unlocked shareholder gains (in target companies alone) of more than $500 billion between 1977 and 1988—more than 50 percent of the cash dividends paid by the entire corporate sector over this period. . . . The widespread waste and inefficiency of the public corporation and its inability to adapt to changing economic circumstances have generated a wave of organizational innovation over the last 15 years—innovation driven by the rebirth of "active investors." (P. 61)

Like so many others, Jensen's (1989) justification of takeovers aligns with the logic of the efficient market hypothesis. Profits from takeovers are self-legitimating: the increase in stock prices following takeovers is "proof" that they were good for industrial production and the U.S. economy. Increased shareholder value is a direct reflection of decreased waste and increased efficiency of production processes in posttakeover firms. Jensen does not consider that a rise in share prices may be disconnected from production processes and follows from the autonomous speculative logic of secondary financial markets. Many speculative management techniques associated with takeovers, including stock buybacks and increases in leverage, have no direct effect on production processes yet clearly increased the price of stock. This study seeks to attain a vantage point of the relationship between corporate reorganization and increased stock prices that does not rely on the presumed mechanism of an efficient market.

Whether takeovers added value to U.S. firms, they created operational challenges for managers of the merged enterprises. After a takeover, the operations of two hitherto disparate organizations had to be integrated in some fashion. Because the legitimating rhetoric of corporate takeovers emphasized cost savings and efficiency, postmerger reorganizations were viewed as an essential part of a takeover, needed to realize potential cost savings resulting from mergers. Without such consolidation, the two organizations would continue a form of parallel production, presumably wasting corporate resources on redundant operations, never achieving any economies of scale. With increasing frequency during the 1980s, managers described postacquisition organizational changes as "restructuring." The following excerpt from the period is a good example:

> Restructuring involves diverse activities such as divestiture of underperforming businesses or businesses that do not "fit," spinoffs directly to shareholders, acquisitions paid with "excess cash," stock repurchases, debt swaps, and liquidation of overfunded pension funds.[7] (Rappaport 1986, p. 10)

Characteristic of writings about restructuring from the mid-1980s is seeing these actions primarily in terms of external transactions—divestitures, spin-offs, acquisitions and the like—rather than in terms of internal organizational change. One of the insights of the current study is that internal organizational change became the focus of restructuring efforts when market conditions for external reorganization plummeted in the early 1990s (see chapters 3 and 8).

Although rhetorically justified as an effort to boost productivity by integrating operations of merged firms, these actions also served to generate cash (from asset sales) to pay down acquisition debt and increase cash generation to meet debt payments, which improved the "creditworthiness" of the firm. Heavily leveraged corporate acquisitions, such as junk bond financed takeovers, place creditors (bondholders) in a powerful position. Bondholders and traders often become part of posttakeover speculative teams. When creditors have a strong hand in corporate governance, the direction of speculative management is altered. Because the value of a bond fluctuates in direct relation to a firm's credit rating, bondholders' interests lie not in the direction of maximum profitability (which benefits equity shareholders), but rather in the direction of maximum creditworthiness. One of the great ironies of the late twentieth century is that the lowest grade debt—junk bonds—often has the greatest potential for appreciation from improvements in corporate creditworthiness. Speculative junk-bond holders realize large gains on their holdings by encouraging firms to take actions that improve their credit rating. High cash flow, sufficient to meet bond payments with a comfortable reserve, was of primary concern to creditors and many posttakeover internal reorganizations were designed to achieve this.

Bond purchasers ride corporate management to improve creditworthiness because purchasers of low graded bonds can realize large speculative gains when the issuing corporation returns to "investment grade." Phillips Petroleum is a good example of a firm that was being speculatively managed to boost bond values as well as stock values in the 1980s. In its annual report to equity shareholders in 1987, the company attempted to legitimate its strenuous efforts to improve the firm's creditworthiness by emphasizing that shareholders would benefit from the improved terms of future debt financing:

> Throughout 1987, despite the difficulties presented by the oil and gas market, Phillips achieved important objectives. We met our debt reduction target for the year, bringing our total debt down to $5.6 billion. Our longer-term objective is to reduce debt and build our equity base enough to regain our investment-grade bond rating, which will allow the restructuring of debt under more favorable terms. Cash flow remained strong throughout 1987. (P. 3)

Many of the reorganizing efforts at Georgia-Pacific in 1990 were related to its acquisition of Great Northern Nekoosa Corporation, "the largest business combination in the history of the forest products industry [which] . . . more important than simply increasing our size . . . gives us improved economies of scale, enhanced strength in our markets and the flexibility required in today's increasingly competitive and global markets" (Georgia-Pacific 1990 Annual Report). In addition to "integrating the operations of the two companies," Georgia-Pacific is also reducing debt and increasing cash flow, which benefit bondholders as much as shareholders. This is a good example of restructuring actions explicitly linked to a preceding transaction:

> Restructuring: We reviewed our operations and sold $1 billion of assets identified as not strategic to the company's goals. On January 31, 1991, we completed the largest of these divestitures with the sale of two containerboard mills, 19 corrugated packaging plants and 540,000 acres of related timberland for approximately $740 million. Also in January, we sold our interests in a containerboard mill and packaging plants in France. In late 1990, we sold four printing paper mills in the United Kingdom, 119,000 acres of surplus timberland and a small paper mill in Reading, Pennsylvania. . . . The asset sales and cash from operations allowed us to retire a significant amount of our acquisition debt less than one year after the acquisition. To continue to reduce debt as quickly as possible, we are managing our businesses to maximize cash flow and are limiting capital expenditures. (N.p.)

One aim of postmerger restructuring, therefore, was the generation of cash and greater cash flow to bolster the creditworthiness of firms. But the most important and consequential motivation for restructuring was the increase in value of corporate stock. The business news media and academic community recognized that restructuring aimed at strategic increases in share prices:

> In many cases, these restructurings are motivated by a desire to foil a takeover bid by so called "raiders" who look for undermanaged companies where changes in strategic direction could dramatically increase the value of the stock, and for companies with high liquidation values relative to their current share price (Rappaport, 1986, p. 10)

The preceding quotation nicely demonstrates early understandings of the links among restructuring, share prices, and takeovers. Companies with less than optimal share prices were at risk of takeover. Management teams that wished to remain in control had to boost share prices to their highest level or lose control to a new team of owners and managers who would. Not all takeover defenses relied on restructuring but, significantly, many firms recording early restructuring charges also engaged in other takeover defenses. Motorola's 1988 annual report contains a complex, but unsubtle, takeover defense plan. The company distributed "preferred share purchase rights" to shareholders that can be converted into rights to purchase common stock at a 50 percent discount to market in the event of a successful takeover, essentially serving as a "poison pill" to destroy pecuniary gains from a hostile takeover.

We can, therefore, clarify two distinct uses of takeover-era restructuring. First, uccessful acquirers deployed restructuring to generate immediate cash to reduce acquisition debt and increase cash flow by integrating operations. Second, successful corporate defenders deployed restructuring to reduce the threat of takeover. In the argot of the time, defending teams of managers and owners made their firms unattractive takeover targets through preemptive restructuring initiatives.[8]

Restructuring programs that aimed to raise cash for share repurchases or special windfall dividends were often deployed to capture easy profits and reduce the attractiveness of the firm to potential raiders. CSX's 1988 annual report describes a complicated and interconnected plan of restructuring and share repurchases aimed at squeezing excess cash from the firm in what was most likely intended as a takeover defense. Furthermore, large accruals (from 1986 and 1988 restructuring charges) helped boost the income of the firm, which should have raised its share price and further reduced any takeover threat. Note that CSX obtained only a portion of the funds necessary for the share repurchase from restructuring; the rest came from the issuance of $1.4 billion of debt. The assumption of debt to buy back shares is a strategic move decidedly aimed at boosting share values, not at raising creditworthiness. The following is from the footnotes to CSX's financial statements:

NOte 2. Restructuring and Common Share Repurchase: In September 1988, the company announced a restructuring program. This plan included the sale of the company's natural gas businesses and certain of its resort properties. Also a part of the restructuring program was the repurchase of up to 60 million shares of common stock. . . 50.1 million shares had been repurchased at an average price of $31.90 per share. The funds required for the $1.6 billion repurchase were obtained from available cash and the issuance and private sale of approximately $1.4 billion of commercial paper. The proceeds from the sales of the natural gas businesses and the resort properties will be used to repay a significant portion of the commercial paper. (Pp. 26–27)

CSX, like many firms during this period, blended shareholder and bondholder interests in its postmerger restructuring. CSX also recorded a $738 million charge to cover severance costs for 8,200 workers in a shareholder-friendly cost-cutting move. Similarly, Textron's 1987 management letter in its annual report displays transactional reorganization alongside debt reduction:

> Since the Avco and Ex-Cell-O acquisitions in 1985 and 1986, respectively, Textron has substantially restructured its operations. More than 20 divisions and other operating units have been sold, nine of them during 1987. . . . Textron . . . completed its second major debt reduction program in three years, . . . achieved through a combination of asset sales, a 6.9 million share common stock sale and funds from operations. The percentage of debt to total capital, which had risen to about 57 percent following the Ex-Cell-O acquisition in late 1986, was 39 percent at the end of 1987. (P. 3)

Although most of these preceding actions favored bondholders, Textron also engaged in numerous shareholder-pleasing actions, including a two-for-one stock split, a dividend increase, and a plan to repurchase 5 million shares of its common stock on the open market.

Restructuring, then, emerged as a subsidiary action tied to takeovers. Internal reorganization (corporate restructuring) was not an autonomous event but was intimately tied to prior reorganizing transactions. Chapter 7 tracks the change in macroeconomic conditions and investor sentiment that encourages speculative teams to pursue internal reorganization as a discrete business activity.

SPECULATIVE TEAMS AND THE RISE OF CORPORATE RESTRUCTURING

Experts have argued that in the late twentieth century corporate governance structures brought together speculative teams comprising senior executives and large owners of their corporate stock. Big, activist shareholders asserted themselves by taking over some of the interests and responsibilities of top managers. Senior executives obtained large stock options and took on the outlook of owners. This inner circle, united by a shared interest in appreciating stock values, constituted a class of united, corporate insiders, separated by their interests from subordinate managers and small shareholders.

The media attention corporate raiders and "defensive" managers received during the 1980s obscured the rise of this form of control within U.S. capitalism. Rather than viewing the 1980s "market for corporate control" as an attack by aggressive owners on entrenched managers, a more accurate view would recognize that rival speculative management teams, each composed of large owners and top executives, waged battles for corporate control. Successful corporate raids required both big owners and top executives. So did successful takeover defenses. The "market for corporate control" affected every large firm in the United States because the most successful defense against a takeover was to raise the price of corporate stock, which contributed to the 1980's and 1990's obsession with shareholder value. This meant that both firms that were "raided" and those that successfully fended off raids were managed by nearly identical speculative teams, using the same corporate practices for the same corporate goal: the maximization of share prices.

One indicator of the spread of speculative teams in U.S. corporations is the rise of executive stock option plans. The annual reports of many of the firms in this study report that equity compensation programs were initiated and strengthened during the mid- to late 1980s. A few examples from late in the period follow.

The following description is from the management discussion and analysis section of Georgia-Pacific's 1990 annual report. It is a good illustration of the type of stock incentive plans implemented during the period when restructuring was on the rise:

> Incentive Compensation Plans: We have implemented compensation programs that we think align our managers' economic interests with those of our shareholders. To reinforce Georgia-Pacific's commitment to increasing shareholder value, compensation under our new Management Incentive Plan depends on the level of free cash flow. Awards of G-P common stock under our 1990 Long-Term Incentive Plan depend upon achieving specified increases in share price and upon the plan participant's continued employment for a specific time. Most of

the awards are based on achieving share price targets of $60, $70, $80, $90, and $100 before the plan expires in March 1995. (N.p.)

Note that Georgia-Pacific's plan contains two separable elements: one incentive plan tied to the delivery of "free cash flow" and the other, "long-term" incentive plan, tied to stock prices. Georgia-Pacific's plan requires "continued employment" for some period after the target price is achieved, which encourages management to use speculative management practices that work not just in the very short run but that will keep share prices lofted for a longer time.

Chrysler's 1990 annual report conspicuously features details of a 1989 stock-option plan. Note that this plan does not just create shared interests between top executives and shareholders, but it makes an obvious attempt to conform to financial market conceptions of good management practice by combining cost-cutting restructuring with stock incentive plans. Note that this emphasis on cost cutting foreshadows market sentiments that dominated the period from 1991 to 1993 (see chapter 7), which is not surprising, given that this annual report was published in April 1991:

> Stock Unit Incentive Program: In 1989, the Company established the Stock Unit Incentive Program to encourage the efforts of eligible executives of Chrysler to support its objective of reducing ongoing annual operating costs of Chrysler by $1 billion by December 31, 1990. Eligible executives, as defined in the Program, were given the option to have a percentage of their monthly base salary deducted during the period from October 1, 1989 through December 31, 1990 and converted into stock units by dividing the amounts deducted by $24.50, the market of the Company's common stock over the 60 days period prior to July 26, 1989. The value of the stock units payable at the end of the Program period were calculated to reflect first, the percentage of attainment of the $1 billion cost restructuring objective and second, any increase over the $ 24.50 market value of the Company's common stock, up to $10 per share, during the final 60 days of the Program. In December 1990, lump-sum cash payments based on a more than 100 percent attainment of the cost restructuring objective and a stock value of $24.50 were made. (N.p.)

Excessive compensation U.S. executives received was a major public issue during the late 1980s and early 1990s and returned to make headlines again in the corporate scandals of 2001 and 2002. Given the public outrage over very high executive compensation, one might question why corporations would feature the details of their generous executive compensation plans so prominently in their annual reports. In the terms of this study, in the late-twentieth-century financial market participants believed that firms controlled by cohesive speculative teams were more likely to experience share price appreciation. Even small, outside holders of corporate stock recognized that they may participate in the increased corporate value that accompanies large grants of shares to powerful insiders.

Some firms went farther than others to demonstrate the link between senior executives and shareholders; International Business Machines (IBM) provides a good example. Although the report from which this excerpt was taken dates from the late 1990s, it is included here because it clearly highlights a claimed convergence of shareholder and senior executive interests in corporations with large stock option plans. The excerpt is from the management letter to shareholders at the beginning of the 1997 annual report:

> Dear fellow investor,
>
> Last year I told you that our strategic vision was beginning to take hold, in the marketplace and inside IBM. I said we planned to stay the course—and to intensify our execution. . . . IBM's market valuation—the ultimate measure of our performance—grew by $23 billion in 1997. Our stock price surpassed its all-time high and continued to climb, rising 38 percent over the year. Since our major restructuring in 1993, our marketplace worth has increased by more than $73 billion. (P. 1)

Although other firms did not address their management letter to their "fellow investors," they did emphasize shareholder value and shareholder interests in corporate communications. Sears Roebuck and Co. devoted a section of its 1989 annual report to a profile of current shareholders. This chart reveals that individuals held only 18 percent of Sears's outstanding shares; the rest were presumably in the hands of professional financial market participants. Nineteen eighty-nine was the first year that Sears recorded a charge for restructuring in its financial statements and the annual report. As with other management discussions of restructuring that were not explicitly tied to external transactions during this period, Sears's management places greater stress on financial matters in its 1989 discussion than it does on operational reorganization. The report contains a section dedicated to shareholder relations (Sears listed its shares on several international stock exchanges during the year) and uses the familiar rhetoric of shareholder value throughout:

> It is a fundamental objective of Sears, Roebuck and Co. to achieve consistent investment growth for our shareholders. To help ensure profitable growth while advancing many business initiatives, realistic performance guidelines are used by management to monitor each new project as well as on-going operations. In this respect, management at every level within the Sears family of companies is accountable for maximizing the return on shareholder investment in Sears. (N.p.)

In 1988 Sears recorded a pretax restructuring charge, labeled in the financial statements as "nonrecurring expenses," to reflect several items, most important the loss on the sale of the Sears Tower in Chicago. Sears's 1989 annual report changed the label of the charge from "nonrecurring" to "restructuring expenses." The reclassification of the sale of the Sears Tower as a restructuring expense in 1989 is a clear illustration of the rise of the legitimacy of corporate restructuring as aggressively good management. As early as 1986, some firms were beginning to relabel earlier corporate actions as "restructuring." For example, MCI restated its 1985 "asset write-down" as "restructuring" (MCI 1986 Annual Report). Such reclassification is also a good illustration of the flexibility of both the term and of the accounting standards for restructuring charges. As a corporation conspicuously aiming to please its shareholders, Sears wished to cast its managerial actions in terms that the financial markets would receive positively. As with many corporations in the late 1980s and early 1990s, Sears uses the term *restructuring* to do so.

One additional point should be made about speculative management teams and corporate restructuring. Individual managers or groups of shareholders may push for or design a restructuring plan, but the board of directors generally approved the restructuring activity, and indeed most other speculative management practices, such as share repurchases, before they were implemented. Despite prominent "production efficiency" rhetoric, corporate restructuring, whether of the transactional variety characteristic of the 1980s or the internal reorganization variety of the early 1990s, was authorized by a team that generally included large stockholders and top managers who held large stock options. A common interest in the market values of equity shares united these teams. It is, at best, incomplete to understand restructuring as attempts of production managers to operate more efficiently in response to or anticipation of a shareholder rebellion.

FINANCIAL ACCOUNTING AND THE RISE OF CORPORATE RESTRUCTURING

During the late 1980s and early 1990s, managers attempted to generate higher market valuations for their firm's securities by announcing corporate restructuring initiatives. As discussed in chapter 4, the financial accounting profession was a decisively important social intermediary through which corporate management affected the financial market valuations of firms. This section describes and analyzes financial accounting rules for internal reorganization. Among the firms in this study, declarations of restructuring charges against earnings, representing the estimated costs associated with the plan, almost always accompanied the announcement of restructuring initiatives.[9]

Internal reorganizations leave a different imprint on corporate financial statements than external, transactional reorganizations. Mergers, disposals, acquisitions, and spin-offs culminate in transactions, the dollar amount of which is readily recorded in financial statements. Although transactional reorganization still provides extensive scope for financial statement manipulation, the potential for such manipulation with internal reorganization is greater. This is because internal reorganizations (corporate restructuring) are discretionary management actions that do not result from transactions. The amount of "cost," the dollar value associated with such actions, is recognized in an accounting entry known as an *accrual*, a "reserve" set aside to cover estimated future costs. The amount and timing of such costs are subject to the discretionary manipulation of management, giving managers a powerful tool to manipulate financial results. This "discretionary" quality of restructuring initiatives is essential for understanding their widespread adoption during the late 1980s and early 1990s.

Most of the restructuring charges I have observed between 1984 and 1990 were connected to external transactions, although a substantial period might have separated the consummation of a merger (or the successful foil of a takeover attempt) and the financial-statement recognition of restructuring charges. Internal restructuring during this period was a discretionary management initiative that followed on the consummation of a reorganization deal. An example of a typical mid-1980's restructuring initiative closely tied to a transactional reorganization and the restructuring charge associated with it is taken from Goodyear Tire and Rubber Co.'s 1986 annual report. The first report for Goodyear in the database for this study, from 1984, also displayed a restructuring charge. The following is the footnote disclosure of the restructuring charge from the financial statements:

> Restructuring Costs: In connection with the Company's restructuring program charges of $334.9 million ($224.6 million after tax or $2.10 per share) were recorded. . . . The Company acquired all of the 12,549,400 shares of the Company's common stock held by the General Oriental Group at a price of $49.50 per share. The Company also reimbursed and charged to1986 income, certain expenses of $37.6 million. The General Oriental Group agreed not to acquire any of the Company's voting securities for five years and to use its best efforts to make certain banking facilities available to the Company. In addition, because the market price of the shares during the time of purchase was less than the amount paid, $34.5 million was charged against 1986 income, . . . [and] includes $81.8 million from the closing of the Cumberland, Maryland and New Toronto, Ontario, Canada tire plants and the Windsor, Vermont shoe products plant. Also included are: $81.5 million for implementation of special employee reduction programs, $67.3 million from the disposal of assets no longer required and the incurrence of certain contractual costs, and other nonrecurring restructuring costs and fees of $32.2 million. (N.p.)

During the late 1980s and early 1990s, restructuring charges sent a signal to financial markets that major reorganization, worthy of a reassessment of corporate value, was under way. Managers often strategically used restructuring charges to influence this reassessment. The content and size of the corporation's restructuring charge often influenced the security market's reaction to restructuring activity. To some degree, the size of the restructuring charge served as a gauge of the severity of the restructuring initiative: large charges signaled extensive reorganization. After a period of turbulent interpretations by financial markets, during the late 1980s and early 1990s, a counterintuitive pattern emerged. The larger the restructuring charge, and hence the lower a firm's reported earnings, the larger the positive stock market reaction. Big restructuring initiatives often triggered a significant upward reevaluation of securities prices (see Table 6.1).

Although quantitatively determining the effect of restructuring on stock prices seems to be an easy matter, it is actually quite difficult. An entire academic management literature has sprung up around "event studies," a popular quantitative method that purports to determine the effect of some class of event on stock values. Event studies are executed as follows. Using the Compustat database of closing stock values, the researcher compares the movement of the stock price of companies experiencing an event (for example, an announced restructuring program) to the overall market. If the stock of companies experiencing the event tracks the overall market, the event is said to have had no influence on stock prices. If the stock has "cumulative abnormal returns," that is, if the price of the stock outperforms the market then the event is said to have affected equity valuations. An impressively large literature in academic accounting, finance, and management uses event studies to track the effect of restructuring on share prices. Yes, this literature does find that restructuring tends to boost share prices. Nevertheless, this study does not rely on them.

This study has sought to avoid several weaknesses of event studies restructuring. First, the sample of firms in these studies is usually quite large and randomly selected from the Compustat database. This means that a few very large firms on the cutting edge of aggressive management practice are compared with many medium, small, and very small firms. Second, the manner in which *restructuring* is defined is either too broad, including any reorganizing activities, which blends together transactional and internal reorganization, or too narrow, capturing only a facet of the overall phenomena. Third, the event studies method does not place restructuring announcements in a context. Many firms announced restructuring on the same day as other news that would affect the share price. In the firms included in this study, corporate restructuring initiatives were announced along with the following: replacement of CEO and management team, recent mergers and divestitures, large losses and earnings surprises, and major stock market action, especially downward movements. Additionally, many firms had already signaled their intention to restructure long before the official announcement. The "event" of announcing a restructuring charge, even from the standpoint

TABLE 6.1
Turbulent Financial Market Reaction to Internal Reorganization: Stock Price Record of 40 Companies that Announced Restructuring, 1989 and 1990

Stock	Date of Restructruing	Stock Price that Day	One Year Later	Change
Data General	8/20/90	$ 5 ¾	$ 16 7/8	+193.5%
Whirlpool	8/24/90	$ 21 ½	$ 36 7/8	+71.5%
Tektronix	5/29/90	$ 15 3/8	$ 22 3/8	+45.5%
Baxter International	4/4/90	$ 24 3/8	$ 35 1/8	+44.1%
Electrolux	8/23/90	$ 32 ¼	$ 43 ¾	+35.7%
Lockheed	5/9/90	$ 32 7/8	$ 43 7/8	+33.5%
Bank of Boston	9/27/90	$ 7 1/8	$ 9 3/8	+31.6%
J.P. Morgan	2/16/90	$ 36 ¾	$ 48 1/8	+31.0%
Northrop	5/16/90	$ 17 ½	$ 22 ¾	+30.0%
Campbell Soup	6/29/90	$ 57 ¼	$ 73 7/8	+&29.1%
Boeing	1/18/90	$ 40	$ 49 ¼	+23.1%
IBM	12/6/89	$ 98 5/8	$ 111 ½	+13.1%
Nat. Semiconductor	8/21/90	$ 5	$ 5 5/8	+12.5%
Chevron	2/28/90	$ 67 ¼	$ 75 ¼	+11.9%
First Fidelity	3/5/90	$ 22 ¼	$ 24 1/8	+8.4%
Grumman	6/22/90	$ 16 5/8	$ 17 ½	+5.2%
United Telecom	7/18/90	$ 27 ¼	$ 28 5/8	+5.0%
Digital Equipment	2/20/90	$ 74	$ 77 5/8	+&4.9%
U.S. West	11/30/89	$ 35 ¾	$ 37 1/8	+3.9%
Goodyear	6/20/90	$ 33 5/8	$ 34 ¼	+1.8%
General Dynamics	4/25/90	$ 36 5/8	$ 37	+1.0%
Centerior Energy	2/28/90	$ 19 3/8	$ 18 5/8	−3.9%
McDonnell Douglas	4/26/90	$ 51 1/8	$ 48 ¾	−4.7%
General Electric	1/24/90	$ 63 ¼	$ 58 ½	−7.5%
Texas Instruments	11/20/89	$ 29 ½	$ 27 ¼	−7.6%
Pacific Telesis	1/4/90	$ 49 ¼	$ 43 ½	−11.7%
Borden	9/28/89	$ 36 ¾	$ 32	−12.9%
Merrill Lynch	1/12/90	$ 24 ½	$ 20 ¾	−15.3%
American Express	2/28/90	$ 29 ¼	$ 24	−18.0%
United Technologies	8/2/90	$ 56 7/8	$ 45 ¼	−20.4%
NYNEX	6/7/90	$ 88	$ 70	−20.5%
Pitney Bowes	12/13/89	$ 47 3/8	$ 37 ½	−20.8%
USAir	8/21/90	$ 16 7/	$ 13	−23.0%
AT&T	10/23/89	$ 43	$ 33	−23.3%
Chase Manhattan	6/25/90	$ 24 ¼	$ 18 1/8	−25.2%
General Motors	1/11/90	$ 43 3/8	$ 31 ¾	−26.8%
Whitman Corp.	9/28/90	$ 19 3/8	$ 12 ½	−35.5%
Chrysler	11/4/89	$ 19 7/8	$ 11 1/8	−44.0%
Wang Labs	11/9/89	$ 5 ¼	$ 2 7/8	−45.0%
Unisys	10/4/89	$ 19 7/8	$ 3 5/8	−81.7%

Adapted from Wloszczyna 1991, 3B.

of the efficient markets hypothesis, will only affect stock prices if the announcement contains a significant "surprise" for the market. The effect of restructuring on stock prices can be diffused over a period of time as the market gleans information about pending organizational changes and because the collateral release of other corporate news can mask the effect of restructuring. Finally, and most serious from the standpoint of this study, event studies lack a time dimension. Events from several years, sometimes a 12-year span, are lumped together and treated as similar events.

The view of U.S. capitalism pursued in this study is sensitive to the changing "meaning" of corporate events and initiatives over time. Restructuring meant something quite different in 1991 than it did in 1997. Event studies of restructuring ignore the changing interpretation of management practice and instead attempt to develop "universal" relationships between specific corporate actions and stock prices. Although typical of quantitative, positivist social science, event studies cannot shed much light on the strategic use of restructuring for speculative management that is pursued in this report, whose methodology is inspired by interpretive sociology. If a corporation's stock decreases when a restructuring charge is announced, it is not necessarily because financial market actors universally view restructuring as a "sell" signal. Instead, the stock price may have gone down because the announced restructuring was seen as too shallow, because poor earnings figures were announced at the same time, because the firm's share repurchase plan has been cancelled, or because recent business news media coverage of a restructuring failure has temporarily cooled financial market enthusiasm for the practice.[10]

A restructuring charge was an important and effective device to trigger increased valuations during the early period of the study because it publicized management's conformity to what the market considered to be good management practice. Restructuring charges were also important for another reason: they allowed corporations to manipulate their earnings, directly enhancing the value of equity securities by artificially boosting the accounting profits of the firm. When corporations began recording charges for restructuring on their books in the 1980s, no clear accounting guidelines governed the financial statement treatment of them. Accounting standards surrounding corporate restructuring were imprecise and flexible as they are for most emergent financial innovations and management practices.[11] This provided management with great discretion and the opportunity for manipulation in its financial reporting of restructuring activities. The lack of clear accounting practices was continued into the late 1980s and early 1990s by a 1986 SEC bulletin that allowed broad latitude in financial reporting of restructuring activity.

The treatment of corporate restructuring remained inconsistent among firms during this period. No single "stereotyped" method of recording and using restructuring charges was employed. Furthermore, not every firm that restructured its operations made use of a restructuring charge to boost income and, indeed, managerial awareness that restructuring charges could be used to manage firms speculatively spread unevenly among corporations. Some firms missed the opportunity to use restructuring activities and charges to their full speculative benefit. In 1986 and 1987, for example, Pacific Gas and Electric engaged in cost cutting and internal reorganization. Despite extensive reorganization, the only cost associated with the restructuring activity identified in its shareholder communications was the cost of early retirement for 2,000 workers. PG&E refrained from aggregating its restructuring costs into a large restructuring charge. They were instead included with administrative and general expenses. Although the company extensively reorganized (reducing 13 divisions to 6), it absorbed the cost of these reductions into its regular, operational expense accounts.

But a significant number of corporations did realize the speculative potential latent in restructuring charges and used them to manage their profits and stock prices. The manipulation of corporate profits through restructuring charges was accomplished in several ways. First, restructuring charges were used to boost return on equity, an important measure of profitability financial analysts used, by lowering the equity in the firm. *Equity* is shorthand for *owner's equity* and refers to the undistributed surplus of assets over liabilities recorded on the firm's books. It is a rough measure of the amount of invested capital employed to operate the firm. Restructuring charges often cleaned up a corporation's balance sheet by removing bad debts, impaired assets, and underperforming facilities, some of which were charged directly against owner's equity. This had the effect of increasing the firm's return on equity even if income figures did not improve. This form of financial-statement engineering, what I term *balance-sheet management*, is important but does not figure prominently in the analysis of restructuring as speculative management.

A second and far more important use of restructuring charges to manipulate corporate earnings was to boost the operating earnings of the firm directly. Early accounting treatment of restructuring charges, before the 1986 SEC bulletin, generally aggregated the costs of restructuring into "unusual or extraordinary" charges, which are excluded from the determination of "ordinary" income. By grouping ordinary operating costs with large unusual charges, managers significantly bolstered operating profits. A fittingly skeptical observer of late-twentieth-century corporate finance describes the power of such large write-offs very effectively, and indicates the way restructuring charges can simultaneously bolster earnings through both mechanisms:

> If, for example, the economy slides into a recession, we can expect to see a number of companies take a "big bath" write-off. The write-off will produce a large, nonrecurring charge to earnings in the year of the bath, which, unlike a decline in current operating earnings, Wall Street is likely to ignore. Investors are thus encouraged to believe that all the bad news is now behind them and to think of the write-off as a positive event. A more forthcoming analysis, one never seen, would be that (1) the earnings were almost surely overstated in earlier years when the company was accumulating the fluff that is now being washed away; (2) by taking an even bigger bath than is necessary, as big as the accountant will permit, the company's earnings in the future may be overstated because depreciation or other charges against income will henceforth be reduced or eliminated; and (3) the one-time charge will also reduce the stated value of the shareholder's invested capital, enabling the company to report seemingly higher returns on a now-reduced level of equity. (Lowenstein 1991, p. 109)

Restructuring charges not only served as an effective cover for the reclassification of current operating costs, but also allowed future costs to be shifted into the unusual charge as well. Market analysts ignored future costs in the year of the charge (because they were not classified as *operating* expenses) and future years' profits were enhanced because future years' costs had already been expensed. The 1986 SEC bulletin did not sufficiently constrain such manipulation, and the EITF of FASB addressed it again in 1994.

SEC SAB 67, *Income Statement Presentation of Restructuring Charges* (1986) constrained accounting for restructuring in the following essential ways:

1. Restricted the classification of restructuring charges under the heading of either unusual items or discontinued operations. Restructuring charges properly classified under operating expenses from continuing operations.

2. Restricted the prominent display of income exclusive of restructuring charges.

3. Recommended extensive description of restructuring activities and their affect on ongoing operations in the management discussion and analysis section of the firm's annual report to shareholders.

4. Placed no constraint on the content and timing of restructuring charges.

Although the bulletin restricted management discretion in the accounting treatment of restructuring charges, it left significant managerial discretion in the content and timing of charges. Corporations soon found ways to circumvent the intent of the first two restrictions by attaching prominent footnotes to every mention of earnings in the annual report. Each time that earnings numbers were presented, a footnote was appended to indicate what profit would have been without the restructuring charges, a functional equivalent of extraordinary treatment.

The SEC bulletin did have an impact on the financial-statement presentation of restructuring charges. Several firms that had recognized restructuring costs prior to the 1986 ruling restated their income statements to conform to the bulletin's recommendations. The most common restatement was the transfer of restructuring charges out of unusual income and into ordinary income. The Goodyear Tire restructuring cited earlier had initially been recorded as unusual income and was reclassified after the issue of SAB 67. Another example follows:

Industry segments and geographic areas have been reclassified in accordance with views recently published by the Securities and Exchange Commission (Staff Accounting Bulletin No. 67) regarding presentation of restructuring charges. Reclassifications made, for all periods presented, incorporate nonrecurring items (see Note 3) within the industry segments and geographic areas to which they relate. (Warner Lambert 1986 Annual Report)

And another example:

Note 5: Restructuring Charges: SEC Staff Accounting Bulletin No. 67 of December 8, 1986 requires "Restructuring Charges" to be included in operating income in the Consolidated Statement of Income. Accordingly, the position of these charges in 1985 and 1984 has changed from a separate line below operating income to a separate line above operating income. (Dow Chemical 1986 Annual Report)

Importantly, no other changes were made to the presentation of restructuring charges other than their reclassification from "unusual" to "ordinary" income. Managers developed, almost immediately, informal means to use restructuring charges as pseudounusual charges. Almost every corporation that declared a restructuring charge in the late 1980s and early 1990s reversed the charges when discussing their earnings for the year. In short, the 1986 ruling allowed managers to use large restructuring charges to signal to financial markets that they were undergoing reorganizations. Furthermore, the ruling allowed managers to take advantage of the flexibility of restructuring charges to reclassify operating costs as unusual expenses and to shift future costs into the present. The restructuring charge, whose concrete effect on current earnings was generally ignored by financial markets who continued to use "operating earnings, or earnings before restructuring charge" as the basis of their computations of value, provided an opportunity to make future earnings appear much higher by including future expenses in the restructuring charge. This resulted in higher reported earnings in later years, the appearance of successful business reorganization, and enhanced stock market valuation.

The central point is that managers exploited the lax accounting rules governing restructuring activities by using these events as opportunities to manipulate their financial results. Future operating costs were often shifted into the restructuring charge, reducing future expenses and improving future profits. This flexibility remained a feature of restructuring until it was constrained by the 1994 EITF ruling that effectively curbed the use of corporate restructuring as a speculative management practice.[12]

BUSINESS NEWS MEDIA AND THE RISE OF CORPORATE RESTRUCTURING

Reviewing articles from the business news media reveals a mixed reception for corporate restructuring during the early to mid-1980s.

Although news of pending takeover bids had the power to increase share prices dramatically, the announcement of restructuring charges might well lower the price of a firm's stock. The business news media also was unsure just what to make of internal reorganization or financial market reactions to it. This was especially true of restructuring initiatives that were not related to a pending or completed takeover. A *New York Times* article nicely illustrates the complicated, collective sense-making of financial analysts and others in the financial community surrounding one very large 1986 restructuring initiative, AT&T's $3.2 billion reorganization. The article reports that analysts expect the restructuring to lower the stock price in the short run (indeed the stock fell 1¼ points on the announcement of the charge); they anticipated that as the cost cutting leads to higher earnings in the future, the stock price will rebound in the long run. Especially important to analysts was the elimination of 27,000 jobs, which were expected to reduce costs by more than $1 billion per year, but they also noted that the majority of the charge accelerated depreciation expenses and inventory write-downs, shifting future costs into the charge. This was anticipated to lower future accounting costs and boosting profits (Wiggins 1986, p. D8).

One of the facets of mid-1980s internal reorganization that puzzled opinion leaders in the financial community was the sanguine reaction of financial markets to announcements of large layoffs and large restructuring charges. Both of these could be readily interpreted as negative news because layoffs are a sign of business contraction rather than growth. The legitimating rhetoric of the time focused in on the slow growth of the overall world economy and the rise of international competition to explain the positive market reaction to these apparently defensive measures. The following excerpt from an article from the *Chicago Tribune*, also from 1986, attempts to make sense of financial market reaction to AT&T's restructuring and other massive layoffs at leading firms by placing these in the context of global capitalism. The tally of 1986 downsizing restructuring announcements in this article is impressive:

> On the same day that IBM announced a 10,000 reduction of staff, AT&T said it would cut 27,400 employees from its payroll, and Gillette said it would lower its worldwide work force by 2,400 workers. In spite of the huge cutbacks—4 percent of International Business Machines Corp.'s domestic force, more than 8 percent of American Telephone & Telegraph Co.'s payroll, and about 8 percent

of Gillette Co.'s worldwide staff—the announcements didn't shock the business and investment communities. They are getting used to it; they had seen and heard such announcements again and again in recent months from some of the biggest names in industry. In the last six weeks, Westinghouse Corp. disclosed plans to cut an unspecified number from its nuclear power operations, Goodyear Tire & Rubber Co. said 3,000 employees would lose their jobs, and United Technologies Inc. announced a goal of cutting its work force by 6 percent, or by about 11,000 workers worldwide. ("Investors Unshaken by Huge Layoffs," p. C18)

Impressively, the article identifies takeovers and changes in global capitalism as the cause of downsizing:

Forcing the restructuring are at least three main factors. . . .—Corporate raids, or the threat of them. Even large companies fear that well-financed groups might offer stockholders a premium to sell their shares. To fend off such efforts, they are seeking to raise profits and market prices for their shares—international competition. The U.S. is the world's biggest market, and it has been invaded by the biggest corporate names in Europe and Asia. Competition demands that domestic companies become lean and mean—a shift in the nature of American industry. Manufacturing is slowly, and painfully, losing its dominant position to the ascending service businesses. The old industries are losing workers, the new ones are hiring them. ("Investors Unshaken by Huge Layoffs," p. C18)

THE DECOUPLING OF RESTRUCTURING FROM TAKEOVERS, 1984–1990

In the early years of this study, internal reorganization was only a part of corporate restructuring and was used primarily as a mechanism for cleaning up operations, paying down debt, and boosting stock values following a takeover. The firms in this study explained their restructuring actions in news releases and annual reports in terms of *production necessity*. Especially toward the end of the 1980s, many presented a vision of saturated global product markets with poor growth prospects. In this environment, profitability could not be restored by growth and expanding capacity but rather only by cutting costs. Financial market assessments of value depended on the cost cutting that the new outside management team initiated.

Production-oriented interpretations of late-twentieth-century corporations emphasized these same familiar product market factors. The interpretation of this study approaches restructuring differently, emphasizing the role of secondary financial markets and the institutions that connect corporations to them. The following summarizes how the pattern of takeovers and restructuring appear when viewed from this angle.

The academic management literature indicates that takeovers came to have a predictable effect on market values of securities (Jensen 1989, for example). The value of targeted firms usually increased dramatically to match roughly the price the acquiring firm offered, which meant that large gains accrued to those who owned shares of stock prior to takeover announcements. Often the value of the acquiring firm, however, increased only slightly or even declined. Raising the value of the securities of the acquiring firm became a central focus of the speculative management team. Restructuring emerged as an important tool to encourage financial markets to reassess and increase the value of the acquiring company. Rather than simply award acquiring firms with high market value on the consummation of a takeover, financial market actors apparently paid attention to the posttakeover changes made in the operations of the firm.

Takeovers led to higher valuations obliquely, as the markets responded to the potential for operational downsizing to bring costs down while maintaining most of the revenue. Financial markets viewed takeovers and the subsequent restructurings as ways to boost profitability in a context where expansion was impossible. For much of the 1980s the ultimate value of an acquiring firm was determined not in the takeover, but in the subsequent restructuring. By the late 1980s, financial market participants realized that internal reorganization, separate from an accompanying transaction, was an important stand-alone strategy to raise corporate value.

This awareness came slowly. Restructuring generally had been seen as a necessity to rationalize the jumble that resulted from combining merged enterprises. Speculative teams gradually came to understand the wonders that flexible restructuring charges could work on the financial statements of merged firms, raising equity values. Financial market participants learned to anticipate the increased accounting profits from restructuring and factored these increased profits into their value assessments. The announcement of a takeover connoted to financial market evaluators a subsequent internal reorganization and increased accounting profits. By the end of the 1980s, news of takeovers and restructurings often, if not always, increased the market value of corporate stock—an increase in fictitious capitalization—as financial markets anticipated increased profits.

Managers and markets both seemed to stumble across the positive effects of restructuring. In the process of implementing and paying for takeovers, markets were clearly responding well to downsizing restructuring actions. As the environment that supported leveraged acquisitions changed in 1990, managers and owners turned to an intensification of internal organizational restructuring as a means to continue boosting market valuations in the absence of transactions. Indeed, some firms, such as General Motors, used internal reorganizations and restructuring charges as a legitimating cover for plant closures during the mid-1980s. The successful reception of these actions by financial markets pointed the way toward internal reorganization as a distinct stand-alone practice of speculative management. Thus evolved the logic of internal restructuring as an end in itself, as a discreet, bounded, managerial action linked not to a prior acquisition, but as an autonomous corporate event. Restructuring became linked not to a prior transaction but rather to a rationalization of the production process.

The General Motors annual report from 1987 is a harbinger of the kind of boastful shareholder communications that made internal reorganization, referred to here alternately as a *restructuring* and *cost reduction action plan*, an effective form of pecuniary reorganization popular with financial markets during the height of the restructuring frenzy in the early 1990s. General Motor's management letter from 1987 reports that the cost savings from these actions are significant and justify the restructuring activity as a necessary step to improve efficiency:

Cost Savings Target Exceeded: Competitive success in the marketplace depends upon our ability to give our customers what they want in terms of style, quality, reliability, safety, and performance. In addition, of course, we must be cost-competitive . . . our cost reduction program receives priority attention. In 1987—the first year of the Cost Reduction Action Plan we reported to you last February—we achieved net cost savings totaling $3.7 billion, substantially exceeding our $3.0 billion goal for the year. . . . Employment was reduced by

over 36,000, representing over 90 percent of our original target. . . .
Net savings totaled $470 million. . . . Corporate staff expenses were
reduced by $49 million toward our objective of a $200 million reduction by 1990. . . . Component cost savings of $500 million will be
achieved by 1990 through our operational effectiveness efforts. . . .
Cumulative savings from restructuring actions to date exceeded our
goal of annual savings of over $200 million by 1990. (P. 4)

The reign of restructuring as a practice of speculative management, wrapped in just such legitimating rhetoric, is the subject of the
next chapter.

Chapter 7

THE REIGN OF RESTRUCTURING, 1991–1993

Let 'em eat stock.
—Sarah Tesliki, executive director of the Council of Institutional
Investors, on the subject of appropriate compensation for
corporate directors.[1]

I passed along a WSJ *story about compensating directors in stock to
our public relations man, Pete Judice. . . . When he contacted Elson
and . . . asked permission to quote him in a press release for an un-
named company, . . . "Tell them their stock will get at least a point jump
when they announce it." He was wrong. The stock jumped $3.125.*
—Albert J. Dunlap, on the boost in share prices that comes from
adopting shareholder friendly policies.[2]

This chapter describes the use of corporate restructuring as a technique of speculative management during the period that began with a
sharp increase in internal reorganization in 1991 and ended with an
abrupt decline in 1994. During the early 1990s corporate restructuring
was widespread among the very large firms in this study and was
widely viewed as an aggressively good management practice. Financial market reactions to restructuring announcements were generally
favorable. Business news media coverage, although recognizing and
sometimes condemning the high human costs of downsizing, often
emphasized good business sense that lay behind these actions. Mergers and acquisitions, the preferred form of pecuniary reorganization
during the 1980s, declined, and internal reorganization emerged as a
leading conception of aggressively good management in the early
years of the 1990s.

One reason for the decline in mergers and acquisitions was a
change in the macroeconomic conditions that had supported them. The
immediate precipitating factor that ended the takeover era was the impending recession of 1990, which lowered the value of existing junk
bonds and cooled financial market reception of new issues of junk
bonds. This eliminated the source of funds that had been used to finance

takeovers. Furthermore, regulators had become more aggressive in the very late 1980s and the business news media became increasingly negative about corporate raids. Even without an external change in economic conditions, the takeover era may have already been on the decline, having run its course as a legitimate management practice.

With the end of takeovers, corporations were unable to demonstrate aggressively good management through external reorganization, and financial market and corporate actors began to search for other means of boosting share prices.

Internal reorganization, under the popular label of *corporate restructuring* emerged in the early 1990s as a leading speculative management practice. Although often intimately associated with takeovers in the 1980s, restructuring decoupled from external reorganization in 1991 to become a separate means of improving corporate value. The years 1991 through 1993 saw the highest restructuring activity among the firms in this study. Fewer than 30 firms announced internal reorganization initiatives in 1990. More than 60 did so in 1991 and 70 in 1993. This peak of internal reorganization occurred in the absence of external reorganization. The annual reports of restructuring firms reflect a dearth of transactional restructuring (acquisitions and disposals, mergers, spin-offs) during this period. Corporations conspicuously proclaimed corporate restructuring activity (internal reorganization) when few mergers, disposals, spin-offs, and other such traditional forms of external reorganization were occurring. Ironically, the high point of corporate restructuring came during a lull in business reorganization, broadly conceived.

The prevalence of restructuring in 1991 is drawn out in the following year-end review of corporate profits:

> [It] will be a long time before anyone forgets 1991. . . . The biggest drag on quarterly and 12-month results can be summed up in one word: restructuring. As the year grew progressively worse, dozens of America's largest companies announced reorganizations. The combined restructuring charges of $ 16.4 billion, excluding the one-time write-offs many companies took to cover retired employees' health care benefits, sliced a whopping $2.40 a share, or 47 percent, off profits for the Standard & Poor's 500-stock index in the fourth quarter alone. That compared with restructuring charges of $2.21 a share for all of 1990, reports PaineWebber Inc. (Hager 1992, p. 64)

Each of the social intermediaries supported the popularity and legitimacy of corporate restructuring during the early 1990s. Speculative management teams were strengthened during the early 1990s in several ways. The continued spread of stock options, which represented a growing share of executive compensation, increased the solidarity of these teams during this period. Not only inside executives, but also outside corporate directors received stock compensation during this period, which blended even peripheral members of the corporate governance structure into a cohesive team with an interest in appreciating share values. Shareholder activism continued to press the viewpoint of secondary financial markets deep into the control structure of corporations. During this period, the SEC removed long-standing barriers, originally implemented during the conglomerate era, which restricted communication between corporate executives and shareholders. These changes in proxy rules improved the flow of communication between big owners and senior executives and improved the effectiveness of speculative management, including the implementation of corporate restructuring.

During the period covered in this chapter, no significant changes were made to accounting rules governing restructuring. Accounting rule-makers, in spite of increased awareness of the use of restructuring charges for earnings manipulation, refrained from tightening the flexible rules SAB 67 established in 1986. Speculative teams recognized the utility of restructuring charges for earnings management. During the economic downturn of the early 1990s, declining profits placed intense downward pressure on stock prices, and speculative teams became desperate either to increase earnings or, at least, to find an explanation for poor results that would preserve high share valuations. Internal reorganizations, and the restructuring charges that accompanied them, enabled managers to accomplish these ends. Restructuring helped many companies improve their accounting results and helped many others legitimately cover their poor, recession-era earnings with market-pleasing restructuring charges.

Positive coverage of restructuring in the business news media suported the early 1990s peak of restructuring activity. Prominent opinion leaders and market analysts developed and articulated a legitimating rhetoric for restructuring that emphasized the necessity for corporate cost cutting and downsizing. Although media reports frequently criticized the social costs associated with restructuring, they also noted consistent increases in stock prices following the announcement of restructuring charges. However brutal, restructuring was considered an effective management practice.

SPECULATIVE MANAGEMENT TEAMS AND THE REIGN OF RESTRUCTURING

The inner circle of big owners and top executives became increasingly cohesive during the 1980s, but cautiously, becaues SEC rules disallowed communication among factions of shareholders or between factions of shareholders and members of management. In 1992 the SEC changed its proxy rules governing shareholder communications in a way that authorized, and formerly institutionalized, speculative management teams in U.S. firms. Although the news media paid little attention to this change in proxy rules, it was an important alteration in the governance of U.S. corporate communications that had remained little changed since midcentury when noninclusive factions of stockholders were banned from communicating with executives or with each other.

The midcentury restriction of factional shareholder communication was consistent with the SEC's view of corporations as a distorted but still recognizable form of representative democracy. Each share represented an equal ownership interest in the corporation; hence, each shareholder, however small, had a right to equal access to the firm's management and to equal information about corporate affairs. From its inception in the 1930s, the SEC was charged with maintaining open, transparent financial markets that ensured fairness for all investors and market participants. Two regulatory cornerstones formed the foundation of the SEC's accomplishment of this goal: reporting requirements and proxy rules. The SEC requires publicly traded corporations to file quarterly and annual financial statements (along with other information). These SEC filings, known as the 10–Q (quarterly) and 10–K (annual) financial statements, are public documents. To enhance their accessibility to geographically dispersed shareholders, the SEC further requires that corporations mail an annual report to the shareholders of the firm, containing the firm's financial statements (three are required: income statement, balance sheet, and statement of changes in financial condition) and any other matters that the firm's management deems relevant, especially the management discussion and analysis of the financial documents. The SEC does not require that annual reports follow the precise form of the 10–K. Until the early 1990s, reports were required to contain complete, audited financial statements. The SEC set minimum standards for annual reports and did not limit corporate management teams from including additional information. As corporations' official, yet flexible, public face, annual reports are important tools for strategic presentation and speculative management. Regulations that govern this reporting process are an important foundation of the SEC's effectiveness as a regulatory agency of modern capitalism.

Proxy rules are a second regulatory protection of shareholder rights, governing relations between management and shareholders. All publicly traded corporations are required to hold annual meetings of shareholders, which management presides. At these meetings, elections are held to choose directors of the corporation (literally shareholders' representatives in corporate governance) and to vote on other matters (including changes in the corporate charter and bylaws). Attending these meetings is not worthwhile for most shareholders, especially geographically dispersed small shareholders, and provisions are made to vote by proxy. Because few shareholders actually attend annual meetings (and because management in the mid-twentieth century went out of its way to ensure that they did not), proxy ballots—rather than the votes of shareholders actually present—determine corporate affairs. Unlike a classical democracy, shareholders of corporations are allowed to cast one vote for each share held, not one vote per person, so those with large amounts of shares have greater power.

Prior to annual meetings, factions mail competing proxy statements and ballots to shareholders that reflect corporate strategies and nominees for corporate directors. The faction that collects the plurality of proxy votes decides the outcome of proxy battles. Proxy ballots are essentially absentee ballots, and the situation at most firms could be likened to a national election in which only small minority of voters go to the polls, the majority casting absentee votes. The outcome of most shareholder votes is determined not by the attendees of the annual meeting, but by the proxy voting of those who do not attend. Given the decisive importance of the proxy process, SEC restrictions in this area are critical to corporate regulation.

SEC proxy rules govern this process and until the early 1990s required that all shareholders have knowledge of all issues facing the corporation at its upcoming meeting: universal information to all shareholders of corporate stock. After the 1950s, proxy rules forbid noninclusive factions of shareholders from special access to corporate officials and information, which provides them an unfair advantage in the securities market and in proxy decisions. It also barred a limited number of shareholders from communicating privately and forming a collusive faction or pool excluding other shareholders. Thus, all communications between management and shareholders and between shareholders are governed by proxy rules that require that these interchanges be made "public" and that all shareholders have an opportunity to be a part of them.

During the early 1990s, changes occurred in both of these cornerstone regulatory areas. Informally at least, the SEC allowed some corporations to release summary annual reports to small shareholders that did not contain the full financial statements included in the 10–K.[3] Firms that distribute summary reports must still make the full 10–K financial statements available to all shareholders (and the public) on request. This increased the stratification of shareholders. At the same time that very large shareholders became intimately entwined in corporate management, small shareholders were no longer provided with the full set of financial accounting data that would allow them effective oversight.

Even more important, changes in patterns of share ownership undermined the effectiveness of SEC reporting requirements. Investing in mutual funds created indirect owners of corporate stock—in many cases the majority of corporate shares are held in mutual funds—and owners of mutual fund shares are not sent annual reports of the corporations whose stock their mutual fund manager has purchased. Mutual funds are required to send out quarterly and annual reports to investors, but they contain relatively scant information about the corporations in which they are invested, certainly insufficient information for effective oversight. Mutual funds centralize ownership in the hands of the fund manager: the ultimate owners of the shares, the holders of mutual fund accounts, have neither legal rights in the firms composing the fund nor are they given access to information that would allow them to monitor corporate affairs effectively. Many commentators and academic analysts view this as a profoundly positive arrangement because professional mutual fund managers make better, more effective owners than dispersed amateurs do (see Useem 1996, for example). The view of this arrangement provided by a speculative management perspective is much less positive because the mutual fund manager, as an agent whose compensation is tied to the short-run performance of the fund, is focused on the question, "When to trade?" rather than, "How to manage?" Those who champion investor capitalism argue that fund managers use their privileged access and position to monitor firms for long-run performance. The speculative management perspective suggests that fund managers use their privileged access and position to gather information and manipulate corporate actions so that they can time their sale of corporate shares to maximum advantage.

In addition to changes in regulatory effectiveness governing reporting, formal changes were also made to proxy rules. In 1992 the SEC issued an amendment to the portion of its proxy rules that governed shareholder communications.[4] The following is the announcement of the rule change from the *Federal Register* on October 22, 1992:

> The Securities and Exchange Commission ("Commission") today announces the adoption of amendments to its proxy rules promulgated under section 14(a) of the *Securities Exchange Act of 1934* ("Exchange Act"). By removing unnecessary government interference in discussions among shareholders of corporate performance and other matters of direct interest to all shareholders, these rules should reduce the cost of regulation to both the government and to shareholders. The amendments eliminate unnecessary regulatory obstacles to the exchange of views and opinions by shareholders and others concerning management performance and initiatives presented for a vote of shareholders. The amendments also lower the regulatory costs of conducting a regulated solicitation by management, shareholders and others by minimizing regulatory costs related to the dissemination of soliciting materials. The rules also remove unnecessary limitations on shareholders' use of their voting rights, and improve disclosure to shareholders in the context of a solicitation as well as in the reporting of voting results. ("Regulation of Communications among Shareholders" 1992, p. 57)

A primary effect of this amendment loosened the restrictions on collusive communications among big owners and between big owners and top executives. One of the most observable changes in investor relations that coincided with this ruling was the creation of separate institutional investor relations departments in many of the firms in this study, often headed by a senior, stock-optioned executive. In many firms, the director of institutional investor relations was integrated into the corporate power structure, their pictures frequently appearing in group executive photos in annual reports. Individual investor relations departments, on the other hand, were essentially absorbed by the firm's public relations function, the head of which was seldom included in the group photos of firms' corporate governance. Useem (1996) provides vivid descriptions of the special access to top executives and corporate files that institutional investors were provided through such departments.[5] After this ruling, the informal access of big owners to top managers (even when not directors of the corporation) was open, frequent, and formalized. In the 1990s groups of large shareholders, mostly institutional shareholders, met regularly with senior management in informational seminars. Additionally, top executives in the 1990s held conference calls to discuss corporate events (reorganizations, earnings releases, and other news) with institutional investors and security analysts. Although such actions were most likely occurring covertly earlier, after 1992 the special access of big owners to top executives (and to other big owners) became more frequent.[6] These activities occurred without the notification of or reporting to shareholders at large. The 1992 amendments to proxy rules greatly facilitated the formation, cohesion, and effectiveness of speculative management teams. They also increased the inequality between big, inside owners and small, outsiders, making manipulating corporate actions easier for insiders to coordinate their speculative trades better to the disadvantage of outsiders.[7]

The stratification of shareowners is significant for successful speculative management. Because speculation yields a profit only when an asset is sold, the realization of the value speculative management creates requires outside shareholders to purchase the shares of insiders. If all shareholders (or potential shareholders) have the same access to information as the speculative management team, purchases of shares at escalating prices are less likely. Unlike pure investing, where profit is realized by holding an asset and enjoying its benefits (as in receiving dividends from shares of stock), speculative profit is realized when the asset is sold. Mutual fund managers must eventually sell their shares to realize gains; hence they are traders, not inert holders, of corporate securities. The inside information that they obtain from their special access to executives, as well as their notable ability to influence corporate actions, provide them with distinct advantages in timing their market trades.

The changes in SEC shareholder protection rules enabled the inner circle of big owners and stock-holding executives to meet, plan strategy, and implement tactics effectively while simultaneously excluding small shareholders and prospective stock purchasers. The amount of information disseminated to smaller, dispersed shareholders and the public was trimmed, which enabled more effective release of strategically timed and slanted information from the inner control circle. Together these changes formalized the corporate control structure that had become increasingly dominant among these very large firms for at least a decade: small groups of big owners meeting with stock-optioned top officials to direct corporate affairs for the benefit of the inside group. Amendments to proxy rules did not change the interests of speculative management teams. They did, however, make effectively acting on their interests easier for speculative management teams.

Speculative management teams also took advantage of these new communication rules in their corporate restructuring activities during the period of peak restructuring activity (1991 to 1993). Both top managers and big owners benefited from the increased communication flow. Large shareholders were able to influence executive decision-making and press for actions that would unlock value from the firm (raise the stock price), whereas executives were brought into close contact with the prevailing culture of the secondary financial market. Big owners and market analysts shared with executives their intimate knowledge of leading conceptions of aggressively good management and the actions that would signal alignment with them, increasing the price of the corporation's stock. In the early 1990s, declaring corporate restructuring initiatives and posting a large write-off, especially framed in terms of cost cutting and downsizing, was one of these signs. Clearly, stock-optioned executives benefited from the announcement of these restructuring initiatives: their total compensation increased sharply in the early 1990s and often in proportion to the severity of their announced restructuring initiatives. Table 7.1 lists the change in total top executive compensation at several firms announcing downsizing reorganizations in the 1993 and early 1994.

During the early 1990s, corporate news releases and shareholder communications about corporate restructuring focused on management of stock values rather than management of production. Seldom did corporate communications provide detailed plans of changes in production that would result from restructuring, but merely the broadest outlines. During peak restructuring activity, almost all firms indicated that cost cutting and production efficiency were primary managerial concerns. The communi-

TABLE 7.1

Speculative Management Teams and Restructuring: Changes in CEO Compensation at Companies Announcing Downsizing Reorganizations

Company	CEO Compensation	Announced Job Cuts 3/91–4/94	Total 1993 Compensation	% Change from 1992
Sears Roebuck	Edward Brennan	50,000	$3,095	198%
United Technologies	George David	10,697	1,479	115%
Citicorp	John Reed	13,000	4,150	90%
General Motors	John Smith Jr.	74,000	1,375	84%
McDonnell Douglas	John McDonnell	10,200	1,055	54%
Martin Marietta	Norman Augustine	15,000	1,651	18%
Pacific Telesis	Sam Ginn	10,000	1,630	18%
General Electric	John Welch Jr.	10,250	4,013	15%
AT&T	Robert Allen	83,500	2,517	11%
Boeing	Frank Shrontz	30,000	1,421	3%
TRW	Joseph Gorman	10,000	1,558	−1%
GTE	Charles Lee	32,150	1,746	−6%
Unisys	James Unruh	10,000	1,573	−15%
Xerox	Paul Allaire	12,500	1,316	−30%

Adapted from *Wall Street Journal*, April 12, 1996, p. R8.

cations detailed changes in corporate finances that would result from restructuring, especially projections of future accounting profits.

An appreciable number of companies simulated restructuring activity by employing restructuring discourse in their shareholder communications without reporting significant organizational change. Simulated restructuring approaches the pure type of corporate restructuring as speculative management, in that restructuring was used for pecuniary manipulation but did not actually result in production reorganization.

An illustration of simulated restructuring is Southern Company, a large utility company whose 1993 annual report brims with the cost-cutting, efficiency idiom associated with restructuring, but describes no planned or completed organizational changes and records no restructuring charge:

We're maintaining intense pressure on costs. We're continuing to drive to improve productivity. And we're sharpening our focus on meeting customer's needs. . . . One such challenge is our strategic goal of being one of the lowest cost providers of electricity. . . . Intensifying competition is requiring all our companies to be flexible and to act quickly in meeting the needs of our customers. (P. 7)

The effectiveness of simulated restructuring as a speculative management technique was predicated on the general legitimacy of restructuring in the business community of the time.

Speculative management continued to be an objective of corporate activity during the peak years. For example, Pacific Gas and Electric's 1991 annual report focuses on the firm's stock price performance. Rather than an in-depth analysis of the market for electricity or the firm's production and distribution process, the management letter to shareholders mentions them only briefly. The bulk of the commentary is a detailed review of the appreciation in share price and the total returns that shareholders have received:

Superior Financial Performance
During the past two years, PG&E has provided shareholders a total return on common stock investment of 62.4 percent. . . . We continued to increase earnings in 1991. Earnings for the year were $2.24 per share, up 6.7 percent over the $2.10 per share recorded in 1990. . . . In January 1991, we increased the dividend on common stock by 7.9 percent. This increase, combined with market confidence in PG&E's ability to continue building earnings, resulted in a higher price for our stock. The stock price began 1991 at $25 per share, and closed the year at an all-time high of $32 5/8 on December 31—an increase of 31 percent. . . . The combination of dividends and stock price appreciation translates to a total return of about 37 percent in 1991. Since 1989, PG&E has provided shareholders an average total annual return of better than 30 percent. (P. 3)

As an electric utility company, the valuation model that would have historically been applied to PG&E is the dividend yield model. This means that management should have been encouraged to maintain steady but unspectacular earnings and to pay steady dividends. What is interesting here is the clear adoption of a high-growth, capital gains strategy by PG&E's control team that is blending in interesting ways with the continuing focus on dividend yield. The focus on share price appreciation is an indication that speculative management had spread even to the utility industry in the early 1990s.

Not only electric utilities were adopting the command structure and orientation to share prices of speculative management; so, too, were the firms that had been purchased in the late 1980s in leveraged buyouts. RJR Nabisco, which was taken over in the largest ever LBO in 1989, had spent the first two years after the takeover focusing on improving the creditworthiness of the firm (paying back debt and ensuring adequate cash flow).[8] Kohlberg, Kravis, Roberts (KKR), the leveraged buyout firm, purchased RJR Nabisco and relisted the firm on the NYSE in an IPO in 1991. After the IPO, the 1991 annual report (published in the spring of 1992) describes a shift in corporate focus away from creditworthiness to speculative management. RJR Nabisco signals this transformation in its annual report by describing its concern with boosting the stock price and neglecting production and operational matters. RJR Nabisco, controlled by KKR, was firmly committed to speculative management in the early 1990s. Management addressed shareholders using the salutation, "Dear fellow investors" and continues to highlight the firm's attractiveness to equity investors and to justify an escalating stock price:

> . . . The LBO is largely behind us. We ended 1991 with total debt of $14.3 billion—down 24 percent from 1990 and less than half the $29.1 billion level we started out with. . . . We've generated almost $5 billion of free cash flow since the LBO—even after meeting significant cash-interest obligations—and delivered a solid operating performance, with operating income last year 43 percent above what it was in 1989. And perhaps most significant, we saw the company's bottom-line performance return to the black, with net income of $368 million. . . . In the process of delivering those results, we've attracted hundreds of thousands of new stockholders, forged new relationships with the banking community and returned to the ranks of "investment grade" credits in the public debt markets. These changes in status are both well earned and essential to our efforts to continue to build value for you. (P. 3)

The rapid decline in RJR Nabisco debt is impressive, funded at least partly through the IPO of new equity securities. RJR's 1991 annual report clearly stated that its corporate governance structure was a fully functioning speculative management team. The senior executives of the firm are referred to as "owner-managers" who have a fundamental interest in boosting the firm's stock price:

> The management team we've assembled is tough and talented, restless and entrepreneurial. They've embraced their assignments as owner-managers enthusiastically, and they've made a difference. As you know, they all have their money (and, for more than a few, their net worth) invested alongside our public shareholders. It's impossible for you to meet them all, but you'll hear from our most senior managers later in this report. (P. 4)

This annual report features the speculative management team—or at least the portion of the speculative management team that are stock-optioned managers and directors—with photographs and quotations throughout the report. This team began RJR Nabisco's 1993 annual report with the following declaration of commitment to speculative management: "RJR Nabisco's mission is to increase the wealth of all its shareholders through stock price appreciation, dividend payments or a combination of the two" (p. 1).

CONSULTING AND THE REIGN OF RESTRUCTURING

During 1992 Morgan Stanley, one of the leading investment banks in the world, created a Corporate Restructuring unit within its Mergers and Acquisitions department. This is not only an indication of the degree of acceptance and institutionalization of corporate restructuring as a management practice in the early 1990s, but it also lead us to a consideration of the role of consultants and other advisors to corporations in their pursuit of successful speculative management.

The use of consultants and outside advisors has grown tremendously during the period the study covers. Table 7.2 lists the 20 largest consulting firms in the United States, their revenues, their revenue growth in 1997, and their affiliation with accounting firms. Importantly, many of the largest business advisory firms in the late twentieth century are affiliates of accounting firms. One analyst of late-twentieth-century

TABLE 7.2

Top 20 Consulting Firms Worldwide as of Year-End 1997

Firm	1997 Revenue (billions)	Change in Revenue	Accounting Firm Affiliation*
Andersen Consulting	$5.73	21	Big Six (spin-off)
Computer Sciences Corp.	3.00	20	—
Ernst & Young	2.68	29	Big Six
Coopers & Lybrand	2.40	25	Big Six
Deloitte Consulting	2.30	30	Big Six
McKinsey & Co.	2.20	10	—
KPMG Peat Marwick	2.01	26	Big Six
Cap Gemini Sogeti	1.65	20	—
Price Waterhouse	1.40	24	Big Six
Mercer Consulting	1.34	15	—
Towers Perrin	1.12	11	—
A. T. Kearney	1.10	22	—
Booz-Allen & Hamilton	1.08	12	—
Arthur Andersen	0.95	22	Big Six
Sema Group	0.89	22	—
IBM Consulting Group	0.88	27	—
American Management Sys	0.79	8	—
Hewitt Associates	0.71	25	—
Watson Wyatt Worldwide	0.67	3	—
Boston Consulting Group	0.66	9	—

Adapted from Schellhardt, MacDonald, and Narisetti 1998, p. A10.
*Big Six firms include Arthur Andersen, Coopers & Lybran, Deloitte Touche, Ernst & Young, KPMG Peat Marwick, and Price Waterhouse.

capitalism articulates the link between business advisory firms and corporate restructuring:

> In the late 1980s and early 1990s, when economic downturns and foreign competition threatened many a bottom line, consultants were the advocates of downsizing for corporations that had become so passionate about quarterly profits that they were willing to lop off their own arms and legs just to keep the money flowing. Behind almost all of those surgeries were consultants advancing a ruthless version of efficiency that rumbled across corporate culture." (O'Shea and Madigan 1997, pp. 12–13)

The growth of management consulting was intimately linked to the rise of corporate restructuring. Internal reorganization, especially downsizing restructuring, often resulted in the layoff of middle managers to cut corporate costs. The management teams of most of the companies in this study did not devise their own downsizing plans; instead, top executives hired consultants to devise and implement corporate restructuring plans. Restructuring actions were often perceived (accurately) as actions that ran counter to the interests of middle managers because they were often the target of downsizing. Restructuring was, however, clearly in the interests of stock-optioned senior executives, who profited from rising share prices in the wake of restructuring actions. The rise of consulting makes clear just how much the interests of top executives and middle managers diverged in the late twentieth century and is a clear signal of the stratification of management. Top executives are compensated by increasing share prices; middle managers, who receive salaries and bonuses not tied to share price, have an interest in keeping their jobs. Although downsizing restructuring was considered a legitimate management practice in the early 1990s, the interests of top executives were realized by firing middle managers. Small wonder, then that top executives relied on consultants for the design and implementation of internal reorganization as a speculative management strategy.

As indicated at several points in this study, the most prominent interpretations of corporate restructuring approach the phenomena from the production side: restructuring was seen as a way to boost production efficiency. This study, however, has emphasized that boosting share prices was a primary objective. The use of consultants as the agents of internal reorganization presents a problem to production-centered interpretations because consultants are corporate outsiders who know little of the detailed production processes and operations of their client firms. If production efficiency criteria drive corporate restructuring, detailed knowledge of production processes, knowledge possessed by existing management, would be essential to successful reorganization.

Business consultants generally do not just give advice but also conduct research to study a company and design custom tailored solutions to their business problems. As O'Shea and Madigan (1997) indicate, however, the information consultants provided to corporate clients is really not all that new or particularly attuned to the needs of client corporations:[9]

Management consultants like to portray themselves as anonymous aides-de-camp devising winning strategies for the generals of free enterprise in the war of the bottom line. Actually, they're smart salesmen who peddle ideas. They wrap their products in elegant brochures, erudite book jackets, or the colorless pages of the *Harvard Business Review*. But strip away the pontificating prose and ubiquitous graphics and a simple formula for the successful consultant remains: Devise an idea, repackage it, give it a catchy name, and then sell the same thing in a new wrapper to another client. (Pp. 147–148)

Consultants who devise restructuring plans produced reports and strategies for their clients that conspicuously claimed would improve their client's operations if enacted. If the primary objective of speculative teams who hired consultants to devise restructuring plans was an increase in stock price, the efficacy of the plans at cutting costs and boosting value was of secondary concern. Successful speculative management of firms in the early 1990s did not require restructuring plans that boosted long-term profitability: it did require plans that satisfied financial markets and raised the stock price.

Consultants are in the business of selling conceptions of aggressively good management to corporations and financial markets. The rise, reign, and decline of restructuring as one such conception is consistent with the fashionlike process to which such conceptions are subject. As business practices begin to lose their speculative effect, consultants and business advisors push them aside advancing the next new management practice to speculative teams seeking advantage in raising corporate stock prices. O'Shea and Madigan (1997) describe the fashion for *reengineering*, a widely adopted form of internal reorganization in the early 1990s, as follows:

The recipe: Get an article in the *Harvard Business Review*, pump it up into a book, pray for a best-seller, then market the idea for all it is worth through a consulting company. . . . The books are all like one another in the sense that they present fat collections of case studies that shore up whatever philosophy is advocated. Some of the fads work for a time, only to be replaced by the next thing that comes along. Some of them don't work at all. . . . Ideas, it would seem, are as perishable as laptops. . . . Offering something different separates the consulting house from the rest of the field. . . . Sometimes, as in the case of reengineering, the idea seems somehow brilliant at birth,

but then backfires. Presented first in a *Harvard Business Review* article by Michael Hammer in 1990, the idea soon became Hammer and
Champy's book *Reengineering the Corporation*, a best-seller that
sparked reengineering projects all across the *Fortune* 500 companies. . . . Reengineering mutated to such a degree in the process that
both authors found themselves writing books and giving lectures
aimed at severing the reengineering philosophy from its bastard child,
downsizing. (pp. 189–190)

During the early 1990s, the speculative management teams that
controlled the corporations in this study closed ranks. The stratification
of both owners and managers increased during this time. Big shareowners were given regulatory permission to collude with each other and
with senior executives, whereas small shareowners lost the right to have
full financial information provided to them automatically by the corporations whose shares they owned. Senior executives received a larger
percentage of their compensation in the form of stock options, whereas
middle managers were increasingly subject to layoff and downsizing.
Senior executives relied on consultants rather than middle managers to
implement restructuring plans. The changes to speculative management
teams that occurred in the early 1990s are inconsistent with interpretations of *investor capitalism* in which corporations are managed for the
long-term benefit of all shareholders. During this period, speculative
management teams strengthened their hold on firms and controlled
them for their benefit, leaving both managers and small owners power-
less, on the outside.

FINANCIAL ACCOUNTING AND THE REIGN OF RESTRUCTURING

> *Restructuring allows companies to bundle up costs that should properly
> be charged against future earnings. That leads to bigger up-front
> charges and flatters future profits. (Perhaps for that reason, it is not un-
> common to see the biggest charges being taken by companies that have
> recently had a change of management at the top.) (Waters 1994b, p. 14)*

Financial accounting also supported the reign of restructuring during
the early 1990s by continuing the flexible accounting rules that gov-

erned restructuring charges. Although some accounting regulators wished to restrict restructuring charges, notably the SEC's chief accountant Walter Schuetze, accounting regulators remained inactive and allowed speculative managers to use restructuring charges strategically. The accounting flexibility restructuring charges provided allowed control teams to manage the bottom line with large accruals. This became especially important during the economic downturn of the early 1990s.

Although from 1990, the following is a good example of the lax reporting of restructuring activity that conformed to SAB 67:[10]

> Note M—Restructuring Charges: In fiscal year 1990, the Company recorded restructuring charges of $550,000,000 on a pretax basis. Included in the charge were $455,000,000 for employee separations, redeployment and related expenses and $95,000,000 for facility consolidations and equipment retirements. (Digital Equipment Corp. 1990 Annual Report, N.p.)

The firms in the study declared a surprisingly large range of items in the restructuring charges. Manpower, Inc.'s 1991 annual report contains an almost classic example of a big bath restructuring charge, in which a firm tries to maximize the size of its charge. Included in its restructuring charge were costs that could reasonably be expected in an internal reorganization: costs to close some Manpower offices and reorganize others, the loss on the sale of a subsidiary, professional fees associated with the potential sale of another subsidiary, costs for reorganizing the corporate structure, and costs for shutting offices and closing the United Kingdom central office. Also included in this charge were costs for a host of other expenses, some of which seem distant from managerial rhetoric about corporate restructuring: writing off goodwill; writing off a bad loan on an industrial development project in Essex, England; professional expenses for a potential share exchange offer with a subsidiary; writing down the value of four buildings in England to their fair market value; and writing off the costs of participating in a joint venture to race a yacht in the America's Cup race.

When financial markets consider restructuring a good management practice, senior executives and big owners have an incentive to record very large charges. Manpower recorded a large restructuring charge that signaled to stock market participants that the corporation was undergoing a severe reorganization. Market actors, who were encouraged to buy the stock because of their substantial restructuring, might be surprised to learn that more than $10 million of the restructuring expense covered the cost of floating a yacht.

Large restructuring charges also allowed firms to engage in maximum earnings manipulation in following years by creating a larger reserve that could be leaked back into income in future years.

When the 1990 recession lowered corporate profits, senior executives awoke to the realization that restructuring charges were useful not only for manipulating financial results but also for explaining poor performance. For many firms, operating profits in 1991 were low already and the declaration of restructuring charges provided a "cover" for the loss. The size, frequency, and prominence of restructuring charges in annual reports grew throughout the early 1990s.

A good example, although from 1995, of the use of restructuring charges to manage financial market interpretations of poor results comes from Monsanto. With restructuring charges, Monsanto's management was able to make a sort of virtue out of necessity, turning poor results into an advantage by drawing attention to the nonrecurring nature of the charges, managers let investors know what to expect in the future:

> Operating income in 1995 of $985 million increased by $62 million from operating income in 1994. If the net pretax restructuring and unusual items of $125 million and $40 million in 1995 and 1994, respectively, were excluded, operating income would have increased by $147 million, or 15 percent, in 1995. . . . If the aforementioned restructuring charges and unusual items in 1995 and 1994 were excluded, operating results would have improved for all segments, with the largest increase occurring in the Pharmaceuticals segment. . . . If restructuring charges and unusual items in 1995 and 1994 were excluded, the Pharmaceuticals segment would have more than tripled its operating income, principally through the success of key growth products and higher income from alliances. (Pp. 32–33)

Lou Gerstner, CEO of IBM, referred to the 1993 restructuring in IBM's 1995 annual report to account for the increase in market value. During the early 1990s (and before the EITF accounting ruling in 1994), restructuring was an effective mechanism to boost share values:

One of the best indicators of our progress—and the one that probably matters most to investors—is market value. Last year IBM's market value grew by $6.9 billion, an increase of 16 percent. Since the summer of 1993, when we announced our restructuring program, through year-end 1995, IBM's market value improved nearly $27 billion. (P. 3)

IBM recorded $25 billion of restructuring charges in the three-year period from 1991 through 1993. IBM's profitability improved in large part because of the cost shifting that these charges allowed. Although operating expenses declined after the charges were taken, whether this occurred because the firm is truly more efficient or, as likely, the restructuring charges taken in 1991 through 1993 contained future operating costs, is difficult to know. The following figures showed investors the stunning turnaround at IBM since 1993 when the new CEO took office. (Incidentally, the new CEO took full credit for the restructuring activities even though they were fully underway by the time he took over.) These figures do not reveal the huge restructuring charges IBM took in 1991 and 1992 and does not allow investors to clearly see that the firm may be cost shifting.

Results of Operations (Dollars in millions)	1995	1994	1993
Revenue	71,940	64,052	62,716
Cost	41,573	38,768	38,568
Gross profit	30,367	25,284	24,148
Total expense without restructuring charges	22,554	20,129	24,000
Restructuring charges	—	—	8,945
Net earnings (loss) before income taxes	7,813	5,155	(8,797)
Net earnings (loss)	4,178	3,021	(8,101)

Restructuring activity allowed managers to manipulate their income and cover their recessionary losses in the early 1990s. The CEO of Halliburton in the 1994 annual report draws the attention of investors to cost savings that resulted from restructuring as an explanation for an "earnings turnaround" between 1993 and 1994. An examination of the Halliburton restructuring charges indicates that the cause of the earnings turnaround might be interpreted as cost shifting instead of production improvement. Halliburton made 1993, an already bad year, look somewhat worse by declaring a restructuring charge that included expenses that might, under other circumstances, have been recorded in 1994. This made the financial results for 1993 look worse, and 1994 much better. Similarly, Kimberly-Clark declared a restructuring charge for the first time in 1992, a year of sharply lower profits ($135,000 versus more than $500,000 in previous years). The restructuring charge gave management a place to point to explain lower profits and it also gave them something to talk about to keep investors on track with the stock. By adopting the legitimating rhetoric of restructuring and declaring a restructuring charge, low profits from operations appeared as an investment in future profitability.

Sears Roebuck and Co. boasts in its 1993 annual report that 1993 was its most profitable year ever. However, the most likely reason this is so is that so many costs were shifted to 1992 when Sears took a large restructuring charge. Sears was unable to sustain the level of earnings it reported in 1993 in the years following, and eventually went through several additional restructurings and an additional CEO. But, in the heady moments after the 1992 charge, the Sears boasted of the newly efficient operations that resulted from restructuring.

BUSINESS NEWS MEDIA AND THE REIGN OF RESTRUCTURING

The recession of the early 1990s lowered corporate profits substantially. Analyses in the business news media were important for guiding corporations toward internal reorganization as a management strategy during the recession by developing a legitimating rhetoric for corporate restructuring that emphasized the importance of cost cutting. Many of the restructuring initiatives launched between 1990 and 1993 were not overtly linked to a triggering transaction, but were instead justified by the need to remain competitive in global markets. The business news media focused attention on the comparative success of Japan and the United States during the 1980s. Japan became the most efficient producer of industrial goods in the world (and also America's creditor), whereas U.S. firms, in spite of takeovers and buyouts, were depicted as remaining bloated and inefficient. During the recession, the business news media helped carry and crystallize the opinions of business leaders, who argued that the primary goal of corporate management had to be shifted from "quality" (which was an important legitimating rhetoric of the 1980s) to "efficiency." Cutting costs in a recessionary period was argued to be the primary means available to boost shareholder value, especially because transactional reorganizations had fallen sharply in 1990.

The business news media often reported the boost in share prices that accompanied announcements of restructuring. Although several reflective articles noted that the affect on stock prices was sometimes only temporary, the pattern of immediate positive stock market reactions to restructuring announcements was widely commented on during this period. The pattern held with sufficient regularity to legitimate restructuring as an aggressively good management practice. The following excerpt from an article from *USA Today* is a good example of the processing of "restructuring mania" that occurred in the popular media. The article is more nuanced than many because it recognizes that the initial enthusiasm for a restructuring initiative might cool:

> Restructuring. The word can work quick magic on Wall Street: In the past few weeks, such companies as Allied-Signal and Compaq Computer announced restructurings aimed at cutting costs. Their stocks jumped sharply on the news—even though the restructurings accompanied disappointing earnings news. . . . Often, the quick stock gains that come with restructuring announcements fail to hold up for a longer period. That's worth knowing because job cuts and other cost-cutting moves are the corporate rage of 1991. And with the economy weak, the rage likely will continue into next year. (Wloszczyna 1991, p. B3)

Summarizing popular financial market reasoning in the early 1990s that favored restructuring activities, the author indicates that financial markets favor closing noncore businesses because "investors don't like complicated stocks. . . . A narrow focus is easier for investors and analysts to understand. . . ." Large, dramatic restructurings lead to larger and more lasting increases in stock prices than small, incremental ones because "investors have to believe the problem is solved before they'll buy." Strategic, focused downsizing might receive better long-term market reception than across-the-board staff reductions because critical areas of the business may be injured in the

process of becoming lean and mean: "Many companies are good at
losing 10 or 20 pounds, but by cutting off an arm or leg rather than
with diet and exercise. The butcher-knife approach may create a set
new set of problems" (Wloszczyna 1991, p. B3).

The positive regard for restructuring in the early 1990s is also apparent in later "renamings" of previous charges as restructuring charges.
Chevron for example had recorded various "special items" as costs
buried its financial statements. In 1990 Chevron relabeled these already
quietly expensed costs as a "restructuring charge," and referred to them
as such in its annual report, apparently with the intention of capitalizing
on the positive regard financial markets held for restructuring efforts.

CONCLUSIONS

Restructuring reigned during this period for several reasons. A recession curtailed transactional reorganization. Speculative management
teams became more cohesive and searched for effective means of
boosting stock prices. Financial accounting rules remained flexible,
allowing speculative management teams to use restructuring to manipulate earnings and cover recessionary losses. Finally, the business
news media transmitted the legitimating rhetoric of cost cutting that
underlie these restructuring efforts. Financial markets in the early
1990s viewed restructuring as a legitimate, good management practice and tended to reward firms announcing restructuring with higher
valuations. Corporate restructuring was an effective practice of speculative management.

Internal reorganization during this time often did lead to large increases in share value. Unisys's 1996 letter to shareholders in its annual
report looks back to the early 1990s as the time when it turned around
through restructuring:

> Where We Are: We have come a long way since 1991 when we an-
> nounced and provided financially for the restructuring of our com-
> pany. Shareowner value then, measured as the market value of our
> common shares, was $6.6 billion; at the end of 1996 it was $17.3 bil-
> lion. Yet, much in your company remains to be accomplished, and our
> tasks are clear. We look forward with confidence, commitment, and
> enthusiasm. (P. 3)

This study suggests that speculative management strongly influenced the rise, peak, and decline of internal reorganization in very large U.S. firms in the late twentieth century. The practice of internal reorganization grew in conjunction with the financially motivated external reorganizations of the 1980s, matured as a stand-alone speculative management practice in the early 1990s, and declined in the late 1990s as social intermediaries altered the effectiveness of restructuring as a speculative management technique. The study is supportive of a broader interpretation of business reorganization in U.S. capitalism that seeks to explain changes in industrial organization in relation to the institutional structure of finance. The social intermediaries linking firms to secondary financial markets are an important channeling mechanism of managerial action and financial market interests.

The next chapter discusses the role of these intermediaries in channeling the decline of corporate restructuring during the mid- to late 1990s.

Chapter 8

THE DECLINE AND DELEGITIMATION OF RESTRUCTURING, 1994–1997

The accounting has really gotten perverted. It's reached the point where managers earn what they think they should earn.
—William Leach, analyst at Donaldson, Lufkin & Jenrette[1]

Companies are not penalized for big writeoffs. In fact, executives are getting big fat bonuses. So other companies' executives say, "What the heck, let's call it a restructuring."
—Lee Seidler, CPA and former accounting analyst at Bear, Stearns[2]

They re-engineered that business to hell.
—Chris Street, major Greyhound bondholder, on the decline of value of Greyhound securities in the wake of a restructuring program[3]

In 1994 the number of internal reorganizations among firms in the study plummeted from 70 in 1993 to just more than 30 in 1994 (see Figure 3.4 and Figure 3.5 in chapter 3). This sharp decline was not caused by a decrease in the corporate imperative for high stock prices: if anything, the pressure on corporations to maintain and increase trading prices of corporate stock grew during the mid- to late 1990s. The rise in restructuring corresponds to a general rise in the importance of speculative management, but its fall lies elsewhere, in two social intermediaries that link firms to markets. Restructuring became superseded as a management practice for several reasons. First, the climate improved for transactional reorganization, which offered greater opportunities for speculative gain than internal reorganization. Second, through the business news media, financial markets began to criticize restructuring: the legitimating discourse of corporate action shifted away from cost cutting toward growth as economic conditions improved. Third, reformed FASB rules curtailed the flexibility of restructuring charges associated with internal reorganization, leaving external, transactional reorganizations such as mergers and spin-offs as the best remaining source of accounting flexibility. Increasingly after 1994 restructuring initiatives of the companies in the study were explicitly related to transactional restructuring events (mergers and spin-offs especially), whereas strictly internal reorganizations declined. As transactional restructurings spread in the late twentieth century, the term *corporate restructuring* appeared in corporate reports less frequently and in business news media less positively.

This chapter explores the decline and delegitimation of restructuring by examining the impact of each social intermediary on the evolution of late-twentieth-century management practice. The chapter begins by reviewing the continued corporate dominance of speculative management teams intensely focused on shareholder value. The changes in financial accounting rules, business mobilization to shape the rule-making process, and the corporate response to the rules are discussed. The chapter ends by examining changes in business news media coverage of restructuring and the development of a business climate favorable to transactional reorganization.

SPECULATIVE MANAGEMENT TEAMS AND SHAREHOLDER VALUE IN THE LATE 1990S

Throughout the late 1990s, shareholder value remained a top corporate objective and speculative management teams remained in firm control of U.S. companies. If anything, references to *shareholder value* as the prime objective of modern corporate life increased during the late 1990s. The pressure to maximize shareholder value encouraged speculative management teams to innovate within the prevailing set of accepted management practices and legitimating discourses in search of new strategies or twists on old ones to increase share prices. The utility of restructuring as a mechanism to boost share prices diminished during the late 1990s (as explained later herein) but other forms of reorganization rose. As internal reorganization declined, speculative teams aggressively pursued higher values through transactional reorganizations (mergers, spin-offs, and divestitures). A few illustrative excerpts from the annual reports and shareholder communications of companies in the study illustrate both the dominance of shareholder value and the innovative pursuit of share appreciation through nonoperational channels, including transactional reorganization.

The following excerpt from Mobil Corporation's 1997 letter to shareholders is a good example of just how central speculative values are to late-twentieth-century corporate discourse. The shareholder communications of the firms in this study reveal that the goal of management was not to increase share prices indirectly by maximizing earnings but to increase the value of corporate stock directly through any available means. The speculative team in control at Mobil placed a top priority on obtaining capital appreciation of shares through nonproduction avenues rather than producing good products efficiently or maximizing the firm's earnings:

> The strong cash flow generation and low debt-to-capitalization ratio provides the flexibility to take advantage of attractive investment opportunities, to increase dividends to shareholders and/or to buy back shares of common stock. . . . Mobil share price appreciation plus reinvested dividends returned 22.4 percent annually, on average, over the last five years—2.2 percentage points above the S&P 500. (Mobil 1977 Annual Report, n.p.)

Shareholder value continued to receive frequent mention in most of the annual reports examined for this period. The Berle and Means–style manager (1968) who ignores shareholders is rare in the late twentieth century. Even genuinely powerful managers, who have little to fear from shareholder rebellion, have an incentive to adopt shareholder value rhetoric because their compensation is so strongly tied to stock performance.

Many annual reports revealed, sometimes prominently, new and extensive executive compensation plans with large equity-based option plans. This indicates that the solidarity of members of corporate speculative management teams continued to tighten during the late 1990s. An example is the compensation plan Dow Chemical instituted in 1997. At Dow top executives received large stock options and were required to purchase substantial additional shares of Dow stock. Prominently described in shareholder communications, the large shareholdings of managers ensure that executives will receive large windfall profits from rising stock values. The following excerpt is from management's letter to shareholders in the 1997 annual report:

> . . . Dow's strategy revolves around four basic themes: (1) changing our corporate culture to an owner/investor mindset and rewarding employees for increasing shareholder value; (2) restructuring our

portfolio in favor of businesses that have world leadership and produce a more stable earnings stream long term; (3) increasing our productivity; and (4) growing our businesses through geographic expansion, new products, acquisitions and alliances. During 1997, we made progress in each. . . . We believe companies that provide maximum value to their owners are best able to serve all of their other stakeholders. . . . To more closely align employee compensation with value creation, we introduced a new compensation plan. Under it, a larger proportion of our top 30 leaders' long-term incentive compensation will be based on economic profit results and on Dow's stock price hitting $150 by 2002 or earlier. In addition, these leaders are required to own three to six times their base salary in Dow stock. (N.p.)

The Dow letter then details the steps that management took to help increase shareholder value and in 1997 that primarily entailed *transactional reorganization:* Dow sold Destec Energy and DowBrands and purchased DowElanco and Mycogen. As the Dow example indicates, internal reorganization was no longer a prominent means of increasing corporate value.

Transactional reorganization also figured prominently in the value creation strategy of Monsanto in the late 1990s. As described later, as the late 1990s progressed and the pace of corporate mergers increased, business combinations ceased to be justified in terms of cost cutting, as they had been earlier in the decade, but rather in terms of synergies and market dominance. Management rhetorically framed merger and spin-off activity in terms of revenue growth, and more directly, stock market appreciation, rather than expense reduction. Because antitrust blockages of mergers rarely occurred in the 1990s, speculative teams openly justified mergers as competition-reducing combinations that will increase their market power, a legitimating discourse that would have been unthinkable during midcentury. But in recent times, financial markets viewed such combinations as aggressively good management, and boosting market shared through anticompetitive mergers became a prime, legitimate speculative management practice. The list of deals that Monsanto completed in the single year, 1997, is astonishing: Solutia, Inc. was spun off to shareholders; joint ventures with Pfizer and Yamanouchi Pharmaceutical Co.; acquisitions of Asgrow Agronomics, Calgene, Inc., Holden's Foundation Seeds Inc., and Sementes Agroceres

S.A. The following is from the opening of the letter to Monsanto's shareholders from the 1997 annual report:

> A New Era of Value Creation
> To Our Shareowners
>
> In 1997, we completed one era of your company's history and made long strides into another. . . . These achievements were only partly reflected in the price of your shares, which began the year at $39 and ended it over $47 on a comparable basis, which includes the spunoff Solutia shares. Total return to shareowners was 23 percent, lagging the Standard and Poor's (S&P) 500 Index, which recorded a 33 percent return. On a three-year basis, however, total return on Monsanto shares was 255 percent. . . . We reduced the dividend after the chemicals spinoff. Many of you didn't like that decision. At this time, for reasons I hope this report makes clear, we strongly believe that the cash we generate is better invested in our future than paid out as dividends. (N.p.)

Monsanto's 1997 management letter focuses on deal-making and growth rather than downsizing and restructuring and largely ignores operational matters, at least in the opening sections. This is a very rapid switch for this company, which was conspicuously focused on downsizing and internal reorganization as recently as 1995. The large cut in dividends is Monsanto's effort not only to save cash for additional acquisitions but also to signal to financial markets that the firm deserves a higher multiple (price-earnings ratio) as a growth company. The apologetic attitude toward shareholders is part of the rhetorical style of shareholder-friendly speculative management.

Philip Morris's 1994 annual report is a good example of the shift away from downsizing and restructuring toward transactional reorganization to boost stock values. Philip Morris reorganized in the mid-1990s by divesting "unfocused" lines of business and acquiring companies in its remaining core businesses to eliminate competition and boost market share. Excess cash was used both to buy back stock and to retire relatively high-cost debt that the firm incurred during the 1980s. The magnitude of Philip Morris's transactional reorganization in the mid- to late 1990s provided many opportunities for financial statement engineering and rhetorical speculative management without resorting to stand-alone internal reorganization. The repertoire of speculative management techniques Philip Morris used is indicated in the following excerpt from the management letter to shareholders in the 1994 annual report:

> Maximizing Shareholder Value
> I want you to know that we are working hard to improve the value of your investment in Philip Morris. The tremendous cash flow generated by our businesses, which topped $6.9 billion in 1994, gives us a range of options-dividend increases, stock buybacks, selective acquisitions and debt reduction—for increasing your total return. In 1994, we took two major steps. First, we raised the quarterly dividend twice, by a total of 26.9 percent. The annual payout now stands at $3.30 per share. Second, we committed $6 billion to buy back our stock over three years, reflecting our unshakable confidence in the future of this company. (P. 8)

In the late 1990s, internal reorganization did not disappear from the sample of firms in the study, but it did decline both in absolute terms and in relative importance as other speculative management practices grew. The following quotation from Mobil Corporation's 1997 annual report describes the orientation of management to shareholder value and indicates the array of speculative management techniques, including stock splits, stock buybacks, and dividend management, employed to deliver capital appreciation. The following is from the beginning of the management letter:

> Our total return to shareholders reached 22 percent in 1997 and has averaged 22 percent over the past five years. . . . We outperformed the average return of our competitors and the Standard & Poor's 500 over five years. During 1997 Mobil split the stock two-for-one and raised the dividend. Then, early in 1998, we announced another dividend increase, of 7.5 percent annualized. This is the 11th straight year of higher dividend payments. . . . We have the flexibility to invest in profitable opportunities that fit our core businesses. . . . We'll consider additional stock buybacks. Over the last five years we've reduced our common shares outstanding by about 2 percent. . . . Our new five-year goals contain as a centerpiece the objective of generating returns to shareholders that are in the first quartile of comparable energy companies. (N.p.)

These examples illustrate that shareholder value remained a top concern of corporate management during the mid- to late 1990s. They also illustrate that internal reorganization of corporate operations receded as a conspicuous speculative management practice. Fewer corporations featured internal reorganization in their shareholder communications and the references that were made were less prominent than they had been in the early 1990s. Many companies engaged in transactional reorganization, a practice that provided management with the benefits associated with internal reorganization during the early 1990s: manipulation of earnings and conformity to prevailing financial market conceptions of aggressively good management.

Why did internal reorganization decline as a speculative management practice? The interests of speculative management teams, although intensifying during the late 1990s, did not change. Two social intermediaries, financial accounting and the business news media, *did* change and the following sections trace how these changes effectively channeled speculative management activity out of corporate restructuring (internal reorganization) and into transactional reorganization.

FINANCIAL ACCOUNTING AND THE DECLINE OF RESTRUCTURING

In the fall of 1994, the EITF, the FASB subcommittee created to address accounting standards for financial innovations, issued a ruling that constrained the timing and content of restructuring charges. It also aimed to make accounting charges and the financial-statement impact of them more transparent. This ruling required full footnote disclosure of specific components of restructuring charges and the timing of the ultimate discharge of these expenses. The ruling further limited the range of items that could be included in restructuring charges and required that severance pay expenses and other costs recognized in the charge actually be expended within a short period of time. Most of the items that were contained in earlier charges were still allowed but had to be described much more thoroughly. The dollar value of restructuring charges was more closely tied to actual (not just potential) expenditures, limiting the effectiveness of restructuring as a tool to engineer attractive financial statements. After this ruling new restructuring charges were drastically reduced because they were no longer as effective for manipulating earnings to enhance stock prices.

Business journalists noticed a change in the power of internal reorganization to increase stock prices in 1994, although they did not often trace its cause to changes in accounting rules. The following excerpt from the article "Just Cutting Jobs Doesn't Impress Wall St. Anymore" clearly notes a difference in the reception of restructuring activity:

> When Sears Roebuck & Co. announced plans to lay off 50,000 workers in January, 1993, its stock took off: Sears' shares finished the year with a 40 percent gain, including the spinoff value of Dean Witter. Stock moves like that were typical; investors pursuing the higher earnings that layoffs would bring routinely pushed stock prices upward for months at a time. No longer. Corporate restructuring announcements this year have barely budged stock prices—and some shares have dropped on cost-cutting news. That despite a stock market that has been generally flat most of this year, with the exception of last winter's turmoil. . . . The days when companies cut jobs and saw a surge in their stock prices are behind us. (Rumbler 1994, p. 43)

The new accounting ruling had been preceded by a warning letter the EITF sent to 300 very large corporations in the summer of 1994, indicating a pending crackdown on abuses of restructuring charges (Pulliam and Burton 1994, p. C1). The SEC's forced reversal of restructuring charges at Borden also preceded the new ruling. Borden was forced to reverse $265 million of a 1992 charge, running some of the costs through ordinary earnings and others through a small 1993 charge. These actions effectively blocked the year-end flurry of restructuring initiatives and corresponding charges that had been announced in the three preceding years. During the 1980s and early 1990s, speculative managers exploited the lax accounting rules for restructuring activities by using these events as opportunities to manipulate their financial results. Future operating costs were often shifted into the restructuring charge, reducing future expenses and improving future profits. The peak activity in restructuring among large corporations in the early 1990s prompted the focus of inquiry into restructuring charges:

> "We've recognized that there has been a great diversity of practice," says Robert Bayless, chief accountant of the SEC's corporate finance division. The issue has become more important, he says, as the agency began to see "more restructurings of greater size and frequency in the last three or four years." (Pulliam and Burton 1994, p. C1)

The 1994 EITF ruling constrained the flexibility of financial accounting surrounding restructuring charges, effectively choking off this episode of business reorganization.

Informed and early reporting of the FASB's interest in restructuring charges came from British journalists who recognized the link, rhetorical if not actual, between restructuring and the U.S. economic recovery from the 1991 recession. Accountancy has greater visibility in Great Britain than it does in the United States, and because the United States and Great Britain share an equity-based financial system and basic accounting rules, the "accounting literate" British business news media recognized the significance of earnings manipulation that accompanied restructuring and downsizing:

> Substantial restructuring charges have been taken by many big U.S. companies in recent months. . . . Such charges, often running into billions of dollars, also serve a useful accounting purpose. By reporting the charges now, in some cases wiping out current period earnings altogether, companies are able to bring forward costs which they may not actually incur for several years to come. The effect: to produce a more flattering profit trend in future. . . . The SEC clearly feels the whole process is open to abuse. "It looks as if some companies are including in the restructuring charges the costs of ordinary operations—for example, advertising, legal settlements and the like," says Mr. Walter Schuetze, the agency's chief accountant. "It may be some of these are ordinary, on-going, necessary, day-to-day costs." (Waters 1994a, p. 12)

The *Financial Times* in London published extensive coverage of the November 1994 EITF restructuring rule changes. The following excerpt gives a sense of the leading edge of business news media analysis of restructuring in late 1994:

> The fashion among U.S. companies for taking big restructuring charges may be drawing to an end. . . . Often, this work has been carried out under the broad-ranging (and fashionable) banners of "reengineering" and "downsizing." Tighter accounting regulations are about to make the process less attractive. Last week, the Financial Accounting Standards Board's Emerging Issues Task Force agreed on a stricter set of rules to govern this area of financial reporting—though

they do not go far enough, according to the securities regulators. (Waters 1994b, p. 14)

The SEC's chief accountant, Walter Schuetze, who played a key role in the EITF, believed that the abuse of restructuring charges was severe and required more extensive standard-setting and enforcement than the EITF agreed to impose. Schuetze is the primary interviewee in the *Financial Times* article.

> The problem until now has been a lack of definition. What future costs should a company recognize in its current liability period? . . . Drawing the net too widely allows companies to bundle up costs that should properly be charged against future earnings. That leads to bigger up-front charges and flatters future profits. (Perhaps for that reason, it is not uncommon to see the biggest charges being taken by companies that have recently had a change of management at the top.) . . . Taking a one-off charge will be limited largely to where companies are shedding businesses. Only those costs "not associated with, or [which] do not benefit, activities that are continued,' will count. . . . At one sweep, this appears to wipe out many of the opportunities for taking restructuring charges that companies have used this year. (Waters 1994b, p. 14)

The EITF attempted to separate the wide range of restructuring activities that were being included in restructuring charges into different types of reorganization with specific types of costs. The EITF specifically identified internal reorganization as a type of management practice that should not lead to special charges for restructuring. Purely internal restructuring initiatives that result from a management decision are problematic from an accounting standpoint because many of the activities completed in these reorganizations are identical to normal, ongoing business practices. The arbitrary nature of restructuring costs, in which management assigns dollar values to them, separates them from ordinary business expenses and aggregates them into special, unusual charges, was central to regulatory concerns. The lack of precision makes prudent, conservative, and comparable accounting problematic. "'I don't know what re-engineering means—it's a fashionable concept,' said Mr. Schuetze" (Waters 1994a, p. 12).

The EITF ruled that *reengineering* and *streamlining* costs should not be labeled as nonrecurring restructuring costs because they are costs associated with the ongoing business of the firm rather than being part of a disposed business and as such the costs of such efforts should be expensed as undifferentiated operating costs. From my own review of the American Institute of Certified Public Accounts (AICPA) manual of practice, the category of restructuring charges clearly grew out of the accounting for *discontinued operations*. Firms in the mid-1980s who were jettisoning businesses sought to label their activities more positively (and in line with emerging conceptions of good management) as restructuring. Once restructuring was "fashionable," companies sought to relabel operating costs as nonrecurring restructuring expenses. The EITF essentially sought to restore the earlier association of restructuring with nonrecurring disposals of discontinued operations. Schuetze found the following diverse, normally recurring expenses had been placed inside the stretched category of restructuring in the early 1990s:

> future expenditures for equipment such as computers, software for those computers or computers already on hand, relocating and retraining employees, advertising and legal services, consulting services, expected adverse factory overhead variances on future production runs, expected increases in returns and allowances on future sales, increased warranty liabilities on future products sales, and the like. (Waters 1994b, p. 14)[4]

Corporations effectively used temporal cost shifting, taking future expenses of the firm and including them in a big-bath restructuring charge in early 1990s restructuring to boost future income. To reign in this practice the EITF introduced new rules that required clear specification of the timing of elements of a restructuring plan. Corporations were required to commit firmly to a formal restructuring plan, to submit the plan for board of directors approval, and to limit write-offs to identifiable costs unambiguously connected to this commitment. Corporations were required to tie restructuring costs to specific, committed actions rather than to a "vague expression of future intention." Furthermore:

> . . . companies will have to have identified the method by which they are going to dispose of the businesses concerned, as well as the expected date they will complete the exercise. The expected completion of the plan has to be soon enough for it to be unlikely that a company's

management will change its mind about the idea. . . . [Restructuring costs] must either be extra costs that a company faces as a result of the restructuring plan, or contractual costs that it cannot get out of. (Waters 1994b, p. 14)

The EITF ruling constrained the use of *restructuring* as a label for business reorganization, reserving the term and the accounting treatment associated with it, to costs associated with the disposal of business lines. In essence, the EITF ruling encouraged speculative teams to engage in transactional business reorganization, especially those culminating in discontinued operations, which enabled firms to use restructuring charges for financial statement engineering. The EITF ruling encouraged both the mid- to late 1990s rebound in transactional restructuring and the decline in internal reorganization. By changing the relative capacity for managers to manipulate earnings using each technique, the EITF accounting consensus effectively encouraged the former while constraining the latter, demonstrating the power of social intermediaries to shape U.S. industry.[5]

A *Wall Street Journal* article, "A Restructuring of Write-Offs Is in the Making," (Pulliam and Burton) broke the story of the EITF ruling in the U.S. business news media. This article brought accounting deliberations surrounding the restructuring issue, hitherto discussed primarily in a few banking journals, to the attention of the public. Even so, the EITF deliberation and ruling on restructuring charges was never a front-page news item. The article on the EITF's pending consensus letter appeared on the bottom of the first page of section C of the *Wall Street Journal:*

The corporate game of pleasing shareholders and boosting stock prices by announcing giant "restructuring" charges is about to become harder to play. New rules are likely to be unveiled Nov. 17 that will crack down on corporate America's habit of seizing upon restructuring as an occasion to take a bushel of write-offs all at once, making an earnings turnaround look speedier and more significant when it happens. (Pulliam and Burton 1994, p. C1)

This article nicely expresses the interpretation the business news media placed on corporate restructuring in late 1994. This article has a clear awareness of the link between restructuring and shareholder value, but not a naïve one:

> Some investors call such charges "the big bath." The routine is familiar: Behemoth Co. announces heavy layoffs and plant closings, and a big charge against earnings to make up for its mistakes. To the uninitiated, it may seem odd when the stock jumps in response. But investors love restructurings because, following a jumbo charge against earnings, a company's profit nearly always improves sharply. That's because lots of companies write off certain expenses all at once that would otherwise be a drag to earnings over a longer period. "This is guaranteed to make future earnings look better—guaranteed," says Robert Willens, an accounting analyst at Lehman Brothers. . . . The stock market obviously likes to see these charges taken all at once so the company can proceed with a clean slate," says one member of the FASB task force. "Under these new rules, that won't be possible any more." (Pulliam and Burton 1994, p. C1)

As Pulliam and Burton reported, the central constraints the EITF imposed were a narrowing of the range of costs approved for inclusion in restructuring charges and a reduction in the chronological flexibility of restructuring costs. Companies had been inflating restructuring charges by including estimated future costs in the charge, costs that were merely planned but not actually incurred. In many cases, firms never actually incurred the expected restructuring costs, and the excess of planned over actual restructuring expense was discretely reclaimed as income in later years. This meant that firms not only could manipulate their income by taking a big bath restructuring charge in year one, but also could reverse overly large restructuring charges to boost income in later years. The EITF ruling sought to eliminate such manipulation.

An example of the effect of the EITF guidelines on restructuring accounting can be seen in the following example of a post-1994 restructuring charge from Digital Equipment Corporation's 1994 annual report. This is the required footnote disclosure to the financial statements that specifies the content and timing of the components of the restructuring charge and is typical of the financial statement treatment of restructuring after the EITF ruling. The new footnote disclosure requirements dramatically increased the ability of sophisticated financial market participants to monitor restructuring activity. Given this level of detailed disclosure, speculative teams have a more difficult task to manipulate earnings shifting operating expenses or future expenses into restructuring charges. The entire footnote from Digital Equipment's 1994 annual report is reproduced here and is quite lengthy:

Note E—Restructuring Actions
Accrued restructuring costs and charges include the cost of involuntary employee termination benefits, facility closures and related costs associated with restructuring actions. Employee termination benefits include severance, wage continuation, notice pay, medical and other benefits. Facility closures and related costs include gains and losses on disposal of property, plant and equipment, lease payments and related costs.

Restructuring costs are accrued and charged to expense in accordance with an approved management plan, supported by an appropriate level of specificity for the planned actions. Actual restructuring costs are recognized as a reduction in the accrued liability in the period incurred.

While expenses continue to decline, the Corporation's cost structure is still too high for the level and mix of total operating revenues. As a result, at the end of fiscal year 1994, the Corporation approved additional restructuring actions and accrued related costs of $1.2 billion. Cash expenditures associated with these actions are expected to be approximately $580,000,000 in the first half of fiscal 1995, $420,000,000 in the second half of fiscal 1995 and $240,000,000 related to facility closures beyond fiscal 1995. These actions do not include workforce or facility reductions that may result from divestments.

The cost of employee separations associated with the fiscal year 1994 charge includes termination benefits for approximately 20,000 employees. A portion of these employee separations occurred near the end of the fourth quarter of fiscal 1994 and the remainder will occur in fiscal 1995. These employees are located principally in the U.S. and Europe. The greatest portion of employee separations, approximately 40 percent, are expected to come from sales and marketing functions, as the Corporation sells more products through indirect channels of distribution. Most other organizations and functions also will be affected by the planned reduction in employees. The fiscal 1994 charge also covers costs associated with closure of 10 million square feet of facilities, including office and manufacturing space, principally in the U.S. and Europe.

Restructuring actions have resulted in termination of approximately 12,000, 17,000 and 10,000 employees in fiscal years 1994, 1993 and 1992, respectively.

Accrued restructuring costs (in thousands)

Year ended	July 2, 1994	July 3, 1993	June 27, 1992
Balance, beginning of year	$ 738,989	$1,546,904	$1,036,704
Charges to operations:			
Employee separations	679,000	—	1,000,000
Facility closures and related costs	527,000	—	500,000
	1,206,000	—	1,500,000
Costs incurred:			
Employee separations	372,450	454,900	759,500
Facility closures and related costs	212,300	314,250	168,480
Other	9,164	38,765	61,820
	593,914	807,915	989,800
Balance, end of year	$1,351,075	$ 738,989	$1,546,904
. Cash expenditures:			
Employee separations	$ 532,000	$ 651,300	$ 822,150
Facility closures and related costs, net of proceeds	67,550	174,700	106,050
	$ 599,550	$ 826,000	$ 928,200

At the end of fiscal year 1992, having fully utilized the balance of restructuring costs accrued at the end of fiscal 1991 and in response to an unanticipated decline in product sales during the second half of fiscal 1992 and resulting operating losses, additional restructuring plans were formulated. These actions resulted in the accrual of $1.5 billion of restructuring costs. (P.41)

The level of detail makes a stark contrast with pre-1994 restructuring charge disclosures, many of which footnotes were fewer than three sentences.

Prior to the 1994 ruling, the presentation of restructuring charges in corporate reports varied widely. Some firms in the late 1980s already disclosed an amount of information about their restructuring activities as extensive as the preceding example, but not most firms, which made strategic disclosures in their own interests. For many firms, this meant providing financial markets with as little detail as possible (to maintain flexibility); for others, this meant the selective disclosure of aspects of the restructuring that would please markets while concealing others. The 1994 EITF ruling imposed standards on this diversity, and most of the restructuring charges after 1994, although not all, met the new requirements.

The EITF further specified proper accounting for termination costs for severed employees, an important component of restructuring costs. These costs were to be included in restructuring charges only if the layoffs occurred within one year of the charge. Because many internal reorganization plans extended several years into the future, charges associated with them included employee severance costs for future years, costs that the EITF indicated should be excluded. The accounting principles that had previously guided these timing issues, contained in Financial Accounting Standard (FAS) 5, indicated that future costs should be recognized immediately if "probable" and "reasonably estimable." Speculative managers, who included vague future costs in big-bath restructuring charges, exploited this long-standing accounting rule, intended to create "conservative" financial statements and limit management's ability to hide potentially damaging contingencies (Waters 1994a, p. 12).

The EITF for a time, however, seemed unable to agree about how to resolve all of the issues surrounding employee severance: ". . . existing termination plans have so many permutations and combinations, we're not sure we can issue" a definitive rule on this by November 17 (Pulliam and Burton 1994, p. C1). The EITF signaled that correct accounting practice only allowed severance costs in restructuring charges if they were incurred within one year of the announcement of the charge, and indeed did resolve the issue at its November 17 meeting.

During much of the summer and fall of 1994, the EITF published its meeting minutes on the restructuring debate and had reached a near consensus that "all people included in a severance plan had to be out of their jobs within a year" (*American Banker–Bond Buyer* 1994f, p. 6). On November 17, 1994, the task force altered its intentions and merely required that employees had to be put on notice that a termination plan existed before the end of one year from the date of announcement.

THE CORPORATE RESPONSE TO NEW ACCOUNTING RULES FOR RESTRUCTURING

One important effect that this ruling had on the evolution of restructuring as a management practice was to accelerate the process of restructuring, especially employee layoffs. To enable severance costs to be included in a large restructuring charge (essential for manipulating earnings), corporations had to restructure in a sort of blitzkrieg. One company that initiated rapid restructuring was Scott Paper in 1994, under the command of "Chainsaw Al" Dunlap. Scott Paper had embarked on a large, multiyear restructuring in 1993, when management announced its plans and declared a sizable restructuring charge. Dunlap was hired as CEO of Scott Paper in 1994, during the period when the EITF sent letters to 300 companies who had taken recent large restructuring charges, warning them about pending changes to accounting rules for restructuring. Scott Paper may have been one of the companies who received the letter because of its large 1993 charge. However, even if it had not received a letter, Scott's accountants would certainly have been abreast of the pending rule changes and Scott's management, like those of other large companies in 1994, would have been cautious about taking large charges over an extended time period.

The EITF letter specifically warned companies that severance costs for employees fired more than one year after the announcement of a restructuring plan would have to be reversed from the charge, and earnings restated (which often has a devastating impact on corporate value). Although the restructuring plan at Scott Paper had already been developed and had begun to be implemented by his predecessor and by the senior management staff that he fired, Dunlap accelerated the pace of the restructuring, especially the employee layoffs and disposals of businesses (which he also increased). Dunlap, who became famous as the icon of corporate downsizing, was not the author of the restructuring plan at Scott Paper. His primary contribution was the acceleration of the layoffs and disposals of facilities. Dunlap boasts in his 1996 book, *Mean Business*, that the acceleration of restructuring was a result of his decisive and commanding character. Dunlap prided himself with the claim that he did not let emotion get in the way of good business decisions, but made tough choices and acted swiftly so that employees and owners of the firm would trust him. In this book, he even embraces the "Chainsaw Al" nickname that the business news media attached to him in the wake of the rapid Scott layoffs (half of the employees were fired within six months, including almost the entire senior management staff).

In light of the EITF warnings, the most important advantage that Scott Paper obtained by the accelerated restructuring plan was conformity with EITF rules, qualifying the severance costs for inclusion in a single, very large restructuring charge. Disposals of businesses and rapid layoffs of employees were necessary for Scott Paper to treat the reorganization as a "restructuring," which gave it the ability to factor these costs out of "ordinary income."

Dunlap claims that accelerating the restructuring process was part of his "Rambo in Pinstripes" style, but it is worth noting that the changed accounting rules for restructuring required it anyway. After 1994 restructuring plans at many firms were made with greater speed and much greater specificity. Dunlap's shift from Scott Paper's initial three-year restructuring plan to a one-year plan ensured that the SEC would allow the 1994 restructuring charge. Furthermore, the rapid layoffs of workers ensured that the SEC would not require Scott Paper to reverse the 1993 charges already taken before Dunlap arrived for failure to comply with the one-year termination rule (as had been done with Borden). Prior to the November 17 ruling, the SEC had left open the possibility that it would be forced to revise the 1993 restructuring charges and recognize the cost of employee severance when incurred. From a speculative management standpoint, much of the value of restructuring is associated with the ability to manipulate accounting earnings. Scott's earnings, and stock price, would have plummeted on earnings restatement, so accelerating Scott's restructuring plan was essential.

Dunlap's arrival at Scott Paper occurred during the interim period before the November 17 ruling, when it must have seemed critical to fire workers before year end or face dire accounting consequences. Thus, the rapid firings that Dunlap conspicuously displays as aggressively good production management appears from the angle of this study as good speculative management.

The change in accounting standards for restructuring charges caused speculative managers, like those at Scott Paper, to change their restructuring plans. Plans aimed primarily at improvements in production efficiency and long-term profitability might have robustly resisted such reformation for the sake of favorable accounting treatment. The fact that so many corporations attempted to avail themselves of maximum accounting benefit by aligning their restructuring activity with EITF guidelines underscores the importance of financial statement engineering to restructuring corporations. Speculative teams desired increased stock prices, and stock prices responded most immediately to attractive accounting reports and conspicuous alignment with market conceptions of good management practice. Actual or real improvements in production efficiency are difficult for financial markets to view and become visible to markets primarily in financial accounting terms.

Because the speculative management team at Scott Paper accelerated the restructuring activity, they were able to employ a large restructuring charge and effectively manipulate company earnings. Scott Paper's shareholder value increased threefold in 18 months under Chainsaw Al's (and the other speculative management team members') command, the largest and most rapid increase in share price occurred when Scott was sold to Kimberly-Clark almost immediately after the restructuring. Kimberly-Clark paid a high price for Scott Paper based on the way Scott looked on paper: the blitzkrieg restructuring at Scott had enabled the company to manage its earnings very effectively and show very high profits in the year after the restructuring. But, from a production standpoint, the reorganization was not a clear success. Kimberly-Clark's management apparently had misgivings about the purchase once the full consequences of the operational cuts prior to the purchase were made known. Business news media articles about Kimberly-Clark and its own shareholder communications lamented the drag on earnings that came from the need to "restructure" further the operations acquired from Scott. The restructuring of Scott Paper, viewed from the angle of this study, is an almost unalloyed case of restructuring for "speculative" rather than "production" effect.

Scott Paper's rapid downsizing had the side effect of riveting the attention of the business news media and, at a time when financial markets enthusiastically embraced restructuring as an aggressively good management practice, dramatically increasing the share price. The rapid appreciation of Scott stock following the restructuring, coupled with the rising celebrity of Chainsaw Al Dunlap, attracted further media attention, which encouraged other firms to expeditiously restructure in pursuit of the same results. Motorola, for example, used the same covering rhetoric of "decisiveness" as Dunlap when it announced rapid layoffs to qualify severance costs for inclusion in its restructuring charge.

As reported in chapter 3 (Figures 3.4 and 3.5), the volume of restructuring activity at the companies in this study fell dramatically in 1994, which coincides with the new EITF guidelines released in November of that year. The question arises: What prevented companies from quickly announcing restructuring activities during the period between the initial media coverage of the impending tightening of accounting rules and the actual release of the EITF consensus? The answer is that the SEC specifically blocked firms from doing so, as reported in these two excerpts from articles in banking industry trade publications:

> The SEC's chief accountant has put companies on notice against trying to sneak in certain types of restructurings before FASB's Emerging Issues Task Force considers these issues on November 17. "If I were a registrant, I would think long and hard about taking those items," Walter Schuetze said Nov. 4 at the AICPA Conference on Banking. Schuetze said the EITF already has made clear it is leaning against permitting companies to take restructuring charges that could bring the firm some future benefit. This matters, the SEC official said, because during the past few years there has been a pronounced uptick in the number and size of restructurings, some of them suspect. One practice that Schuetze looks askance at involves taking charges for severance payments when no severance plan was in place. (*American Banker–Bond Buyer* 1994c, p. 5)

> Just in time for the expected wave of consolidations in the banking industry, the accounting profession is moving ahead on its controversial rules covering restructuring charges. (*American Banker–Bond Buyer* 1994c, p. 7)

The new constraint accounting authorities placed on restructuring activity did not end restructuring, but encouraged speculative managers to be innovative within the boundaries the new rules established.

Although the total volume and dollar amount of restructuring fell sharply in 1994, as did write-offs of most kinds, in the years that followed, managers found new ways to obtain the earnings manipulation and market legitimation that restructuring had provided before 1994.

First, companies employed euphemisms for restructuring to avoid the EITF accounting rules. Because transactions were required for restructuring accounting treatment, some firms relabeled their restructuring efforts as *streamlining*, *rationalization*, or some other euphemism. In several cases, avoiding the label *restructuring* apparently allowed the corporation to avoid triggering the 1994 EITF accounting ruling. For example, Occidental Petroleum took a "reorganization charge" and not a "restructuring charge" in the 1995 fiscal year. Its decision to avoid the word *restructuring* is interesting because the company had conspicuously labeled earlier internal reorganizations with the word *restructuring* and had employed the term widely in its 1991 annual report. The content of the 1995 charge, as much as can be determined from the information available in shareholder communications, is similar to the restructuring charges recorded earlier at the firm and seems to fall within the EITF guidelines. Yet, Occidental does not conform to EITF rules for restructuring charges, despite the material size of these charges. By using *reorganization* instead of *restructuring* as a label for its activity, Occidental was able to avoid rigid accounting standards and disclosure requirements.

When Lockheed Martin was formed in a large merger in 1995, it incurred substantial expenses and embarked on an internal reorganization. However, the internal reorganization seemed unnecessary as a mechanism to boost shareholder returns, which were already enormous as a result of the external reorganization:

> This strong overall financial performance was clearly reflected in the investment community's confidence in Lockheed Martin stock, which increased in value by more than 78 percent during 1995. The total shareholder return for 1995, including dividend reinvestment, topped 81 percent, well above market averages. (Lockheed Martin 1995 Annual Report, p. 4)

When Lockheed Martin's management described the internal reorganization in the annual report, the word *restructuring* was not used. Instead, the reorganization was referred to as a "consolidation" that resulted in a "consolidation charge." Despite using *restructuring* as a label for internal reorganization in previous reports and taking numerous restructuring charges, management avoided the term in 1995. Note however that the reorganization was completed very rapidly, which was necessary for effective earnings management under the new EITF guidelines:

> Consolidation : On June 26, just three months after our merger and on our original schedule, we announced a corporate-wide consolidation plan. . . . By year end, we had met all key decision dates; all consolidation activities are on or ahead of schedule; and we had made substantive progress toward realizing the significant cost savings anticipated. In the first five years of the plan, we expect to realize net savings of about $5 billion; when fully implemented, by 1999, we expect to achieve annual savings of $1.8 billion. By increasing economies of scale, capitalizing on corporate-wide synergies and leveraging our added financial strength, consolidation will benefit shareholders, customers and employees. . . . (Lockheed Martin 1995 Annual Report, p. 6)

The consolidation charge did not conform to the new EITF restructuring disclosure requirements. The footnotes to the financial statements did not breakdown the details of this rather hefty charge and by avoiding the language of restructuring, the flexibility associated with pre-1994 "restructuring" charges was extended to the consolidation charge. For Lockheed, speculative management was directed away from internal reorganization into transactional reorganization. The consolidation charge drew attention to future cost savings to follow from the merger without triggering the disclosure requirements of restructuring charges, allowing for significant earnings manipulation. In fact, management used the size of the consolidation charge in the letter to shareholders to account for the decline in earnings fully:

> The Corporation's operating profit (earnings before interest and taxes) decreased in 1995 to $1.4 billion from $2.0 billion in 1994. Operating profit in 1995 included the effects of pretax charges totaling $690 million representing the portion of the consolidation plan and merger related expenses not expected to be recovered under future pricing of U.S. government contracts. (Lockheed Martin 1995 Annual Report, p. 6)

Although Boeing's 1998 reorganization is another example of a firm avoiding both the term *restructuring* and the accounting rules for them. On December 3, 1998, Boeing announced that it would lay off

20,000 workers and reduce production targets by 25 percent, but declined to use either the language or the accounting of restructuring in the announcement of the reorganization.

The search for innovative language to describe reorganizations that would not trigger EITF disclosure requirements may have led Philip Morris to describe its 1997 reorganization as "Food Realignment Charges." The content of this charge is quite similar to pre-1994 restructuring charges at this firm. The change in terminology not only allowed Philip Morris to avoid accounting strictures, but also enabled the company, which recast itself as a "growth" stock firm, to avoid the downsizing and layoff connotations associated with the term *restructuring* in the late 1990s (Philip Morris 1997 Annual Report).

Occidental's 1997 special charges are consistent with the pattern the preceding companies established. Its financial statement contains a restructuring charge in all but name. Occidental's "special charge" avoids the detailed restructuring disclosures. Rather than employing restructuring as legitimate management practice, Occidental emphasizes "refocusing of the firm" and "growth" through acquisitions in each of the major product lines in which the firm remains. The firm also uses stock repurchase programs extensively to manage share prices to increase its potency as a merger currency (Occidental Petroleum 1997 Annual Report).

Companies that attempted to avoid the EITF strictures were not the only firms that sought euphemisms for their activity. Firms that conformed to EITF restructuring guidelines often avoided using the label *restructuring* as well, even when they had employed the term in earlier years. The large insurance and financial firm Traveler's used "simulated restructuring" during the late 1980s and early 1990s. Traveler's shareholder communications are laden with restructuring rhetoric as well as frequent detailed references to specific restructuring actions in an illustrative manner. Although its late 1980s and early 1990s reports to shareholders teem with words such as *restructuring, streamlining,* and *reorganization,* management made no effort to aggregate these actions into a "special charge." Despite management's willingness to employ *restructuring* as a label for its actions in the early 1990s, when Traveler's reorganized its operations after a 1997 merger, it conspicuously labeled the aggregated expenses a "merger-related restructuring charge" in the financial statements.

In the late 1990s corporate management displayed a studied avoidance of the label *restructuring,* to avoid accounting strictures. As the legitimating rhetoric of management practice shifted, from cost cutting to growth, restructuring was no longer aggressively good management. General Motors' 1997 annual report to shareholders entirely avoided the word *restructuring*. GM instead packaged its intraorganizational changes as competitiveness studies. Goodyear's 1997 annual report included a footnote to the financial statements that also avoided restructuring language. Goodyear labeled its special charges for internal reorganization "rationalizations" instead of "restructuring," as it would have done a few years earlier. Likewise, Kellogg's management completely avoided the word *restructuring* (the term does not appear in its 1997 report) and instead used "nonrecurring charges" and "streamlining" to describe its internal reorganizing activities. Kmart took extensive restructuring charges in the early 1990s, but labeled its 1997 internal reorganization a "voluntary early retirement program." Mobil Corporation used the phrase "staff redesign project implementation" to refer to its internal reorganization in the late 1990s.[6]

Figure 3.4 in chapter 3 depicted the decline of internal reorganization and the rise of transactional restructuring in the late 1990s. Internal reorganizations, described in terms of downsizing, restructuring, and reengineering peaked in 1993 and fell sharply in 1994, the period when restructuring initiatives conspicuously linked to a transaction began to appear more frequently. The decreasing legitimacy of internal reorganization is manifested both in the avoidance of the "corporate restructuring" label for business reorganization in the late 1990s and a rise in transactional reorganizations.

RESURGENCE OF TRANSACTIONAL REORGANIZATION

A second response of firms to the new accounting guidelines for restructuring was to engage in transactional reorganization. Business reorganization deals have been a consistent source of speculative profit in American capitalism at least since the great corporate revolution of the 1890s. Mergers, acquisitions, and divestitures generate huge price breaks and hence opportunities for deal makers to extract very large reorganizer's profits. The use of internal restructuring, conspicuously packaged to capture the reorganizer's profit through equity appreciation, was a possibly unique and short-lived innovation of the late 1980s and early 1990s. The increased use of transactional reorganization to generate and capture speculative gains in the mid-1990s represented a return to business-as-usual for American capitalism.

Beginning in 1994, companies engaged in a flurry of mergers, spin-offs, acquisitions, divestitures, and disposals. This occurred just when preferential accounting rules for internal restructuring were eliminated, creating an advantage for firms engaging in transactional reorganization. Merger-related accounting charges began to replace restructuring charges as a source of earnings manipulation. Because a transactional reorganization made comparing financial results from year to year difficult, this form of restructuring provided an even greater scope for financial engineering than did internal reorganization. Even without large merger-related write-offs, the construction of financial statements after mergers and divestitures provided substantial opportunities to make accounting results attractive to financial markets. The mid-1990s recovery of an active merger-and-acquisition market, especially the prevalence of stock-swap mergers, provided a lucrative forum for speculative management. The growth in mergers and acquisitions had other, important, macroeconomic causes that need not be developed here. But an important contribution to the late 1990s merger mania was eliminating internal reorganization as a means to manipulate earnings and please financial markets.

The following charge was taken in 1999 and it illustrates the continued evolution of business reorganization in the late twentieth century.

Albertson's Says Purchase Charges to Hit $700 Million
Albertson's Inc. said that it expects $700 million in merger-related charges and other expenses as part of its acquisition of American Stores Co. . . . . Albertson's said it would divest itself of 145 stores. . . . Albertson's said a significant portion of the $700 million charge would be taken in the second fiscal quarter, which ends July 29. Analysts expect combined income from continuing operations for the quarter to be about $250 million. . . . Cost savings from the merger are greater than originally expected, totaling more than $100 million in the first 12 months, $200 million in the second full year and $300 million for the third. . . . (Berner 1999, p. A11)

These actions would most likely have been characterized as restructuring during the early 1990s, but were specifically identified as a "purchase charge" to link the reorganization conspicuously to a preceding transaction. Albertson's language and treatment of its special charge conformed to post-1994 rules for restructuring charges (that require a transaction to trigger restructuring treatment). It also aligned the firm with the climate of financial opinion in the late 1990s, which rewarded firms for engaging in mergers and divestitures, or in Albertson's case, both.

After the EITF constrained restructuring charges for internal reorganization, financial-statement manipulation became more difficult unless accompanied by a transaction. Speculative teams in the mid- to late 1990s continued to seek out such charges. Because external, transactional reorganization became a precondition for large special charges, the speculative demand for these charges contributed to the wave of external reorganizations in the mid- to late 1990s.

BUSINESS MOBILIZATION AND ACCOUNTING RULES FOR RESTRUCTURING

> . . . *The ingredients and amounts included in restructuring charges ran from A to Z. . . . Now they're reining it in: it runs from A to G, or maybe A to I.*
>
> —Walter Schuetze, chief accountant for the SEC, describing the incomplete accounting regulation that resulted from business lobbying efforts. (Waters 1994b, p. 14)

Business interest groups pressured the EITF to soften the new restructuring rules and leave sufficient flexibility in place so that this important means of financial statement engineering would not be completely foreclosed. The rules were softened, apparently much to the dissatisfaction of the SEC's chief accountant, who retired one week after this consensus was reached:

> There are those who think the rule-makers have not gone far enough—among them Mr. Schuetze at the SEC. Speaking earlier this week, he said: "In my opinion, they have allowed for the recognition of liabilities that do not meet the FASB's definition of a liability, and which are more in the manner of contingencies." Liabilities should only be recognized when there is some contractual or legal obligation to make a payment, he says. "Obligations do not arise because a board of directors decides something." (Waters 1994b, p. 14)

That business news mediaure was also apparent in the November 1994 changes that the EITF made to the earlier consensus it had reached in May 1994. The EITF "deleted an earlier requirement that all people included in a severance plan had to be out of their jobs within a year" (*American Banker–Bond Buyer* 1994f, p. 6).

Clearly business opposition to tightened restructuring accounting standards was considerable and important for shaping the rules that eventually emerged, however, good descriptions of the business lobbying activity on this issue are scarce. The *Wall Street Journal* indicated rather than described such opposition. The pressure organized business groups applied to the FASB during the stock option controversy (as described in chapter 5) was also aimed at influencing restructuring charge rulings. Retrospectively, SEC Chief Accountant Walter Schuetze's opposition to restructuring charges was cited as a major cause of his contentious relationship with business interests.

Once the 1994 election gave business interests such unchallenged political power, business regulators such as the SEC and quasi-regulatory institutions such as the FASB and EITF worried that legislation might be introduced to reduce their regulatory power.[7] Such legislation was threatened by organized business groups and legislators that supported them (or that they supported) if regulators constrained business interests too much. The EITF and the FASB were not immune to business lobbying and political pressure. When Walter Schuetze resigned as the SEC's chief accountant, his opposition to restructuring charges and his consistent skeptical stance toward large write-offs was cited as a contributing factor to his resignation (Berton 1994, B5).

The spread of special charges to manage income in the late 1990s, in spite of the accounting profession's efforts to curtail such practices, leads to a more general consideration of financial accounting as a social intermediary. The accounting profession, especially in its role as auditors of the nation's corporate financial statements, should be and is a constraining force for managers wishing to manipulate financial statements to influence security prices. But several factors limit its oversight role. First, corporate pressure to beat quarterly earnings targets is intense. As discussed elsewhere, the consensus opinion of analysts who follow a company is widely publicized (of course, executives themselves have some control over these "targets" because the analysts base their estimates largely on accounting information and rhetoric management provides), and meeting, beating, or failing to meet these targets becomes "news" that is quite capable of moving the market. The speed with which earnings surprises affect stock prices has accelerated in the 1990s with most of the market response occurring in the first few hours after the surprise has been announced.[8]

Managers are quite aware of this, and if they are unable to match the earnings target often issue an "earnings warning," a preannouncement of the upcoming quarterly results with a covering narrative that seeks to soften the impact of the earnings failure, especially stories that make the failure appear nonrecurring. But because even these preannounced earnings failures have negative effects on corporate stock prices, far better to bend the accounting rules to meet the target.

Auditors are less likely to stand in the way of such bending because the quarterly results of publicly traded firms are not audited, only the year-end financial statements. But even when auditors are in a position to limit this kind of rule stretching, they are increasingly reluctant to do so because their fees for auditing are quite low. In fact, in the 1990s auditing services became a loss leader for accounting firms, a service that is sold at a loss to establish a relationship with corporations that can lead to more lucrative consulting contracts. Accounting firms are among the largest management consultants and advising clients on reengineering and restructuring programs generated a substantial part of their 1980s and 1990s business activity. Currently, about half of the revenues and most of the profit for accounting firms are coming from their consulting divisions, rather than the low-margin auditing side (MacDonald 1998e, p. A4).

When clients ask auditors to approve aggressive accounting, auditors have a strong incentive to comply unless clear accounting guidelines or unambiguous injunctions from regulators contrain them. Clear rules provide auditors with powerful reasons to constrain creative accounting without risking the wrath of clients and the potential loss of audit and consulting fees. In an article detailing the SEC's role in designing new guidelines for acquisition write-offs, the *Wall Street Journal*'s Elizabeth MacDonald notes that, "Auditors increasingly are asking the SEC to bless certain dubious accounting practices that their corporate clients demand" (MacDonald 1998c, p. A2). Another business news writer notes from the late 1990s:

> A nice, fat write-off can help your stock. . . . Despite its recent tightening of some accounting rules, the Financial Accounting Standards Board (FASB) has left definitions of "one-time" and "restructuring"

vague. Managements would be less than human if they did not exploit the ambiguities. . . . Since one-time charges don't penalize current or future earnings and don't hurt stock prices, it is tempting to overstate them. Why? Because you can later restore some of the write-off, running it through the [profit-and-loss] statement, thereby bolstering reported net income in a year when you might need it. (Condon 1998, p. 129)

BUSINESS MEDIA AND THE DECEGITIMATION OF RESTRUCTURING

GM's most recent "one-time" charge will be the fourth major one it has taken in seven years. GM's charges total a staggering $7 billion, about one-third as much as the company earned during the period. Examining GM's reports, it is darned hard to figure out just how much the company earned or lost over the last decade.[9]

—Bernard Condon, reporter for *Forbes*

Shareholders get rewarded beyond their wildest dreams, but there's a cost . . . through stagnant wages, through downsizing and layoffs, through widening inequalities. Capital wins but at a cost. . . .[10]

—Stephen Roach, economic analyst for Morgan Stanley, early guru of the voluntary restructuring movement, who turned negative on restructuring in 1996

Restructuring was widely accepted as a legitimate business practice among large corporations in the early 1990s in part because it allowed managers to boost the trading price of the firm's securities. This was accomplished by management's capacity to conform conspicuously to prevailing conceptions of aggressively good management—downsizing and restructuring were all the rage on Wall Street and announcing such actions was almost certain to produce "buy" recommendations from analysts covering corporate stock. Financial market support for restructuring was also based on the capacity for managers to boost future earnings by shifting future costs into the current period, thus making earnings shine for several years into the future.

From the viewpoint of this study, the decline in restructuring activity that occurred in 1994 was caused by changes in accounting rules for restructuring rather than by a radical change in product markets that made the operational changes brought about in a restructuring initiative no longer attractive. Indeed, restructuring remained an attractive management practice throughout much of 1994 and announcements of restructuring actions had the capacity to boost share prices well into the late years of the decade, albeit on a more selective basis than earlier. The image of restructuring that emerges from this study is one of accounting rule changes constraining restructuring activity that the financial markets were still encouraging. Changes in financial market assessments of restructuring came later, most famously in 1996 with Stephen Roach's declaration of an impending worker backlash against downsizing. Restructuring charges were further discredited when the SEC launched a 1998 assault on special accounting charges as a mechanism to manipulate earnings. Furthermore, in the late 1990s, that many companies that had previously restructured had lingering operational problems became increasingly clear. In retrospect, the era of restructuring in the early 1990s created more paper profits than real efficiency improvements.

Whereas some negative articles accompanied neutral and glowing reports of restructuring in the early 1990s, in 1994 the balance tipped toward criticism of restructuring as a management practice. In part this was due to the EITF controversy, which helped bring the accounting manipulation possible with restructuring into at least partial light. After 1994 downsizing, reengineering, and corporate restructuring were searchingly scrutinized in the business news media, not only by those opposing restructuring on humanitarian grounds but also by those opposing restructuring on strictly financial grounds. Many analysts found the long-term positive benefits of restructuring to be nonexistent and the short-term costs of restructuring to have been considerable. Many firms recorded one-time and special charges for restructuring every year or two during the early 1990s.

For example, when Kellogg, the Michigan-based cereal maker, recognized a $126 million streamlining initiatives charge on its financial statements in 1998, it was the ninth such charge in 11 quarters. A news reporter asked a Kellogg spokesperson if charges such as these should simply be recognized as "operating expenses" instead of being taken routinely as "one-time" charges (because these clearly were not one-time but nine-time charges). Richard Lovell, Kellogg spokesperson, responded, "This is unprecedented in the history of the company. We certainly have no intention of continuing these one-time charges. This doesn't mean that if a situation comes up where the accountants indicated that's the way to treat the charges, we wouldn't have one" (Condon 1998, p. 127).

Serial restructuring such as this undermined investor confidence in the production and profitability improvements that were to result from reorganization. By 1995 shareholder activists were becoming skeptical of corporate restructuring as a technique to boost share prices. Schwartz (1995) lists "chronic restructurings" as one of the "red flags" of a poor management team that is destroying corporate value:

> As I write this, I am in the midst of watching a local Michigan company that is undergoing its third reorganization in five years. Amazingly enough, this firm's stock price has gone up at each reorganization announcement (even though it falls shortly thereafter). Hope springs eternal among institutional investors, and the market is quick to interpret reorganization as a sign that management has admitted its mistakes and is about to fix them. . . . Constant reorganization is a sign of frustration and panic. Almost always, it is an indication that a company has lost its focus. . . . (Pp. 139–40)

Another late 1990s analyst of corporate restructuring describes the decreasing legitimacy of the practice as follows:

> Downsizing efforts may have brought corporations into the most dangerous company of all. The consulting companies were eager to tap the trend for all it was worth, and executives they were dealing with were obviously not hard to convince, a formula that came in some cases with built-in blinders. Millions upon millions of dollars of investment in employees and their experiences over the years walked out the door in the bid to improve short-term gains by cutting overhead. But it was a devil's bargain, particularly for the businesses that found themselves unable to meet increasing demand from customers as the economy improved. The new message in corporate America is growing businesses. But it takes experienced, valued employees to do that. (O'Shea and Madigan 1997, p. 13)

As Walter Schuetze predicted in 1994, the changed accounting rules of the EITF did not put an end to financial statement engineering, although it certainly did put an immediate damper on the volume and size of restructuring charges. However, by 1998, accounting regulators again expressed concern over the use of restructuring charges and other large write-offs to manipulate corporate earnings. In the fall of 1998, SEC Chairman Arthur Levitt gave several speeches outlining five types of "accounting hocus-pocus" managers currently use to manipulate their financial results. Restructuring charges were one of the accounting treatments that still allowed managers significant latitude to manipulate earnings (see Table 8.1). Levitt's speeches were framed in terms of concern about what this study calls speculative management, rather than as corporate fraud against investors. The following is an excerpt from a news article covering a speech Levitt delivered to an audience at New York University in September 1998:

> Increasingly, I have become concerned that the motivation to meet Wall Street earnings expectations may be overriding common sense business practices. Too many corporate managers, auditors and analysts are participants in a game of nods and winks. . . . I fear that we are witnessing an erosion in the quality of earnings." . . . Mr. Levitt said the SEC in particular will crack down on "big bath" restructuring charges, in which companies overstate one-time write-offs for things such as layoffs in order to make future earnings glow. . . . Companies, he said, are initially padding these charges, which are then "miraculously reborn as income" when "future earnings fall short." (MacDonald 1998e, p. C18)

A perceived rise in financial manipulation associated with "acquisition write-offs" triggered the refocus on restructuring charges in 1998 by the SEC:

> The SEC is worried that a rising tide of companies are abusing acquisition charges for purchased research and development, goodwill and restructuring costs. Accounting critics say some acquiring companies are reporting dubious write-offs for these costs to artificially "manage" subsequent earnings. . . . The SEC is worried about the rise in reported restructuring charges, Mr. Lane said. Such charges are usually taken for things like layoffs or plant closings, and can temporarily depress profits, but make earnings glow in subsequent years. They are "often characterized as one-time unusual events, but if they are one-time unusual items, then why are they becoming more usual?" Mr. Lane asked. (MacDonald 1998c, p. A2)

TABLE 8.1
"Aggressive Accounting" Targeted by the SEC in the Fall of 1998

1. "Big bath" restructuring charges: Companies have an incentive to overstate the cost of restructuring their businesses—or to take as a big a charge as possible— because they know investors will swiftly refocus on future earnings. By overstating the reserves with future operating expenses, they can more easily hit their earnings targets.
2. Creative acquisition accounting: Companies chalk up too much of an acquisition price to ongoing research and development—a cost that can be immediately written off in a one-time charge removing any drag on future earnings from goodwill.
3. Miscellaneous "cookie jar" reserves: Companies use overly pessimistic assumptions to estimate liabilities such as sales returns, loan losses, or warranty costs. In doing so, they stash accruals during good times that they can use as needed in bad times.
4. Materiality: Companies intentionally record small errors on the assumption that auditors will not scrutinize any variance that falls within a certain percentage of revenues or profits. These small errors can add up and mislead the market if they allow a company to meet earnings estimates.
5. Revenue recognition: Companies boost earnings by putting revenues on their books prematurely, either because a sale is incomplete, the product has yet to be delivered, or the customer still has ways to walk away.

Adapted from Petersen 1998, p. C8.

The *Wall Street Journal* noted a study by First Call that found the number of U.S. companies taking one-time charges had increased to 230 in 1997, up from 96 in 1995.[11] The *Wall Street Journal* further notes that the *Analyst's Accounting Observer* reported that in the nine-month period ending in September 1998, companies recorded a total of $40 billion in write-offs of all kinds, including restructuring charges (MacDonald 1998e, p. C18).

Some firms' use of special charges in the late 1990s was pronounced. Mobil Corporation's financial statements in the late 1990s has eight separate "special charges": restructuring provisions, asset sales gains/(losses), employee performance award, litigation, LIFO/other inventory adjustments, asset impairment, staff redesign project implementation and others (Mobil Corporation 1995, 1996, and 1997 Annual Reports).

DISTANCING LATE 1990S REORGANIZATIONS FROM RESTRUCTURING

Restructuring is an invention by Wall Street. It's a term used to cover up debits. We don't play that game. It's shortsighted. It delays the inevitable."

> —Gerard Johnson, chief financial officer of V.F. (maker of Lee and Wrangler jeans), explaining why no "restructuring charges" were taken in association with 1998 layoffs of 2,000 workers and consolidation of 17 offices into 5 (total cost of $400 million)

In spite of efforts to constrain restructuring charges, businesses in the late 1990s found paths around these constraints to continue to engage in reorganization for pecuniary purposes. As restructuring became delegitimated and criticized more heavily by the news media, speculative teams used other special charges to manage their earnings and boost stock prices. In fact, some teams conspicuously distanced their reorganizations from the news media's criticism of restructuring, a clear signal of the decline of restructuring as a legitimate management practice.

In the 1997 annual report of Rockwell International, for example, the CEO describes the successful sale of its aerospace division to Boeing as the culmination of a long series of business reorganizations at the firm that are not to be interpreted as restructuring:

> Over this period [the past 5 years] we have made more than 50 strategic acquisitions and 30 divestitures to reshape our company. Prudent acquisitions to strengthen our businesses are a fundamental element of our strategy going forward. . . . Clearly, major changes have taken place at Rockwell. *We take pride in the fact that this significant transformation has been accomplished without massive restructuring charges or disruption.* (N.p.)

Another example of the changing business climate for restructuring appeared in the language CEO of Fleming used in the 1994 annual report. Although this company is clearly engaging in internal reorganization that is linked explicitly to shareholder value, the term *restructuring* is used only as a pejorative, while the *reorganization initiative* is characterized with other terms:

One of Fleming's key strengths is the breadth and depth of experience possessed by our associates and management team. We are dedicated to creating value for our shareholders. . . . Our ultimate objective is to reward our shareholders with higher returns when our initiatives are completed. The consolidation, reorganization and re-engineering plan is expected to produce estimated net pre-tax savings of $65 million per year by 1997. . . . We begin implementation of re-engineering while assimilating Scrivner. *This is not a superficial restructuring or downsizing.* It will impact the way we charge for goods and services, unique to the industry. We believe the implementation of this new program called the Fleming Flexible Marketing Plan will result in a sustainable, competitive advantage. (P. 5, emphasis added)

Unisys's 1997 annual report contains excerpts from an interview with the new CEO, the former head of Andersen Consulting and someone familiar with the cutting edge of aggressively good management practices. His comments are illustrative of the sophisticated (and subtly critical) views toward restructuring that were being expressed in some corporate circles in the late 1990s:

We will continue to make changes to successfully attack the marketplace. Every successful company must do that. But it will be incremental change. *I'm not interested in a "change day" where everyone stops work in anticipation of a major reorganization and then spends months putting the new structure in place.* We must harness the momentum we have and continue to move forward with all eyes turned to our customers' needs. (N.p., emphasis added)

Companies who had recently recorded restructuring charges also attempted to distance current managerial practices from restructuring. This was often accomplished with an overt statement that restructuring was in the past, other managerial actions are in the present and future. The following is from Emerson Electric's 1994 annual report (published in April 1995):

As we focus on growth, we are challenged with defining the path from restructuring—a difficult process of cutting, consolidating and reducing resources—to a revitalizing process of creating value through renewed growth resulting from increasing and leveraging resources.

Restructuring is a finite process and, at some point, management must refocus on growth. In other words, eventually management must create an environment for revitalizing the top line in the same manner in which it protected and enhanced the bottom line (P. 4)

Many companies that used the legitimating discourse of cost cutting to justify their restructuring charges and restructuring initiatives in the early 1990s employed "growth" as the legitimating rhetoric for late 1990s reorganizations. Unable to use restructuring charges to manage the firm speculatively in the wake of the EITF standards and a turbulent business news media, firms began to search for the next practice that financial markets would view positively and reward with high valuations. The search for growth seemed the next most likely direction for speculative management to turn:

> Midway through the 1990s, the philosophy of downsizing, with the tremors it sent across industry, began to change, and the agendas of consulting companies changed with it. Increasingly, CEOs began to realize that downsizing may not have been a panacea. It improved the bottom line, but it did nothing to increase revenues and grow businesses. If slash and burn was the previous theme, the new direction was to value employees and help them become more productive, a far cry from the mandate of a few years earlier to get rid of everything that didn't produce a profit. (O'Shea and Madigan 1997, p. 13)

Chevron's 1994 annual report further illustrates the positive, growth-oriented rhetorical framing of special charges during this period:

> Looking Ahead at New Opportunities
> I'd like to concentrate on the future in this letter. From where I stand, it looks very good. Our intense period of major restructuring is over. We've made fundamental changes in how we manage our businesses, moving decision-making and accountability closer to the operations. Since 1991, we've also saved about $1.3 billion by cutting operating costs, trimmed our work force by about 10,000 people and sold about $2.7 billion in non-essential assets. Now, we're more than ready to capitalize on our many growth opportunities. (P. 3)

TRW Inc.'s management letter in its 1995 annual report also contains a typical postrestructuring framing: "growth" features prominently in the rhetoric describing future managerial strategy. TRW even boasts that it has hired, not laid off, workers, a clear sign of change in the business climate from 1991:

> With several years of restructuring and downsizing behind it, TRW's space and defense business began to grow in 1994 and continued that growth in 1995. TRW has revitalized this business and positioned it for long-term growth. New contract awards in 1995 totaled $3.8 billion, with an additional $1.8 billion in options. Backlog reached a record $4.9 billion. The company hired more than 1,100 people in its space and defense operations. Growth is expected to continue, fueled by several company accomplishments and advantages. (P. 14)

The following strategy statement from Tenneco's 1995 annual report, written in the spring of 1996, illustrates the intertwining of three facets of speculative management in the mid- to late 1990s. First, Tenneco's reorganization actions, in fact all of its managerial actions, are justified and explained in terms of shareholder value. Second, management indicates that it intends to pursue several transactional reorganizations to increase shareholder value, including mergers, acquisitions, and spin-offs. The list of planned future reorganizations does not include restructuring, especially of the cost-cutting variety. Third, Tenneco's management is apparently aware of negative assessments of restructuring in the news media and took pains to distance its actions from restructuring's darker connotations. This statement illustrates the fashionlike, evolutionary process of speculative management:

> The Future
> We have created impressive value in each of our companies, and we now have a credible set of strategic actions available to us to realize that value. These include dispositions, initial public offerings, merger tax-free spinoffs, and outright sales. Others include reinvesting in our primary businesses to support growth and expansions into new businesses, as well as stock repurchases, increasing common dividends, and providing special dividends to shareowners. . . . We have been dedicated to three basic operating principles as we have restructured and refocused this company. . . . First, we have built

strong companies by virtue of performance. We have engaged in prudent restructuring and downsizing mainly by attrition and early retirement. *We have not created real or perceived value by virtue of excessive job reductions.* When job reductions have been necessary, we have done them right: with severance job placement, retraining and early retirement benefits among the best in American business. (P. 12, emphasis added)

The decline of internal reorganization was due to both changed accounting rules and a changed business climate, especially stock market conceptions of aggressively good management practices. During the recession years of the early 1990s, a legitimating business culture that encouraged corporations to eliminate excess employees supported restructuring. Given the imperative to deliver shareholder value and the inability of firms to increase profits through business expansion during the recession, financial market actors viewed cutbacks and layoffs positively. The economic expansion of the 1990s altered market sentiments about what constituted good management practice. In the mid- to late 1990s, many firms faced a shortage of good workers rather than a downsizable excess, and the market response to internal reorganization and downsizing became tepid and highly dependent on the specific circumstances of each company.

TRANSACTIONAL REORGANIZATION AND SPECULATIVE MANAGEMENT IN THE LATE 1990S

[They are] often characterized as one-time unusual events, but if they are one-time unusual items, why are they becoming more usual?[12]
—Brian Lane, director of the SEC's Division of Corporate Finance, on the rise in reported restructuring charges in the wake of mergers and acquisitions

A neglected but important line of thought in socioeconomics focused on a special kind of "market magic" through which the value of the corporations increases at the moment equity securities are floated on financial markets. IPOs generate a peculiar form of one-time gain known as promoter's profit, the increase in corporate value that results from securitization (Harvey 1982, Hilferding 1981, Veblen 1932). It has been a central argument of this book that the rise of transactional finance has permanently linked corporations to speculative financial markets. This has created tremendous opportunity for firms to generate gain by dipping into financial markets for additional promoter's profit: spin-offs not only provide corporations with cash from the sale of a business unit but also harvest this profit.

This book has also argued that social intermediaries continuously mediate between corporations and secondary financial markets, creating high-tension, perpetual monitoring and revaluation of corporate value. In recent times, opportunities to generate or destroy corporate value in security markets are perpetual. Value capture through securitization—in IPOs or periodic spin-offs—is now an unceasing activity. This book has argued that speculative teams restructured corporations to generate reorganizer's profit by triggering a revaluation of the firm by stock market actors, through the intermediation of accounting and business news media. Once generated, the increase in value that results from business reorganization deals—conceptualized in this study as reorganizer's profit—is available for capture through deft financial market action. Speculative teams generate and capture reorganizer's profit as well as key brokers and deal-makers. Investment bankers, lawyers, and consultants feast on fees derived from reorganizer's profit, as well as stock holders, arbitrageurs, speculators, and the stock-optioned or golden-parachuted managers of the corporation.

As we have seen, transactional reorganization accelerated in the mid-1990s and eventually surpassed internal reorganization as a leading speculative management technique. Many factors caused the shift to transactional reorganization, including changes in accounting rules, changes in financial market assessment of good management practices, and macroeconomic changes in the business climate that made transactional reorganizations possible.

The *Wall Street Journal* reported that the 1993 economic recovery spilled over into a recovery of transactional reorganizations as well:

> U.S. merger activity took off unexpectedly last year after three slack years, surging 80 percent on a crescendo of ever-larger deals aimed at bringing the information superhighway into American living rooms, . . . announced 1993 U.S. merger volume to $275.2 billion, up from $153 billion in 1992. . . . The U.S. volume was only 18 percent below the record of $336 billion set in 1988 by the heady mix of corporate raiders, junk bonds and leveraged buyouts. (Smith 1994, p. R8)

In chapter 3, Figure 3.4 depicted the relationship between transactional and internal reorganization and indicated two periods of heightened transactional reorganization in the 1980s and 1990s. Transactional reorganizations in the late 1990s exhibited greater diversity and, often, financial complexity than did the takeover-dominated 1980s. The legal transformation of U.S. corporations from the multidivisional form to the MLSF greatly facilitated a wider range of transactional reorganizations (Prechel 2000, Prechel and Boies 1998). Restructuring divisions as subsidiaries enabled corporations to spin off, in whole or in part, business units through IPOs. Spin-offs proliferated in the 1990s, facilitating speculative management by generating cash and accounting profits for industrial firms.

AT&T's forced breakup in the early 1980s demonstrated to financial market actors and speculative management teams the pecuniary potential of spin-offs. Although the telephone monopoly was operationally disrupted, AT&T shareholders profited greatly from the breakup. They received shares of each of the Baby Bells and have participated in excellent capital appreciation of these shares.[13] Spin-offs, especially after the booming IPO market of the mid-1990s, have become a way for speculative management teams to realize large increases in corporate value. This occurred directly through the capital appreciation of the combined shares, as well as because spin-offs provided corporations with the currency, in the form of highly valued stock, necessary for further business reorganization, especially stock-swap mergers. Transactional reorganization could be built up in a wavelike pattern: the increased valuation that accrues to reorganized firms provides them with the means to engage in further reorganizations, which increases the value of their stock. This was the dynamic of conglomeration, an episode of business reorganization in the 1950s and 1960s that depended on successful speculative management of equity share values. In the 1990s the ultimate source of the capital that fueled the wave of corporate transactional reorganizations was the tremendous inflow of funds into the capital markets from the expansion of retail investing. As millions of Americans continued to pour money into the stock market, transactional reorganization emerged as an effective means to "harvest the value" in the market, to use a phrase from McKesson's CEO (McKesson 1995 Annual Report).

In the late 1990s, mergers and spin-offs were important means to boost shareholder value and were heavily deployed by speculative management teams. McKesson's 1995 annual report indicates just how powerfully transactions could boost equity value:

> Shareholder value has more than quadrupled since 1990: McKesson's recent record is one of significant value creation for shareholders. When we began to revitalize the PCS Health Systems business in fiscal 1990, McKesson's market value was $1.2 billion. Five years later, PCS had become the largest pharmaceutical benefits management company, covering more than 50 million lives. We had planned to continue to manage PCS's growth—until we received a $4 billion offer from Eli Lilly & Company. As a result, we harvested the value for our shareholders and returned $3.4 billion to them in cash. Over those five years, total value created for shareholders exceeded $4.5 billion including the incremental increase in market value, dividends and the value of stock repurchases. That's an annualized 34 percent return on shareholders' 1990 investment. (P.1)

The sale of PCS Health Systems for $4 billion was a greater source of revenue for McKesson than the entire earnings of the firm from 1990 to 1995. In other words, the transactional reorganization provided more shareholder value than the combined earnings of all McKesson's businesses, including PCS. The language the CEO used neatly expresses the logic of speculative capitalism in which value is not produced by industrial operations, but is harvested in reorganization deals.

Increasing the market value of corporate stock is an important objective of management and a prime motive behind transactional reorganizations in the mid- to late 1990s no less than it was a prime motive of restructuring in the early 1990s. This is illustrated in the following excerpt from CPC's (Bestfoods) management letter to shareholders in its 1997 annual report:

> We measure our company's performance the same way you do—by total shareholder return. Of course it is not possible to show a shareholder return history for Bestfoods alone. Until now, its results have been combined with corn refining results in the record of our predecessor, CPC International. . . . Over the past 10 years, total return to shareholders of CPC International (share price appreciation plus dividends) was 586 percent, compared to the average return of 491 percent for our 15-company food industry peer group and 426 percent for

the Standard and Poor's index. In fact for that period, CPC was among the top four food companies in our peer group in terms of the number of times we achieved top quartile growth rates. In other words, we are superior performers not only in terms of total return, but also in terms of consistency. (N.p.)

A second way that transactional reorganization differs between the 1980s and 1990s is in the type of mergers and acquisitions that dominate each market (see Table 8.2). While 1980s mergers and acquisitions generally involved cash purchases of firms, often under hostile conditions, mid- to late 1990s mergers and acquisitions often involved exchanges of shares of stock under "friendly" terms. The turnaround in mergers that began in 1993 continued throughout the 1990s, and beginning in 1994, merger volume set new records each year (see Figure 3.6 in chapter 3).

The case of Waste Management illustrates the relationship among mergers, internal reorganization, accounting manipulation, and speculative management. Founded by Wayne Huizenga and Dean Buntrock in 1971, Waste Management created a network of local trash hauling companies. Now the nation's largest trash hauler, Waste Management grew to its current size primarily through stock-swap mergers. As we have seen, the currency for these mergers was highly valued stock, and maintaining a high stock price was critical to continued growth. Accomplishing this required management to maintain a steady pace of acquisitions of companies that had a low price-to-earnings ratio allowing the corporation to post ever-improving earnings, which leads investors to assign ever-increasing value to the firm's stock, enabling the continuation of the cycle through additional profitable acquisitions. If ever the firm failed to deliver new acquisitions or increased earnings, its high valuation was jeopardized. Devaluation was fatal because it took the firm out of contention for additional bargain acquisitions. The whole key to growth through acquisitions was successful speculative management to maintain high valuation of the acquirer's stock.

Huizenga became somewhat of a master of the stock-swap strategy, sometimes called "acquisition-stock" strategy, buying up scores of local companies in a similar business, combining them into a national empire. When Huizenga left Waste Management in 1984, he began stitching together local video stores into the national Blockbuster Video franchiser, and he currently runs Republic Industries, a national string of car dealers, auto parts, and car rental franchises. Waste Management re-

TABLE 8.2
Mergers Compared: 1960s, 1980s, and 1990s

	1960s	1980s	1990s
Rationale for Merger	Diversification, conglomeration	Undervalued assets, takeover opportunity	Strategic growth, cost efficiencies, market share
Currency for merger	Stock	Cash	Stock
Merger type	Friendly	Hostile	Friendly
Size of firms	Large acquirers, small targets	Large and small acquirers, large targets	Large acquirers, large targets
Mechanism of deal-maker profit	Boosted earnings per share leads to stock appreciation	Selling assets and loading debt, reselling at higher price	Larger market share and rapid growth leads to stock appreciation
Accounting methods	Pooling	Purchase	Pooling

mained successful in maintaining high market value for its shares, and indeed was "obsessed with its stock price," working aggressively to send appropriate signals to Wall Street to maintain its high valuations. One of the most important signals was steadily increasing earnings, which increased from $1.3 billion in 1984 to more than $6 billion in 1990. The market valuation assigned to shares of the firm's stock increased from $3.41 in 1984 to $46.63 at its peak in 1992. "The stock enjoyed a growth-company multiple, its P/E breaking into the mid-30s. . . . The company was doing upwards of 100 acquisitions a year—while analysts wrote glowing buy recommendations" (Elkind and Rao 1998, p. 130). The challenge with a stock price based on expectations of rapid growth, however, is that eventually meeting market expectations becomes impossible. Eventually, growth companies mature, and as growth slows, the stock is devalued.

Waste Management forestalled this market devaluation by purchasing ever-larger companies in diverse fields such as hazardous waste disposal, recycling, and water treatment. It also expanded internationally. These purchases came at a higher price than local trash firms and proved less profitable than was hoped. Aiming to keep the stock valued in "growth" territory, Waste Management promised continued revenue and earnings growth, but failed to deliver. When in 1993 profits fell by 50 percent, the stock also declined to half of its 1992 high. "'We are a growth company!' [CEO Buntrock] protested to angry investors at the 1994 annual meeting" (Elkind and Rao 1998, p. 130).

In an effort to report high accounting earnings, Waste Management engaged in two types of earnings management activity. First, the company began changing business practices to boost earnings. To reduce expenses, trash trucks were depreciated over a longer life (which backfired due to high maintenance costs). Increasing the salvage value of garbage trucks to $25,000 per vehicle and increasing the assumed useful life of dumpsters from the standard 12 years to 20 years further reduced depreciation expenses. In total, reduced depreciation added $716 million to profits. Second, the company engaged in transactional restructuring, spinning off four subsidiaries, representing its four basic business units. Then, Waste Management began taking a series of one-time charges to mask operating losses. None of this really helped the firm, however, whose stock price fell.

In 1995 Nell Minow of LENS, a firm that specializes in buying minority stakes in troubled companies and forcing them to engage in bloodletting at the executive level and cost cutting among the rank-and-file, began to buy an interest in the firm. George Soros, a global financier and philanthropist, backed her. This team forced existing management to resign and installed a new management team, who quit when they found that the firm's meager performance was based on inflated accounting reports. In early 1998, Waste Management announced that it was taking a $3.54 billion charge against earnings to restate earnings from 1992 to 1996, in essence reducing the earnings of the firm during the period by 40 percent. By this point, the Soros team and other large stockholders were looking to sell the firm, believing that an acquirer might pay more than the firm's current market value. USA Waste acquired Waste Management in 1998, just months after the accounting announcement was made (Elkind and Rao 1998; Holland 1998).

This firm's story illustrates the relationship among speculative management, mergers, and the operations of industrial firms. Speculative management is consequential not only because it is a means to increase the wealth of the principals in a firm, the inner circle of top managers and senior owners, but also because it affects the capacity for a firm to grow. Speculative management also can affect the firm's capacity to remain an independent enterprise. Waste Management's failed speculative management led to its acquisition by a rival firm.

This is an important lesson for corporate managers in the late twentieth century. In the 1960s speculative management was important only to a handful of high-growth companies that engaged in stock-swap mergers—the conglomerateurs. It was an optional area of management attention for all other firms. But in the 1980s speculative management became an imperative. An active market for corporate control, in which firms with low stock market values were susceptible to hostile takeovers, meant that managers who ignored speculative management would be replaced on buyout. In fact, the most successful defense against hostile takeovers was maintaining a high stock market valuation. Managers worried about declines in their share price not only because it lessened their wealth, but also because it put their firm's continued existence in jeopardy.[14]

Although hostile takeovers did not recur with great frequency in the 1990s, the imperative of speculative management remains. Rather than buying out an entire firm, a successful strategy for somewhat smaller players, such as LENS, has been to purchase a minority interest, and through networking with other large institutional holders of stock, knit together a powerful controlling interest in the firm, forcing changes that will lead to enhanced values.[15] Chief among these have been restructuring and cost cutting, changes in management, divestitures of business units, and mergers with competitors. The shareholder rights movement has kept corporations focused on speculative management.

As long as reorganizer's profits can be captured through business reorganization that boosts market valuation, management will be pressured to engage in actions to realize it. If current management fails, then large, powerful, speculative holders of stock will replace them with others who will.[16]

CONCLUSIONS

In this chapter we have seen that speculative management remained a primary focus of U.S. corporations throughout the 1990s. We have also seen that restructuring lost its effectiveness as a speculative management practice during the 1990s, first, because of changed accounting rules that constrained the capacity of managers to manipulate earnings with restructuring charges, and second, because of changed assessments of restructuring as a legitimate management practice. Restructuring became increasingly less relevant for the speculative management of firms, and many corporations conspicuously distanced themselves from this label for their reorganizing activities. In the late 1990s, pleasing financial markets with "signs of aggressively good management" and generating flexibility in financial reporting were accomplished more effectively with transactional reorganization, such as mergers, acquisitions, spin-offs, and divestitures, than with internal reorganization. The volume of internal reorganization peaked during a sharp decline in transactional reorganization, the period between the LBO and junk bond frenzy of the 1980s and the stock-swap mergers of the mid-1990s. Restructuring essentially filled the gap. It had enormous appeal for financial markets because it pointed toward the maximization of shareholder value on the cost side rather than the revenue side and provided "career" managers with the portable honor and immediate profit that major reorganizations had provided in the past and are providing again.

This chapter explained the decline and delegitimation of corporate restructuring by showing how the social intermediaries of financial accounting and the business news media altered the capacity for speculative management teams to boost stock prices with internal reorganization. Tightened accounting rules, increasingly negative media coverage, and a favorable climate for transactional reorganization (bull stock market, sustained economic recovery) encouraged corporations in search of aggressively good management practices to put their focus elsewhere than on internal reorganization. Accounting flexibility and positive financial market opinion accorded to transactional reorganization hastened the displacement of restructuring as a preferred technique of speculative management. Pooling of interest mergers not only provided great accounting elasticity, but also received glowing media coverage in the mid- to late 1990s. The reign of internal restructuring as a conspicuous speculative management technique ended by the mid-1990s, and by the end of the decade, companies well behind the leading edge of aggressively good management primarily employed restructuring as a desperate measure.[17]

Corporate restructuring is one type of pecuniary reorganization that rose in the 1980s, prevailed in the early 1990s, and then declined under the constraint of financial accounting regulators and the business news media. The interest of speculative management teams propelled them to look for innovative forms of pecuniary reorganization, such as stock-swap mergers and spin-offs, to generate and capture reorganizer's profits. The next chapter turns to the consideration of the relationship of corporate restructuring to other speculative management techniques and succeeding phases of pecuniary reorganization.

Chapter 9

THE SPECULATIVE MANAGEMENT OF CORPORATE
VALUE: SUMMARY AND CONCLUSIONS

This study conceptualized the structure and functioning of a cluster of institutions within late-twentieth-century American capitalism: secondary markets for corporate equity securities and social intermediaries that link industrial corporations to them. Experts have argued that certain changes in the size and organization of finance have given the institutional order of secondary equity markets a special significance. In recent times, speculation reached beyond the stock market to affect the management of the largest corporations in the United States. Orienting their activity toward the stock market, speculative managers employed the logic and viewpoint of stock market participants in their direction of U.S. corporate life. American firms were conspicuously managed to maximize shareholder value, which stated most baldly, meant maximizing the trading price of equity shares. In practical terms, this meant that the rules of evidence used within secondary equity markets to assess corporate value became the rules of corporate management.

THE HISTORICAL CONTEXT

This book highlights speculation on secondary security markets. These markets occupy a special prominence in recent economic affairs in the United States. More important historically were primary security markets that placed new security issues to fund productive investment. In the late nineteenth and early twentieth centuries, financiers who controlled corporate access to primary security markets were important power brokers (Chernow 1994). Secondary markets displaced primary financial markets as a critical environment for corporations and their managers. As described in chapter 2, boundaries separating primary and secondary security markets have become indistinct in recent times. Even traditional investment banking, the issuance of securities to obtain investment capital, requires rapid transactions on secondary markets for its successful execution. The stock market and the social intermediaries that link firms to them form the basic institutional structure of this new *transactional finance*.

Transactional finance refers to a system of financing corporations dominated by secondary market trading and organized on a transaction-by-transaction basis. Relationship-based investment banking foundered in the late twentieth century as money markets and deregulation enabled corporations to bypass bankers, reducing their power and influence. Deprived of traditional banking service fees, investment banks adapted to the new market-based system by developing trading and speculative capabilities. In a short period, banking was transformed from a relationship-based services business into one of trading and speculation for profit on stock markets.

The consequences for corporate management were significant for the operation of late-twentieth-century U. S. capitalism. Transactional finance culminated in the 1980s "market for corporate control." Takeovers and other external reorganizations required adept trading in equity securities for their profitable execution. Takeovers exposed the vulnerabilities of industrial corporations in the age of transactional finance, where powerful persons could, and often did, purchase sufficient shares of corporate stock to realize speculative profits from radical corporate changes that they induced. The expansion of the retail market for corporate securities in the late twentieth century further bolstered the newly realized power of shareholders in transactional finance. Millions of Americans purchased securities for the first time while others increased their holdings. The participation of the masses in the stock market not only swelled the value of securities but also concentrated financial power in the hands of other big owners: managers of mutual funds and pension plans.

Together, takeovers, the threat of takeovers, and large, institutional shareholders created an imperative for managers to incorporate the logic of secondary financial markets into their decision-making. Managing relations with shareholders and, particularly, situating the firm to conform ostensibly to shareholder expectations became crucial late-twentieth century corporate tasks. Takeovers and institutional shareholding are evidence that corporate finance, in addition to being an instrument for raising productive capital, had evolved. Corporate finance became a powerful control apparatus within capitalism, available for the powerful to exploit for the capture of economic value.

THE SPECULATIVE MANAGEMENT FRAMEWORK

Transactional finance placed an imperative on the *speculative management* of U.S. firms. Speculative management, the orientation of corporate actions and results to affect stock prices on secondary markets, extends the values, logic, and legitimating discourse of secondary financial markets into corporate governance structures.

Experts have argued that *speculative teams*, composed of a firm's stock-optioned executives and largest owners, oriented corporations to financial markets. These teams directed corporate actions and results to conform *to conceptions of aggressively good management* that were considered especially legitimate by actors in secondary securities markets. Raising corporate stock prices was the prime goal of speculative teams. To be executed effectively, speculative management required conformity to and a mastery of the rules of evidence that govern the imputation of value to corporate securities. Because most market participants valued securities as "capitalized earnings," the most important information for the imputation of value was accounting data presented in the firm's financial statements.

Corporate restructuring emerged as an important speculative management practice because it presented opportunities to manipulate accounting profits and because it came for a time to be the prevailing conception of aggressively good management, both of which were central to the determination of stock prices on secondary markets. The impact of corporate restructuring on stock prices was channeled through *social intermediaries*, institutions that link corporate organizations to secondary financial markets. These include corporate governance structures, financial accountancy, and the analytic business media (which includes stock analysts). Corporate restructuring was executed by persons bound together in a special form of corporate governance structure characteristic of the late twentieth century, a speculative team composed of stock-optioned top managers and active, big owners with shared interest in equity appreciation.

Market participants viewed corporate activity through the rules of evidence and procedures of financial accounting. Flexible accounting rules surrounding corporate restructuring provided the opportunity for the manipulation of accounting profits. Restructuring charges enabled managers to shift "ordinary" costs to "extraordinary" restructuring charges, effectively removing them from analyst's calculations of future profitability. Restructuring charges also allowed managers to shift costs from future periods into the current period, making the firm appear more profitable in future years. Restructuring charges further allowed managers to directly manipulate income, as overlarge restructuring charges from prior years were reversed to create income.

The business media recognized and promoted corporate restructuring as an aggressively good management practice. Managers sought to manipulate stock value strategically by signaling conformity to or innovation within current conceptions of good management. Opinion leaders in the financial community, especially securities analysts, and articulated and dispersed through the financial media the charade that cost cutting justified restructuring. Corporate restructuring spread through large U.S. firms in a fashionlike process.

THE RESTRUCTURING WAVE

Results of this study confirm that restructuring was a major preoccupation of managers and financial markets during the last decades of the twentieth century. The vast majority of industrial firms in this study restructured during this period, some many times. Corporate restructuring spread through large industrial firms in the late twentieth century in a wavelike pattern. In particular, internal reorganization of U.S. firms began before 1984, grew slowly during the 1980s, peaked during 1991 through 1993, and then sharply declined beginning in 1994.

Internal corporate restructuring arose in conjunction with takeovers and other external corporate reorganizations in the 1980s. The decline in external reorganizations in the early 1990s encouraged managers to employ internal organizational restructuring as an autonomous strategy. In management and financial market discourse, corporate restructuring began to signify downsizing and internal reorganization rather than takeovers and buyouts, effectively decoupling internal and external corporate restructuring for the remainder of the 1990s.

Internal corporate restructuring had a powerful impact on the earnings of large U.S. firms in the early 1990s. The average restructuring charge was greater than 100 percent of the profit of firms in this study during this period (see chapter 3). By strategically employing restructuring charges, managers were able to impact the valuation of the firm's securities significantly by signaling the onset of enhanced accounting profits. Restructuring charges allowed managers to shift routine costs to extraordinary accounts and improve future profitability by including future costs in a big-bath charge.

Corporate governance structures, financial accounting, and the business media contributed to the rise, reign, and decline of restructuring by functioning *as social intermediaries* linking corporations and stock markets. The alteration of corporate governance structures during the 1980s facilitated the rise of restrucutring as takeovers strengthened the bonds tying top managers to big owners, creating speculative teams united by an interest in equity appreciation. Accounting rule-making bodies legitimated restructuring charges and left managers with substantial flexibility in their application. Flexible restructuring charges allowed managers to manipulate profit strategically to affect share prices. Opinion leaders in the financial community articulated the positive contribution of internal reorganization to productivity and profits in the business media.

The peak of restructuring activity during 1991 through 1993 corresponded with a sharp decline in external corporate reorganization. Speculative teams, which were blocked from engaging in takeovers and buyouts due to unfavorable economic conditions, switched their focus to internal reorganization to manage corporate relations with financial markets. A 1992 change in proxy rules enabled managers and big owners within speculative teams to collude without threat of SEC intervention, and combined with expanded executive stock options, further tightened corporate control structures. Financial accounting regulators refrained from changing rules governing restructuring charges, leaving managers to continue their strategic use of these charges to manipulate corporate profits. Opinion leaders in the financial community articulated the sharp increases in stock values that accompanied the announcement of corporate restructuring plans. Considered during this period as an aggressively good management practice, restructuring became widespread.

Internal reorganizations fell by more than 50 percent in 1994, dramatically marking the decline of corporate restructuring as a speculative management practice. The decline was prompted by the FASB's EITF adoption of stricter accounting rules for restructuring charges that made using restructuring to manipulate corporate profit more difficult for managers. This ruling placed bounds on the content and timing of expenses included in the charge and required much more complete disclosure of the restructuring plan. The decline in announced restructuring initiatives corresponds to this restriction. Because restructuring was no longer as effective for manipulating earnings, its capacity to enhance market evaluations was reduced. Also, opinions about restructuring expressed in the business media shifted during this time, as analysts detected that the anticipated benefits of restructuring often did not materialize. The legitimacy of restructuring as good management practice was increasingly questioned in the business media. Speculative teams, still needing to increase and maintain stock prices, shifted their activity from internal reorganization to a new round of external reorganizations. Throughout the late 1990s, mergers and acquisition activity were at record or near-record levels as corporations channeled their speculative management activity in this direction.

Although the systems of rules and procedures financial markets use to assess corporate value constrained managerial action, they also enabled action of other kinds. Managers exploited lax accounting rules for restructuring to manage the financial statements and market value of their firms. Managers also packaged their restructuring activities to correspond with prevailing views of legitimate corporate management key players in the financial community held and the business media transmitted. Despite the refined constraint of financial accounting rules and procedures and the more diffuse constraint of the business media, ample play remained in modern capitalism for the strategic manipulation of indicators of value in financial markets.

Efficiency-driven, production-centered restructuring most likely formed the basis of the legitimacy for speculation-centered restructuring. Technical and organizational changes associated with production-centered restructuring sometimes did lower costs and improve production processes and profit at some firms. Financial market observers responded so positively to restructuring, at least at moments, precisely because production-centered restructuring sometimes worked. The prominence of firms that experienced enhanced profits after restructuring helped make possible the exploitation of restructuring for speculative management.

As discussed in chapter 6, in the late 1980s and early 1990s, managers and markets awoke to the power of internal restructuring to boost stock prices. The conception of downsizing and other internal restructuring as aggressively good management arose in the 1980s because of real improvements in profits, at least in the short term, in significant, prominent cases. But once restructuring was viewed as a legitimate management practice, the opportunity was created for managers to obtain a financial profit using the legitimacy of restructuring by announcing restructuring initiatives and enjoying the increased share value. By the early 1990s, restructuring activity could be expected to enhance stock prices. In the short run, financial markets had an opaque view of production changes within firms and could not definitively determine whether restructuring was improving production. The speculative management perspective also highlights how restructuring was oriented toward and shaped by the responses of financial markets during this period.

The wave of downsizing restructuring had largely subsided by 1998. In many ways, the late-twentieth-century wave of corporate restructuring was not a radical discontinuity with corporate practices of the past. Rather, it was one of a series of episodes (vertical integration, conglomeration) of pecuniary reorganization, when financial markets have viewed disruptive change as aggressively good management.

This report has interpreted corporate restructuring as one practice of speculative management, but a broad range of corporate practices can be interpreted from this perspective. Mergers, acquisitions, and other transactional reorganizations, as well as corporate practices such as stock repurchase plans, security listing changes, and dividend policy and pension policy changes, affect the valuation of corporate stock and hence can be exploited speculatively. The speculative management model sheds light not only on corporate restructuring, but also on these other consequential corporate practices of recent years. The role of financial accounting, opportunistic and self-interested speculative teams, and the analytic contingent of the financial media in the corporate scandals of 2001 and 2002 are clarified when viewed from the perspective of speculative management.

THE ANALYTICAL CONTEXT: OTHER VIEWS OF RESTRUCTURING

The perspective taken in this report interprets the restructuring wave as a result of speculative teams' attempts to affect stock market values. At moments in earlier chapters, the ideal-type model of speculative management has been placed in the context of other perspectives currently employed in the study of corporate restructuring. Michael Useem's (1996) "investor capitalism" perspective and managerialism were compared to speculative management in chapter 5. In this chapter, additional viewpoints of corporate restructuring are reviewed to sketch how a fuller awareness of speculative management might add to their interpretations of corporate restructuring. Constructive connections between two such perspectives, post-Fordism and the "conceptions of control" perspective, and speculative management are suggested.

POST-FORDISM AND SPECULATIVE MANAGEMENT

The diverse body of writings collected under the post-Fordism rubric situates restructuring in the context of a radical, late-twentieth-century transformation of the world capitalist system (Amin 1994). These writings attempt two interrelated tasks: adequately theorizing Fordism, the stable system of mass-production capitalism that prevailed during the mid-twentieth century, and theorizing transitions to "post-" or "neo-" Fordist capitalism. Fordism is generally characterized in terms of scientifically managed industrial production, mass product markets, and unionized labor markets. Industrial production under Fordism was centrally coordinated, standardized, and employed "inflexible," dedicated production facilities to maximize economies of scale. The "crisis" of Fordism is generally bound up with the late-twentieth-century rise of competitive, global product markets, multinational corporations with global dispersion of production processes and falling productivity in the West.

In *Post-Fordism: A Reader* (1994), Ash Amin discerns several branches of post-Fordist writings, distinguished by their explanation for the transition from Fordism to post-Fordism. The regulation approach, built on Michel Aglietta's (1979) *A Theory of Capitalist Regulation*, interprets the crisis of Fordism in terms of contradictions and imbalances within a stabilizing "regime of accumulation" that supported the long expansion of the mid-twentieth century. Stagnant productivity, product market saturation, state fiscal crises, and changing consumer tastes ran counter to Fordism's mass production, intensive accumulation, and mass consumption. The *flexible specialization* approach, which Piore and Sabel (1984) clarified in *The Second Industrial Divide*, views the crisis of Fordism in terms of a macroeconomic shift favoring flexible specialization or craft production for niche markets over Fordism's mass production for mass markets. The neo-Schumpeterian approach, anchored by the work of Freeman and Perez (Amin 1994), emphasizes the role of technological underpinnings for long "Kondratiev" waves of sustained capitalist accumulation. In this view, Fordism was based on electromechanical technologies whereas post-Fordism is being constructed around new, information technologies.

Each strain of post-Fordism, although specifying different causes of Fordist crisis or distinct mechanisms of capitalist transition, focuses on an analysis of production and product markets.[1] Although changes in corporate finance appear at the margins of some of these writings,[2] production transformation remains at the center. This leads to a view of corporate restructuring as a discontinuity in *production management*. Restructuring is seen as part of the transformation to new, flexible production systems sharply distinct from the stabilized, rigid processes of Fordism. Oriented toward improving competitive positions of firms, newly globalized, niche product markets conditioned restructuring activity.

Incorporating a fuller awareness of the implications of speculative management into post-Fordist discourses would augment this view of restructuring in several ways. Speculative management suggests that changes in corporate finance and stock markets also contributed to the crises of Fordism. The destabilization of mid-twentieth-century corporate finance preceded the Fordist production crisis by nearly a decade. The transition to transactional finance—financial deregulation, global financial markets, and rise of speculative trading—contributed to the transformation to flexible accumulation. Speculative management, a perspective alive to the importance of secondary financial markets as a critical environment for industrial firms, suggests additional nuances little explored by post-Fordist theories.[3]

Some post-Fordist writings have been criticized for being overly deterministic (Amin 1994, pp. 10–11), especially those interpreting the crisis of Fordism as the result of inherent, internal contradictions and limits within the Fordist system (Aglietta 1979). The speculative management perspective emphasizes that powerfully positioned speculative teams actively produced corporate restructuring. Enabled by transactional finance and constrained by accounting and the business media, these teams strategically manipulated corporate actions and results for speculative gain. Incorporating this perspective, sensitive to the active role of powerful groups in the production of corporate restructuring, balances the sometimes-deterministic logic of some post-Fordist writings.

MANAGEMENT CONCEPTIONS OF CONTROL AND SPECULATIVE MANAGEMENT

Neil Fligstein's historical studies of U.S. corporate change, especially *The Transformation of Corporate Control* (1990) and *The Architecture of Markets* (2001), are prominent works in a developing literature linking industrial reorganization to changes in managerial culture.[4] This viewpoint argues that a legitimating conception of control within firms is consequential for alterations of corporate form. What are considered to be legitimate management practices are built up and subject to change contingent on medium- to long-range fluctuations in the environment of corporate firms. This perspective interprets broad changes in management conceptions of control over relatively long time spans that correspond with major periods of change in industrial form. Fligstein (1990) identifies four conceptions of control in U.S. corporate history: control of competitors, manufacturing control, sales and marketing control, and finance control. Each conception of control led to strategies compatible with four dominant industrial forms: horizontal integration, vertical integration, divisionalization, and conglomeration (p. 12).

The management culture and speculative management perspectives align most closely in their shared focus on legitimating cognitive frameworks: "conceptions of control" in Fligstein's work and "conceptions of aggressively good management" in speculative management. Conceptions of control guide *operational* decisions and are primarily used to frame strategies to cope with competitors in *product* markets. This is easily seen in the first three types of control: competitors, manufacturing, sales and marketing. It is somewhat less apparent in the fourth type, finance control, but even this type, which denotes the use of "financial" decision-making tools (portfolio management techniques using return on investment decision-making programs), is used to make operational decisions about diversified production units. Fligstein's latest work (2001) adds the development of a shareholder value conception of control, corresponding to the period of takeovers and restructuring, signaling an end of management use of return on assets and return on equity in decisions and the substitution of decision-making models to enhance long-term value to shareholders. Fligstein works within the legitimating discourse of corporate management, and each conception of control, including the finance and shareholder value conceptions, are an element of *production.*

Speculative management promotes a search for gains by conformity to or innovation within prevailing financial market conceptions of aggressively good management. These are cognitive frameworks of *financial market actors,* articulated and carried through business media. Although speculative managers seek to exploit these frameworks, they arose largely outside the corporation in its financial environment. This contrasts with Fligstein's conceptions of control, which are cognitive frameworks of *managers* that arise within management culture. Conceptions of aggressively good management point to the importance of the adaptation of management strategies to prevailing legitimating cultures in the speculative environment of firms. By conceptualizing the dominant actors in modern corporations as speculative teams, the perspective of this report gives an account of how the cognitive frameworks of managers and financial markets are brought into direct, mutual influence within the control structure of firms. Incorporating a fuller understanding of the market origins and speculative direction of manager's cognitive frameworks significantly extends Fligstein's interpretation of the place of finance in managerial decision-making.

Fligstein highlights how legitimate management practices interact with medium- to long-run alterations in the competitive production environments of firms. Speculative management draws attention to much *shorter term* fluctuations in an important element of business culture: financial market conceptions of aggressively good management of stock values. Speculative teams manipulate corporate actions and accounted expenses and profits to match or advance this conception within a given set of institutional constraints financial accounting imposes, market structures, trading rules, and so forth. Whereas the conceptions of control perspective sheds light on the way changes in manager's cognitive frameworks are linked to epochal moments of industrial transformation, speculative management appreciates the way shorter run innovations become essential and bear on both transformative and mundane corporate action. This draws attention to the way corporate restructuring was one practice speculative teams used to orient corporations *within* a given institutional environment that formed and maintained a given legitimating discourse.

SPECULATIVE CAPITALISM

This book has been concerned with the *technical* machinations of capitalism and here, at the end, it might be well to turn to larger social concerns.

A central argument of this study is that the stock market, or more precisely the secondary market for corporate securities, was central to the management of American capitalism in the late twentieth century. The viewpoint and interests of actors on this market were injected into and adopted by the controllers of American industry, so that U.S. corporations in the late twentieth century were managed with eyes fixed on the trading price of corporate stock. This study has attempted to develop an apt image of how stock market interests penetrated into corporate affairs and affected U.S. capitalism.

Many theories of capitalism, even those normally opposed (such as Marxism and neoclassical economics), share a view of capitalism as a system of firms managed to extract maximum profit through *production*. To understand capitalism in these models is to understand production management. The spread of transactional finance and the dominance of secondary stock markets change the strategic action of those who control U.S. firms: capital gains from increasing share prices on stock markets becomes a primary goal of managers. Profit from production, at moments, becomes a secondary means of capturing value for owners and owner-managers. American-style transactional finance is achieving a kind of global hegemony in recent years: virtually every economy in the world is moving toward the adoption of American-style financial institutions. As these economies adopt the institutions of transactional finance, they also, unwittingly perhaps, adopt the enabling structure for speculative management. External reorganization is transforming industries in Italy, Germany, and other European countries, where the adoption of transactional finance has led to an active market for corporate control and industrial reorganization. Many European economies are experiencing their first shareholder rebellions, using the tactics and legitimating rhetoric that accompanied the shift to transactional finance in the United States. The elevation of shareholder value or more simply, raising stock prices, becomes a top priority of corporate governance wherever transactional finance is instituted.

To date, the consequences of such a transformation of capitalism have not been adequately understood, in part because the current U.S. financial system is so often interpreted in terms of production management. Given the rapid global adoption of American-style financial institutions, one of the most important tasks of twenty-first century economic sociology is the specification of the institutional structure of American speculative finance.

Downsizing, layoffs, plant closures, and other actions associated with restructuring caused considerable pain for a broad section of U.S. society. The legitimating culture that accompanied restructuring claimed benefits that were distributed at least as broadly. In this discourse, restructuring transformed corporations into lean, efficient, profitable global competitors that rewarded shareholders, including the rapidly expanding ranks of small retail investors, with maximum share value. This study raises questions about these claims. A considerable portion of downsizing and internal reorganization was probably unnecessary to improve production efficiency and, indeed, may have been counterproductive. This report casts doubt on the extent to which corporate control teams carefully engineered improvements in industrial production, but instead exploited positive financial market regard for restructuring to capture quick speculative gains.

The speculative management perspective raises questions about the way the pecuniary interests of powerfully situated speculators affect productive organizations imperatively coordinated for efficiency and profit. This concern is reminiscent of Thorstein Veblen's (1904) analysis of pecuniary and industrial orientations in his incisive writings on unproductive, industrial reorganizations that occurred a century ago. Financiers and speculators, positioned to profit from industrial reorganization, encouraged business reorganization deals that disrupted industrial output and often led to a reduction rather than an enhancement of productivity. Reorganization served the pecuniary interests of financial interests more than the efficiency imperative of industry (pp. 28–29). Although late-twentieth-century business discourse often emphasizes the virtues of managing corporations to maximize shareholder value, the perspective of this report, as Veblen's, questions those virtues.

We come full circle, then, to reconsider John Maynard Keynes's (1935) statement that appears at the beginning of the first chapter of this book, regarding the potential disruption of industry by speculative activity:

> Speculators may do no harm as bubbles on a steady stream of enterprise. But the position is serious when enterprise becomes the bubble

on a whirlpool of speculation. When the capital development of a
country becomes a by-product of the activities of a casino, the job is
likely to be ill-done. (P. 159)

In recent times in the United States, although stock ownership expanded through retail investing, stock ownership remained quite unequally distributed with a small group of wealthy individuals and
stock-compensated executives owning the bulk of corporate shares (see
chapter 2). Furthermore, the value of corporate stock escalated throughout the 1990s, creating large capital gains for shareholders. Capital
gains receive preferential tax treatment. This unearned income is taxed
at roughly half the rate of earned income from employment. Political
opposition to this preferential treatment has been mild, possibly because
a broad spectrum of Americans receives some form of capital gains. But
the inequality of stock ownership in the United States means that the
prime beneficiary of this preferential treatment is the small percentage
of the citizenry that owns the bulk of corporate stock.

The taxation of unearned gains has been a long-standing concern
in the socioeconomic literature, but whereas contemporary debates generally focus on the macroeconomic benefits of preferential treatment of
unearned income, earlier debates focused on the moral right of individuals to unearned income, which might be best considered to belong to
the larger community. John Stuart Mill (1848), for one, advocated the
confiscation of unearned income through taxation:

Suppose that there is a kind of income which constantly tends to increase, without any exertion or sacrifice on the part of owners. . . . It
would be no violation of the principles on which private property is
grounded, if the State should appropriate this increase of wealth, or part
of it, as it arises. This would not properly be taking anything from any-
body; it would merely be applying an accession of wealth, created by
circumstances, to the benefit of society, instead of allowing it to become
an unearned appendage to the riches of a particular class. . . . (P. 818)

Mill (1848) was not targeting big owners of corporate stock, but
rather the propertied class of his time, the landowners. But considerable
similarity exists between the situation of absentee landlords and absentee owners of corporate stock:

The ordinary progress of a society which increases in wealth is at all times tending to augment the incomes of landlords; to give them both a greater amount and a greater proportion of the wealth of the community independently of any trouble or outlay incurred by themselves. They grow richer, as it were, in their sleep, without working risking or economizing. What claims have they on the general principle of social justice to this accession of riches? (P. 818)

As the view of restructuring advanced in this report has described, the beneficiaries of restructuring did not grow rich in their sleep, but were quite active in bringing about the generation and capture of speculative gains. Furthermore, their gains did not steadily accumulate over time, but came through pecuniary reorganizations that triggered financial market reevaluations of their stock. Mill wrote about the unearned income of a passive, leisure class of absentee landlords. This study has reported on the pecuniary gains of active, professional speculative teams. Despite these differences, the moral question Mill raised is a fitting counterpoint to the almost unquestioned glorification of the shareholder and capital gains in contemporary corporate and political discourse. The Enron scandal, arguably the most destructive episode of speculative management, led not to a criticism of managing corporations to maximize stock prices, but rather to an intensification of political pandering to shareholders. Every political response to the corporate scandals in the early 2000s was framed as a protection of shareholders. Preferential tax treatment of capital gains and dividends is said to promote industry, enterprise, and full employment, but this is predicated on the notion that capital gains and dividends are generated by activity that leads to these socially desired ends. This study suggests that speculative teams may generate gains and distribute dividends through socially undesirable practices that harm workers, communities, and the long-run viability of productive organizations. Stock price appreciation and dividend payouts result not only from good production management, but also from savvy speculative management.

NOTES

1. Keynes 1935, p. 159.

2. Byrne 1999, p. 35.

3. All of the preceding are from Smith 1998.

4. Journalist John Byrne's book, *Chainsaw* (1999), describes the restructuring of the Sunbeam plants at Bay Springs and McMinnville. This section draws on Byrne's book and on a clippings file on Sunbeam that I have maintained since 1996 (including *Baltimore Sun* wire reports 1998, Bloomberg News 1998, Byrne and Weber 1996, Dunlap 1996, Lublin and Lipin 1995, Ryan 1998, Serwer 1996, and Smith 1998). Byrne conducted interviews with workers in both Bay Springs and McMinnville and interviewed Sunbeam managers and executives, and I draw on his account of these interviews in the description of Sunbeam.

5. This legitimating rhetoric is evident in this 1992 clip about downsizing, one of restructuring's folk synonyms:

> Downsizing, a word that the dictionary hasn't even caught up to yet, was the word of the year in St. Louis. The third college edition of *Webster's New World Dictionary* says "downsize" means "to produce smaller models or styles of." But in 1992, *downsizing* was the term corporations used to describe shrinking their operations by cutting staff, usually by layoffs or attrition, to meet the demands of a continuously slipping economy. . . . The reasons for the cuts varied, but most were related to the economy's anemic recovery in the face of a huge federal deficit and increasing pressure from foreign competitors. . . . Big companies that dominated U.S. business after World War II still shrinking to improve efficiency in a new era of global competition. (Linstead 1992, p. 10)

6. Laing 1997, p. 29.

7. Frank 1996b, p. A4.

8. *Production management* refers to corporate actions oriented toward product and labor markets. Good production management is generally aimed at improvements in the operations of the firm that will increase production efficiency and profitability. Production management is contrasted with speculative management, defined as corporate actions oriented toward financial markets, often with the intention of influencing the trading price of corporate equity shares (stock).

9. Academic treatments of restructuring are surprisingly diverse, and include Alkhafaji 1990; Barker and Duhaime 1997; Barmash 1995; Bergquist 1993; Bonanno and Constance 1996; Bowman, Singh, Useem, and Bhadury 1996; Brickley and Van Drunen 1990; Clark 1993; Cornett and Varaiya 1992; Donaldson 1994; Elayan, Swales, Maris, and Scott 1998; Gordon 1996; Harrison 1994; Harrison and Bluestone 1988; Harvey 1989; Head 1996; Kose, Lang, and Netter 1992; Markides 1992; Rock and Rock 1990; Schoenberger 1997; Sirower 1997; Smart and Waldfogel 1994; Wright and Thompson 1992.

10. A prominent group of socioeconomists views the late-twentieth-century reorganization of U.S. business as a sharp discontinuity with the past. Events in the early 1970s ruptured the long run of Fordist capitalism, which led to the emergence of post-Fordism. I do not agree with this view. I argue that disruptive business reorganization is a nearly constant theme in U.S. capitalism and has a special, underappreciated significance. My conception of business reorganization is rooted in an examination of the history of U.S. capitalism over the last two centuries. Reviewing this history, assuming, as I do, that business reorganization is a fundamental activity of American capitalism seems reasonable. The late-twentieth-century episode of corporate organizational restructuring is one variation on this constant theme. Indeed, the era of deindustrialization begins as the previous major wave of reorganization, conglomeration, ends. Deindustrialization shades off into the transaction-based reorganization of 1980s takeovers. Takeovers lead to late 1980s and early 1990s corporate organizational restructuring, which itself gives way to the new transaction-based reorganization of the late 1990s mergers. This study points toward the important position business reorganization occupies in U.S. capitalism.

11. Prechel (2000) provides a chart tracking rate of return on equity after taxes for American Steel that shows a very sharp decline in profitability in the late 1970s and early 1980s with a sharp rebound between 1985 and 1989 (p. 183).

12. The broad restructuring of American Steel, especially its restructuring into a multilayered subsidiary form, was aimed at boosting capital generation and by extension, share prices. But the internal reorganization segment described previously relates closely to the conception of restructuring as production management (Prechel 2000, pp. 232–49).

13. Lublin and Brannigan 1996, p. B2.

14. And profit he did. The price of Sunbeam's shares jumped more than 50 percent on the day his appointment was announced. Collectively, Dunlap's stock grants gave him more than 2 percent of the ownership of the firm: He was Sunbeam's largest individual shareholder and third largest shareholder overall.

15. Lublin and Brannigan 1996, p. B2.

16. *Wall Street Journal* 1996, p. B6.

17. Byrne 1999, pp. 155–56. Details of the executive stock compensation plan are to be found in Sunbeam Corporation's 10–K (annual report to the SEC) for 1996, p. F14.

18. Business news articles reported that Sunbeam had hired investment bankers to find a buyer for the firm as early as the summer of 1997. Conventional wisdom held that no acquirer could be located because the price of the stock was driven too high. At the trading price of the firm's stock, Sunbeam was a poor bargain.

19. Laing 1997, p. 29. Byrne (1999) agrees:

> Dunlap, who had built his career on Draconian Downsizings, understood that Wall Street handsomely rewarded companies that shuttered plants and laid off workers. The more people a company fired, the more Wall Street seemed to applaud, sending a company's stock price higher and higher. In the 1990s, when corporate downsizing seemed almost trendy, Dunlap had emerged as one of the most celebrated executives on the Street. (pp. xiii–xiv)

20. Sunbeam's financial situation deteriorated rapidly in 2000 and 2001. In early February 2001, Sunbeam Corporation filed for Chapter 11 bankruptcy protection. The company had accumulated more than $1.4 billion of losses since Dunlap took over the firm. Shares of Sunbeam's stock have now ceased to trade on the NYSE and are worthless. Terms of the bankruptcy were not finalized at the time of this writing, but it is expected that Sunbeam will be taken private and full equity ownership will reside in the hands of its creditors.

21. Cited in Baran and Sweezy 1966, p. 14.

22. Cited in Baran and Sweezy 1966, p. 218.

23. The focus of this study is the comprehension of a "historical individual" in Weber's terms: a culturally significant historical-social object. The particular features of historical individuals are worthy of comprehension because of their cultural significance. The wave of corporate restructuring in the late twentieth century was an important phenomenon worth understanding in

its uniqueness. The interpretation of restructuring developed in this study is saturated with the uniqueness of the case it is meant to interpret and is not a "pure type." Many of the ideal type concepts formed in this study—including speculative management, pecuniary reorganization, and social intermediaries—are less historically saturated and are useful for larger comparisons. These concepts were formed through comparative-historical research.

24. Kahlberg's book, *Max Weber's Comparative-Historical Sociology* (1994), helped to clarify this methodology for me. Weber is the best-known practitioner of ideal-type research, but other major sociologists, including Herbert Blumer, worked in a sufficiently similar fashion. Weller's (2000) characterization of Blumer's empirical research made me aware of similarities (and some differences) between Weber and Blumer.

25. Locating adequate, comprehensive guides to the construction of ideal types is difficult. Weber's methodological statements describe what ideal types *are*, and often what they are not, but tell little about how ideal types are to be constructed. Kahlberg's (1994) thorough and useful book on Weber's comparative-historical sociology gives only a few paragraphs to the question, "How are ideal types formed?" Weller (2000) provides insight into the complex concepts Blumer advocated in his methodology and presented in several of his articles.

26. Much will be made of this distinction as the study unfolds. Takeovers and mergers require a business deal, a transaction, to complete them. Internal reorganization (corporate restructuring) requires none. These management practices are discretionary: management can time the announcement of these actions strategically. Transactions generate a "trading price" that determines the financial accounting recognition of the event. Internal reorganizations generate no fixed price and therefore management can exploit strategically the financial-statement recognition of them (an accrual of future costs).

27. My conception of reorganizer's profit was tested against materials on corporate reorganization, including: Cole 1996; Dechow, Huson, and Sloan 1994; Frank 1997; Greenwald 1996; Jenkins 1996; Lipin 1996; Maremont 1997; McGeehan 1997; O'Shea and Madigan 1997; Tully 1996, 1998a, 1998b; Ziegler and Naik 1996.

28. Weber (1949) notes that concepts useful for understanding a social object "significant for its unique individuality" cannot be developed in the manner of taxonomic classification schemes, in which conceptual attention is directed toward the definition of boundaries that separate classes of phenomena (p. 47).

29. American Steel's production-oriented restructuring was part of a larger legal and financial reorganization of the firm that is amenable to a speculative management interpretation. The internal cost accounting component,

had it been packaged and marketed to financial markets as an "aggressively good management practice" justifying higher valuation, could have had a speculative management impact as well. Some firms in the study, particularly "engineering" driven firms, engaged in stealth restructuring, where details of changes in production and even layoffs were masked from outsiders, including financial markets.

30. The following sources provided financial data: Investment Company Institute 1998, New York Stock Exchange 1999.

31. The 2001 recession, exacerbated by the terrorist attacks in New York City and Washington, D.C., triggered a flurry of downsizing announcements at large firms in the fall of 2001. In corporate news releases, these workforce reductions were often explicitly tied to the weakening economy and were often rhetorically justified as a defensive management move rapid economic slowdown made necessary rather than an offensive move aimed at the maximization of stock prices. Internal reorganization and downsizing may regain legitimacy as an aggressively good management technique.

CHAPTER 2

1. Smith 1998.

2. Smith 1998.

3. Smith 1998.

4. McGough 1999, p. C1.

5. Important aspects of late-twentieth-century finance are explored in a large literature, including Abolafia 1996, Adler and Adler 1984, Blair 1993, Herman 1981, Herzel 1992, Kareken 1992, Lowenstein 1988, Monks and Minow 1996, Morck 1992, Sametz 1992, Schwartz 1999, Schwert 1992, Sobel 1987, and Tonks and Webb 1992.

6. Among the many academic and news media sources on takeovers and leveraged buyouts include Auletta 1986; Bruck 1988; Chatterjee and Meeks 1996; Herzel and Shepro 1990, 1992; Jensen 1992; Johnston 1986; Manne 1992; Martin and Kensinger 1992; Michel and Shaked 1986; Nizer 1944; Platt 1994; Roe 1993; Shapiro 1992; Singh 1992; Stein 1992; Stevens 1987; Stewart 1991; Taggart 1992; and Winter 1993.

7. Michael Jensen summarized the benefits of takeovers as follows: (1) shareholders of acquired firms receive a 30 percent to 50 percent increase in "value," (2) shareholders of acquirers receive a small increase in value of up to

4 percent, and (3) value of the merged companies is about 8 percent higher than market value of companies before the takeover. Jensen claims that managerial action to avoid takeovers harms shareholders, whereas the actions of aggressive raiders help them. Jensen puts forth the claim that the increased value of takeovers does not come from monopoly power (in Coffee, Lowenstein, and Rose-Ackerman 1988, pp. 314–15).

8. The first company for which Michael Milken underwrote a junk bond offering was Texas International, Inc. (TEI), in April 1977, a $30 million subordinated bond issue. The bond paid 11.5 percent interest, fully 150 percent of the prime rate at the time. In April 1988, TEI filed for bankruptcy, and after reorganization, the bonds were valued at only 20 percent of their initial face value. In the reorganization, all of the equity in the reorganized company, Phoenix Resource Companies, was given to the holders of TEI bonds. Equity holders of TEI were given mere warrants to buy shares of stock in the new firm. Financial markets understood that junk bonds could be used to obtain an equity stake in a firm: "When a company gets into trouble like this, let's admit that we have equity. Equity is ultimately where we're going to get value out of the company. Subordinated debt really is equity, and that's coming out more and more today" (Platt 1994, p. 148).

9. Broad and economically significant ownership of corporate securities has had a political impact as well. Those who participate most heavily in the market, upper- and middle-class Americans, have also remained the most politically powerful group in the country. This group has become even more conservative financially and socially, in part because its interests are largely co-extensive with the interests of finance. Market participants recognize that economic or social policies harmful to the interests of elite financiers would also be destructive to their security values, the preservation and advancement of which becomes a prime political goal.

10. For all of the hype over the egalitarian participation in the New Economy and the stock market in the 1990s, benefits have been very unequally skewed toward elites. Harms and Knapp (2001) provide an interesting analysis of the rhetorical framing of the New Economy in the late 1990s and the divergence of this framing from economic reality.

11. Other contributing factors included mass losses in the market, which cooled enthusiasm for Wall Street, a general "taint" to stock trading that lasted well into the 1950s; the powerful industrial position of the U.S. leading producers in the wake of World War II; and the producers' incredible growth; and benefit from the war itself. The government carried on and managed war production and the financing of war production, largely accomplished through the "reconstruction finance corporation." During World War II, the government

assumed the central position financiers played in arranging the financing of World War I.

CHAPTER 3

1. Several good overviews of the Fordist and post-Fordist debate have been written, including Vallas's 1999 article in *Sociological Theory*, "Re-thinking Post Fordism: The Meaning of Workplace Flexibility." An authoritative overview of this literature is Ash Amin's (1994) introductory chapter to *Post-Fordism: A Reader*. I follow Amin's parsing of this literature throughout this report.

2. Aglietta (1979) identifies a crisis of productivity within labor markets in the West expressed in terms of dissatisfaction with the intensification of the labor process, with high-consumption lifestyle and with grueling and degraded work that was unattractive to workers. This crisis was only partly autonomous from the saturation of global product markets.

3. The conceptualization of social intermediaries falls between two literatures: economic theories of markets and sociological theories of firms and their environments. The economic theory of markets emphasizes traditional economic categories such as profit maximizing. They are deductive theories, and although they are increasingly including larger portions of an organization's environment in complex, situated explanations, they often rely on network associations and relatively flat conceptions of power. Sociological theories of organizations have moved toward the inclusion of ever-greater aspects of an organization's environment to explain organizational structure and action.

4. 1993 was the last year *Fortune* had a separate listing for industrial and service firms. Beginning in 1994 the *Fortune* 500 ranked the largest firms from all industries and economic sectors. I used the 1993 ranked for my study for several reasons. First, I had conducted an early study using this listing in 1994, so I already had the physical reports for these companies. Second, 1993 represented an important watershed year: internal reorganizations seemed to be at a peak of activity and the external mergers and spin-offs that so reshaped the composition of the 500 rankings had not yet begun. Using the 1993 sample seemed the best way to view corporate restructuring as a social object.

5. The simulated nature of W. R. Grace's early 1990s restructuring was further revealed by the lack of detailed provision for restructuring costs and the identification of formal restructuring plans in its annual reports. The business news media was also noticeably silent about downsizing and other restructuring activities at the firm.

6. Piore and Sabel (1984) and Harvey (1989), for example, pointed to changes in work and work processes as the most important feature of late-twentieth-century economic change. Post-Fordists and other writers focused on rationalization of work and the increased intensity of labor process as the center of the post-Fordist shift, the primary consequences of the end of the Fordist system of accumulation and the beginning of the post-Fordist system.

7. The predominance of industrial firms among restructuring firms seems consistent with a production-centered interpretation, presuming industrial firms are more likely to be Fordist than nonindustrial firms, and hence are undergoing a more pronounced transition to a post-Fordist regime of accumulation. However, a finance-centered interpretation is also required. An examination of nonindustrials indicates that other techniques of speculative management to stimulate their stock prices were available to them (mergers and other transactional reorganization, and moves to conform to market expectations for high technology). Internal reorganization is only one technique of speculative management and was only a favored technique under a particular set of circumstances.

CHAPTER 4

1. MacDonald 1998d, p. C18.

2. Condon 1998, p. 128.

3. Lublin and MacDonald 1998, p. B1.

4. Lowenstein 1991, pp. 99–100.

5. Lowenstein 1991, p. 106.

6. Although this report focuses on financial accounting, corporate governance, and business media, a comprehensive treatment of social intermediaries might expand this list or separately conceptualize elements that are worthy of independent examination.

7. This example points to only the most tepid and defensive speculative management action possible. It is important to keep in mind the wide range of speculative management as it applies to accounting and mediated information. Speculative management holds more potent and underhanded options than begging for mercy by reducing the "surprise" element of bad news.

8. Accruals are adjustments to the financial statements of the firm that do not result from transactions. The goal of financial statements is to reflect the economic reality of the firm. Transactions constitute the bulk of entries in

bookkeeping: sales and purchases. However, additional adjustments, called accruals, are necessary to make the "transactional" picture conform to economic reality. Long-lived assets, for example, have a useful life that extends beyond the year of purchase. Such assets are recorded in the financial accounts of the firm and the cost of acquiring the asset is expensed (or accrued) over years, roughly corresponding to the asset's useful life. Accruals are "estimates" and are subject to discretionary adjustment.

9. Ronen and Sadan (1981) distinguish between two types of smoothing techniques: (1) classificatory smoothing, where "ordinary" income is managed with extraordinary charges and unusual items, and (2) intertemporal smoothing, where revenue and expenses are shifted to various time periods to yield smooth income. Interestingly, restructuring charges allow managers to accomplish both of these goals in a single throw (p. 59).

10. In a 1992 study of 100 United Kingdom companies, a researcher found that one company used nine of the 12 techniques to manage their income listed in Table 4.1, two used 8, four used 7, and fifteen used 6. Only a handful of companies did not use any of the techniques to manage their accounts (Samuels, Brayshaw, and Craner 1995, p. 38). The most frequently used techniques: (1) depreciation of buildings and intangible assets, such as goodwill); (2) capitalization of costs, for example, interest, start-up costs, research and development; (3) writing off costs direct to reserves; (4) treatment of acquisitions and disposals; (5) extraordinary and exceptional items; and (6) income recognition, such as timing issues (Samuels, Brayshaw, and Craner 1995, p. 37).

11. My research into the history of the accounting profession confirms my own opinions (as a former auditor) that the profession reached a zenith of power during the period of "regulated finance" in the mid-twentieth century. Business political mobilization as well as the globalization of business has eroded the power of virtually all regulatory bodies in late-twentieth-century capitalism. The EITF does not so much mandate accounting policy, but negotiates workable compromises with organized business interests. As stated later in this chapter, the compromise most often used when speculative interests are threatened is footnote disclosure rather than financial statement recognition.

12. It is probably significant evidence of speculative management that stock options, once a covert form of managerial compensation, became conspicuously proclaimed in the 1980s and 1990s. In a sustained bull market, the speculative dynamic somehow outweighed the potential for outrage at the extraordinary levels of windfall executive profits, except when speculative management did not work.

13. Lowenstein (1991) reports that during the years of GM's most aggressive income-statement management (which included early restructuring charges and other accounting accruals), chairman Roger Smith "was leading a fight on behalf of the Business Roundtable to scuttle the FASB because, he argued, its rules were too rigid" (p. 109).

14. In the era of speculative management and transactional finance, accounting regulators also sought to constrain unrecorded use of derivatives, an issue that was implicated in the 2001 Enron scandal. Managers in their efforts to manipulate the bottom line relied more heavily during the late twentieth century on derivatives and other off-the-book transactions to generate income and hide risk. With derivatives, firms invested large amounts of surplus cash in derivative instruments, sometimes to hedge against currency fluctuations or interest rate changes and sometimes as a speculation. Accounting rules did not require the disclosure of derivative exposure in the financial statements. Only when derivative positions were closed out did the gain or loss on these instruments become realized; only when realized were they recognized on the financial statements of the firm, thereby giving management significant control over earnings.

CHAPTER 5

1. Lowenstein 1991, p. 209.

2. Evans 1998, p. H3.

3. Cited in Coffee, Lowenstein, and Rose-Ackerman 1988, p. 31.

4. Dunlap 1996, p. 29.

5. Dunlap 1996, p 122.

6. One sign that financial news became mainstream during this period was the rising celebrity of financial reporters and news anchors. Louis Rukeyser, of PBS's *Wall Street Week*, and Paul Kangas, of the *Nightly Business Report* achieved celebrity status, and one reporter for CNBC, Maria Bartiromo, made several guest appearances on talk shows, including David Letterman's program, *The Late Show*.

7. The *Wall Street Journal* and other well-funded organizations with a well-connected reporting staff, continued to deliver investigative scoops on financial events, such as the merger of Daimler-Benz with Chrysler in 1998.

8. Standard & Poor's Stock Report for McLeodUSA, Inc., July 22, 2000.

9. The source of this quote is a detailed exposé of stock swindles and their relationship to the overall secondary security market, Watson Washburn and Edmund S. De Long (1932), *High and Low Financiers*, pp.18–19.

10. Issues of corporate governance in late-twentieth-century capitalism are discussed in Schwartz 1995; Taylor 1987; and Useem 1993, 1996.

11. Other strands of socioeconomic thought also emphasize management power and management control. In the monopoly capitalism viewpoint of American Marxists Paul Baran and Paul Sweezy (1966), managers of a few powerful, large firms dominate product markets, eliminate competition and leave managers largely in control of American capitalism.

12. Roe (1994) argues that late-twentieth-century institutional investing leads to investor passivity not investor activism because of the diversification of the holdings of institutional investors. Because fund managers have only a small percentage of their total holdings in any single corporation's securities, becoming an activist owner is less profitable than careful selectivity in the choice of stocks. Fund managers are disposed, however, to favor and advocate state and market policies that benefit the corporate sector as a whole, such as lower taxes.

13. Both the Fordist image of midcentury American capitalism and many post-Fordist images of late-twentieth-century capitalism are essentially managerialist views. Corporate managers, although forced to restructure their firms in the late twentieth century by internally generated changes in global product markets, nevertheless remain firmly in control of the corporations they run in each period.

14. Ironically, many of the academic and business media apologists for the shareholder rebellion of the 1980s and 1990s ground their critiques of "managerial capitalism" in the writings of Berle and Means (1968). Monks and Minow (1996), leaders of this movement, cite long passages from Berle and Means and use their work as a foundation for the shareholder rights movement. This is ironic because Berle and Means do not defend shareholder rights. To them, shareholder control of corporations for the sole benefit of shareholders is no better than management control of corporations for its benefit. Instead, Berle and Means argue that the community as a whole should control because corporations are responsible to and consequential for the entire community. Theirs is really a stakeholder approach rather than a stockholder approach and lies close to the German codetermination system. What is clear is that Berle and Means's arguments undermine support for shareholder value as a governing principle of U.S. capitalism.

15. The most important shareholder rights association is the Council for Institutional Investor, formed in 1985. Other groups that are important include the United Shareholders Association (founded in 1986), Analysis Group (1981),

Institutional Shareholder Services (1985), Institutional Shareholder Partners (1990), and Investor Responsibility Research Center (1972). This study does not fully develop the significance of these associations. The foundation and political activism of these groups, as well as the important networking function they provided for the spread of shareholder rights rhetoric and of corporate restructuring as aggressively good management is worthy of exploration.

16. In an unusual passage that conflicts with the overall view of divergent investor/manager interests, Useem (1996) acknowledges that big owners and top executives share control of late-twentieth-century firms:

> Under investor capitalism, both charts are turned on their side. Here, shareholders, directors, and managers coexist in an uneasy but more coequal alliance. Rather than one overseeing the other's overseeing of the firm, they oversee the enterprise together. Though the rubric of investor capitalism might seem to imply the owners are back on top, it is meant here to connote that a new kind of engaged owner is back in the picture and working closely with— though also sometimes against—company management. (P. 7)

Even though Useem (here at least) correctly recognizes that managers and owners "oversee the enterprise together," he draws the wrong conclusions about the direction of this control. The investor capitalist view argues that late-twentieth-century managers and investors are focused on the creation of long-term value. This study argues that speculative management teams are focused on the creation of short- to medium-term increases in stock price.

17. This study suggests that any shareholder can benefit proportionately if he or she adopts a short-term speculative outlook in valuing shares. So, a bull market makes even small holders winners in the short term. The long-term, profit-oriented valuation of shares is diluted by watering. And, small speculators, of course, do not have the capacity to sustain setbacks that large investors do, so their life chances are placed more at risk by speculative management of corporations than for elite owners.

18. There are "outs" available to top executives to recover their lost compensation when share prices decline. The repricing of options is one, as is granting even larger megaoptions in the current year, at a new, lower strike price (Lublin 1998, p. B1).

CHAPTER 6

1. Rappaport 1986, p. 10.

2. Rappaport 1986, p. 10.

3. EITF Issue 87-4, *Restructuring of Operations*, essentially confirmed SAB 67 as the working standard for restructuring charges.

4. For example, the term can be found in Bluestone and Harrison's (1982) *The Deindustrialization of America*.

5. In the academic management literature, *restructuring* literally refers to shifts from one organizational structure to another: geographic to functional structure and so on (see, for example, the discussion in an organizational behavior textbook by Schermerhorn, Hunt, and Osborn 1997, pp. 230–32). In a narrow, technical sense restructuring signifies altering the organizational structure of the firm for enhanced communication, efficiency, and productivity.

6. This article captures the flavor of an era. Jensen's (1989) article integrates the takeover phenomena into a coherent framework. This article is cited so often in the literature because it is a convenient summary of the main actions and the primary interpretation of takeovers.

7. This book labels not only transactional reorganization but also other speculative management techniques such as stock repurchases as "restructuring." In this study, the term *corporate restructuring* is primarily reserved to refer to the type of internal reorganization that the term signified during the peak period between 1991 and 1993: intraorganizational changes of hierarchies, work processes, communication flows, and so forth.

8. During this period, the distinction between voluntary and involuntary restructuring that Donaldson (1994) uses is blurred because many of apparently voluntary restructuring activities are undertaken in pressure situations, for example, when aggressive and powerful ownership groups threatened to install members of their team in upper management. Donaldson recognizes this in his list of preconditions for voluntary restructuring: (1) an awareness on the part of investors that management's current strategy is not yielding maximum value; (2) shift in the balance of power toward shareholders over entrenched managers—especially the rise of pension and institutional investment managers; (3) existence of a clear strategic alternative that will yield "substantial transformation of performance with the degree of speed and certainty sufficient to change the perceptions of investors"; and (4) change in leadership or change in the attitude of current leadership. (pp. 44–46).

9. A thick literature on restructuring charges includes the following academic sources: Bunsis 1997; Elliot and Hanna 1996; Elliot and Shaw 1988; Francis, Hanna, and Vincent 1996; Pearson and Okubara 1987; Waymire 1988; Wilson 1996; and Zucca and Campbell 1992. Articles from the business media include: *Accounting Today* 1998; *American Banker–Bond Buyer* 1994a–g; Bellinger 1997; Berton 1994; Blackmon 1997a, 1997b; Burton 1996; Condon

1998; Elkind and Rao 1998; Evans 1998; Harlan 1994; Ip 1998a–e; Jenkins 1998a, 1998b, Lublin and MacDonald 1998; MacDonald 1998a–e; McCafferty 1996; Morgan 1996; Myers 1995; Petersen 1998; Pulliam and Burton 1994; Springsteel 1998; Storck 1995; Waters 1994a, 1994b, 1998; and Whitford 1998.

10. Among the articles on earnings management and event studies are: Barth, Elliot, and Finn 1997; Bitner and Dolan 1996, 1998; Capie 1992; DeAngelo 1988; Dechow, Sloan, and Sweeney 1995; Ferris 1989; MacNeil 1970; Mautz and Sharaf 1961; McNichols and Wilson 1988; Meigs 1953; Newman 1988; Perry and Williams 1994; Pourciau 1993; Rees and Sutcliffe 1992; Scott 1931; Smith 1912; Trueman and Titman 1988; and Tully 1999.

11. Often standards-setting boards do not establish accounting rules until a pattern of accounting practice has been established for a financial innovation. When restructuring emerged as a management practice, accounting practitioners fit the activity into corporate financial statements by stretching the preexisting rules for comparable business activity. Practitioners often used accounting conventions for "exited businesses" to record restructuring actions before 1986.

12. In 1994, the EITF, a subcommittee of the FASB expressly designed to address accounting issues in financial innovations, issued a ruling that constrained the timing and content of restructuring charges. This ruling also required full footnote disclosure of the details of the component costs within the restructuring charge. Although the EITF still allowed corporations to take charges, they became far more transparent and had to be linked to real expenditures. Because the ruling limited the use of restructuring for the management of earnings, it effectively reduced corporate restructuring.

CHAPTER 7

1. Dunlap 1996, p. 127.

2. Dunlap 1996, p. 222.

3. Levi Strauss, in the early 1990s, sent shareholders very brief summary annual reports that contain more product information and marketing materials than it did financial data. Using these reports to monitor Levi Strauss' corporate performance or to assess its value analytically is difficult. The financial statements do not contain footnotes or detailed breakdowns of expenses.

4. The 1992 proxy rule changes are discussed in Anand 1992, Chernoff 1992, Dobrzynski 1992, Dow Jones Investment Service 1992, and Pound 1992.

5. At Sunbeam, Chainsaw Al Dunlap's second act, Rich Goudis was Dunlap's handpicked head of investor relations. From all appearances, he was the one of the most powerful persons in the company. When Goudis resigned from his position in the spring of 1998 in the middle of an accounting scandal at Sunbeam, the value of Sunbeam's shares fell sharply.

6. I must be emphasize that collusive communication between big owners and the special access of big owners to corporate executives and information was occurring prior to the 1992 rule change. Apparently, the SEC had been lax in its enforcement of these rules (which do seem difficult to enforce). The amendment to proxy changes simply eliminated any threat of SEC punishment for such behavior.

7. Enough small, outside shareholders were aware of their disadvantaged position vis-à-vis large, insiders to pressure effectively the SEC into changing some of the rules that govern shareholder communication again in 2000. Regulation FD (for fair disclosure) governed "selective disclosure" of company information, in which insiders to the firm were no longer allowed to receive corporate news releases one day earlier than the general public. The SEC allows individuals to comment on proposed rule changes, and the response to this particular revealed a great deal of resentment from small shareholders about unequal access to management and information in late-twentieth-century American capitalism.

8. The holders of RJR Nabisco bonds profited enormously from the increase in creditworthiness of the firm as the value of their bonds increased with RJR Nabisco's resumption of investment grade status.

9. An extreme illustration of the prepackaged nature of consultant's advice occurred in a scandal involving Towers Perrin, the eleventh largest consulting firm. In addition to other advisory services, Towers Perrin devised custom-fit workplace diversity plans for corporate clients. In 1995, Towers Perrin landed an extensive assignment at Nissan Motor, Co. USA. Consultants interviewed 55 executives, gave surveys to several hundred workers, and reviewed company documents and charged for this research at a rate of up to $360 per hour. After four months of study involving hundreds of Nissan's employees and a final bill of $105,000, a report was delivered to Nissan in June 1995 that disappointed Nissan officials, who complained that the 121-page report they received made generic recommendations that were not customized to Nissan's situation. Nissan officials later learned that Towers Perrin had delivered an identical report to a second client, Thompsen Consumer Electronics, on the same day. All nine major recommendations, supporting tactics and objects and a 13-element proposed implementation plan were word-for-word identical between the two reports. The only change was the company name used

throughout. A *Wall Street Journal* reporter reviewed 11 other Towers Perrin reports that were delivered to clients about the same time and found that seven were nearly identical. Towers Perrin's defense is that the delivery of such off-the-shelf reports is a general industry practice (Blackmon 1997a, p. A1).

10. Compare this footnote to the long post-1994 footnote disclosures the EITF required in 1994 (see chapter 8).

CHAPTER 8

1. Condon 1998, p. 125.

2. Condon 1998, p. 126.

3. Tomsho 1994, p. A1.

4. The range of costs that companies were including in these charges remained large in 1994. The following costs were included in the EITF consensus letter as types of expenses that had been included in restructuring charges in the past, costs that would no longer be allowed:

•Relocation costs for employees not actually incurred.

•Training of employees who will replace those being let go, before actually incurred.

•Taking as expenses future capital costs for personal computers that will be used to replace terminated employees.

•Accruing costs of dismissing employees related to future business combinations in acquisitions not yet completed.

•Charging against profits the future costs of advertising, new logos or names and other steps meant to enhance the company's image after restructuring—costs that haven't yet been incurred.

•Accruing future costs of developing software to make the company more efficient after the restructuring—also costs not yet incurred.

•Hiring outside consultants to identify future corporate goals, strategies and organization changes after restructuring.

•Packing and moving inventory from one facility to another if these costs don't benefit continuing activities.

•Expected higher premiums for unemployment insurance in future periods.

•Increases in customer service costs expected after restructuring.

•Unfavorable "overhead variances" resulting from operating a closed plant for additional time to meet existing orders.

•Subcontracting warranty work after closing a plant, because such costs are really associated with generating future revenue." (Pulliam and Burton 1994, p. C1)

5. There are important public policy implications of social intermediaries, implications that policy practitioners did not effectively exploit in the late twentieth century. Changes in a social intermediary—accounting rules for restructuring—profoundly reduced restructuring activity. Policymakers seeking to reduce the social costs of downsizing pursued several policy areas but, to my knowledge, none pressed for changes in accounting rules. Speculative teams have a clearer understanding of the power of social intermediaries to shape industry and control industrial action than regulators do. Accounting rule changes are an important and underutilized arena of public policy.

6. Not all firms prior to 1994 employed the term *restructuring* to designate their reorganizing activity. In the early 1980s, a variety of terms competed as a label for restructuring actions, in large part because *internal restructuring* had no clear name at the time. Not until the late 1980s and early 1990s did restructuring emerge as the dominant label for internal reorganization of industrial operations both in the business media and in shareholder communications. Even in this period, however, numerous terms were employed. During the peak restructuring period, however, managers who chose other labels also used descriptions to indicate clearly that they were engaged in internal reorganization of the type *restructuring* connoted.

7. FASB had good reason to worry about business and Republican attacks against it. The IRS was also targeted by such attacks during this period, threatened with complete dismantling, and was ultimately downsized and restructured by 1998. After the restructuring, the percentage of high-income returns audited was halved and the burden of proof for tax fraud was shifted from the taxpayer to the government, making it much easier for high-income taxpayers to underpay their taxes.

8. See Ip 1998a.

9. Condon 1998, p. 126.

10. Smith 1998.

11. Note that this is a different sample of firms from my study and the object of their count, one-time charges, differs from mine. The figures for

my sample show an increase of reorganization charges between 1996 and 1997 as well.

12. MacDonald 1998c, p. A2.

13. Long-time holders of AT&T stock have had an interesting investment experience. Original, pre-1984 shares of AT&T have multiplied exponentially. After the breakup of AT&T in the early 1980s, a holder of AT&T stock also held shares in each of the Baby Bells as well. Each of these has split and merged in an ever-changing array of companies. These stocks appreciated after the initial breakup of AT&T, they appreciated during the 1980 bull market, they continued to appreciate during the 1990 downsizings, and they continued to appreciate during the 1990s as some of the Baby Bells merged again and additional high-tech subsidiaries were spun off. The telecommunications sector experienced dramatic devaluation after 2000. Fortunes have been won and lost through reorganization of telecommunications.

14. Aspects of the relationship between corporate stock and mergers appears in Binkley, Kirkpatrick, and Lipin 1997; Blackmon 1997a, 1997b; Brooks and Murray 1997; Browning 1997; Burrough and Helyar 1997; Deogun and Frank 1996; R. Frank 1996; S. Frank 1996; Keller and Lipin 1997; Lipin and Frank 1997; Lisser 1997; Lohse 1997; Lowenstein 1996; MacDonald 1997; Pulliam 1997a, 1997b; Sandler 1996; and Sandler and Suris 1997.

15. Between 1987 and 1993, pension funds moved away from pushing takeover-related proposals and instead focused on governance-related proposals, such as changes in board of director elections, as well as nonproxy proposals, which include restructuring (Wahal 1996).

16. The relationship between the hostile takeover and leveraged buyout reorganizations of the 1980s and current techniques of speculative management is apparent in the Cendant case. In May 1999, more than a year since Cendant's market value was halved by disclosures of accounting improprieties, shareholder activists pushed to remove the "classified board" of directors at Cendant, on which directors serve three-year terms, with only one-third of directors up for election each year. Instead, shareholders voted to elect all directors each year. "An institutional shareholder, which introduced the proposal, said the change was warranted due to the erosion of Cendant's stock price in the wake of an accounting scandal last year" ("Shareholders Decide to Alter the Way Board is Elected" 1999, p. A9). Classified boards were a popular and effective takeover defense of the 1980s. Classified boards make hostile takeovers more difficult because they delay the exercise of power of those seeking to takeover the firm because three election cycles are

necessary to realize full representation in corporate governance. Shareholder activists in the 1990s have targeted classified boards and other takeover defenses because they insulate management from "shareholder power." Sources on this issue include Bases 1998, Bigness and Blumenthal 1996, *Business Wire* 1998, Fox and Rao 1997, Franecki 1998, Granahan and Ip 1998, Healy and Palepu 1995, Intindola 1998a, 1998b, 1998c; Lipin and Scism 1998; Miller 1997; Nelson and Scism 1998; Nelson 1998a–d; Olster 1998; Pulliam 1996, 1997a, 1997b; Reuters 1998a–d; Rudnitsky 1996; Schay 1998; Scism, MacDonald, and Nelson 1998; *Wall Street Journal* 1997a, 1997b; and Wettlaufer 1998.

17. The success of restructuring as a speculative management practice is highly contextual and as economic conditions change, curtailing other business reorganizations, restructuring (or something very like restructuring with a new twist) might well reemerge.

CHAPTER 9

1. Amin (1994) organizes the *Post-Fordism: A Reader* by the major themes of post-Fordism: macroeconomy, industrial organization, policy and politics, and culture and lifestyles.

2. Changes in finance are thrown into the mix of post-Fordist phenomena, for example, in the following description of the major changes underway:

A shift to the new "information technologies"; more flexible, decentralized forms of labour process and work organisation; decline of old manufacturing base and the growth of the "sunrise," computer-based industries; the hiving off or contracting out of functions and services, . . . a decline in the proportion of the skilled, male, manual working class and the rise of service and white-collar classes, . . . an economy dominated by multinationals, with their new international division of labour and their greater autonomy from nation state control; and the 'globalisation' of the new financial markets, linked by the communications revolution. (cited in Amin 1994, p. 4)

3. David Harvey's (1989) *The Condition of Post-Modernity* and Frederic Jameson's (1998) *The Cultural Turn* recognized the importance of changes in corporate finance, including speculative trading, in their accounts of the crisis of Fordism (see also Antonio and Bonanno 1996, 2000).

4. See also Fligstein 1985, 1996; Fligstein and Dauber 1989; Davis, Diekmann, and Tinsley 1994; and Davis and Thompson 1994. These writings

square in a general way with the new institutionalism in organizational research, which emphasizes the role of legitimating discourse, myths, and rituals in organizations, such as Czarniawska and Sevon 1996, Donaldson 1995, Hirsch 1986, Meyer and Rowan 1977, and Powell and DiMaggio 1991. For an insightful critique of the utility of this approach, see Prechel and Boies 1998.

BIBLIOGRAPHY

BOOKS AND ACADEMIC ARTICLES

Abolafia, Mitchell Y. 1996. *Making Markets: Opportunism and Restraint on Wall Street*. Cambridge, MA: Harvard University Press.

Adler, Patricia and Peter Adler, ed. 1984. *The Social Dynamics of Financial Markets*. Greenwich, CT: JAI Press.

Aglietta, Michel. 1979. *A Theory of Capitalist Regulation: The U.S. Experience*. London: New Left Books.

Akard, Patrick J. 1992. "Corporate Mobilization and Political Power: The Transformation of U.S. Economic Policy in the 1970s." *American Sociological Review* 57:697–15.

Alkhafaji, Abbass F. 1990. *Restructuring American Corporations: Causes, Effects and Implications*. New York: Quorum Books.

Amin, Ash. 1994. "Post-Fordism: Models, Fantasies and Phantoms of Transition." Pp. 1–39 in *Post-Fordism: A Reader*. Oxford, England: Blackwell.

Antonio, Robert J. and Alessandro Bonanno. 1996. "Post-Fordism in the United States: The Poverty of Market-Centered Democracy." *Current Perspectives in Social Theory* 16:3–32.

———. 2000. "A New Global Capitalism? From 'Americanism and Fordism' to 'Americanization-Globalization.'" *American Studies* 41:33–77.

Auletta, Ken. 1986. *Greed and Glory on Wall Street: The Fall of the House of Lehman*. New York: Random House.

Baker, Wayne. 1984. "The Social Structure of a National Securities Market." *American Journal of Sociology* 89:775–811.

———. 1990. "Market Networks and Corporate Behavior." *American Journal of Sociology* 96:3, 589–625.

Baran, Paul A. and Paul M. Sweezy. 1966. *Monopoly Capital*. New York: Monthly Review Press.

Barker, Vincent L. and Irene M. Duhaime. 1997. "Strategic Change in the Turnaround Process: Theory and Empirical Evidence." *Strategic Management Journal* 18:13–38.

Barmash, Isadore. 1995. *A Not-So-Tender Offer: An Insider's Look at Mergers and Their Consequences.* Englewood Cliffs, NJ: Prentice-Hall.

Barth, Mary E., John A. Elliott, and Mark W. Finn. 1997. "Market Rewards Associated with Patterns of Increased Earnings." Stanford University Graduate School of Business Research Paper: 1423, Standord, CA.

Baskin, Jonathon Barron and Paul J. Miranti. 1997. *A History of Corporate Finance.* Cambridge, England: Cambridge University Press.

Bergquist, William. 1993. *The Postmodern Organization: Mastering the Art of Irreversible Change.* San Francisco: Jossey Bass.

Berle, Adolph A. and Gardner Means. [1932] 1968. *The Modern Corporation and Private Property.* Reprint, New Brunswick, NJ: Transaction.

Bitner, Larry N. and Robert C. Dolan. 1996. "Assessing the Relationship between Income Smoothing and Value of the Firm." *Quarterly Journal of Business and Economics* 35:16–36.

———. 1998. "Does Smoothing Earnings Add Value?" *Management Accounting* 80:44–48.

Blair, Margaret M. 1993. "Financial Restructuring and the Debate about Corporate Governance." Pp. 1–18 in *The Deal Decade: What Takeovers and Leveraged Buyouts Mean for Corporate Governance*, edited by Margaret M. Blair. Washington, DC: Brookings Institution.

Bluestone, Barry and Bennett Harrison. 1982. *The Deindustrialization of America.* New York: Basic.

Bonanno, Alessandro and Douglas Constance. 1996. *Caught in the Net: The Global Tuna Industry, Environmentalism, and the State.* Lawrence, KS: University of Kansas Press.

Bowman, Edward H., Harbir Singh, Michael Useem, and Raja Bhadury. 1996. "When Does Restructuring Work?" WP 96–27, Reginald H. Jones Center, Wharton Business School, University of Pennsylvania, Philadelphia.

Brewster Stearns, Linda and Kenneth D. Allan. 1996. "Economic Behavior in Institutional Environments: The Corporate Merger Wave of the 1980s." *American Sociological Review* 61:699–718.

Brickley, James A. and Leonard D. Van Drunen. 1990. "Internal Corporate Restructuring: An Empirical Analysis." *Journal of Accounting and Economics* 12:251–80.

Brooks, John. 1958. *The Seven Fat Years: Chronicles of Wall Street.* New York: Harper.

———. 1984. *The Takeover Game.* New York: Dutton.

Bruck, Connie. 1988. *The Predator's Ball: The Junk-Bond Raiders and the Man Who Staked Them.* New York: American Lawyer/Simon and Schuster.

Bunsis, Howard. 1997. "A Description and Market Analysis of Write-Off Announcements." *Journal of Business Finance and Accounting* 24:1385–401.

Burgstahler, David and Ilia Dichev. 1998. "Earnings Management to Avoid Earnings Decreases and Losses." *Journal of Accounting and Economics* 24:99–126.

Byrne, John A. 1999. *Chainsaw: The Notorious Career of Al Dunlap in the Era of Profit-at-Any-Price*. New York: Harper Business.

Capie, Forrest. 1992. "Window Dressing." Pp. 803–4 in *The New Palgrave Dictionary of Money and Finance*, edited by Peter Newman, Murray Milgate, and John Eatwell. New York: Stockton Press.

Chandler, Alfred. 1978. *The Visible Hand: The Managerial Revolution in American Business*. Cambridge, MA: Harvard University Press.

Chaney, Paul K. and Craig M. Lewis. 1995. "Earnings Management and Firm Valuation under Asymmetric Information." *Journal of Corporate Finance* 1:319–45.

Chatterjee, R. and G. Meeks. 1996. "The Financial Effects of Takeover: Accounting Rates of Return and Accounting Regulation." *Journal of Business Finance and Accounting* 23:851–69.

Chernow, Ron. 1990. *The House of Morgan: An American Banking Dynasty and the Rise of Modern Finance*. New York: Simon Schuster.

———. 1994. *The Death of the Banker*. New York: Vintage.

Clark, Gordon L. 1993. *Pensions and Corporate Restructuring in American Industry*. Baltimore: Johns Hopkins University Press.

Coffee, John C., Louis Lowenstein, and Susan Rose-Ackerman. 1988. *Knights, Raiders and Targets: The Impact of the Hostile Takeover*. Oxford, England: Oxford University Press.

Collins, Daniel W. and Linda DeAngelo. 1990. "Accounting Information and Corporate Governance: Market and Analyst Reactions to Earnings of Firms Engaged in Proxy Contests." *Journal of Accounting and Economics* 13:213–47.

Cornett, Marcia Millon and Nikhil P. Varaiya. 1992. "Assessing Corporate Restructuring: An Empirical Investigation of Acquisition and Divestment Decisions." *Research in Finance* 10:151–72.

Czarniawska, Barbara and Guje Sevon. 1996. *Translating Organizational Change*. New York: deGruyter.

Davis, Gerald, Kristina Diekmann, and Catherine Tinsley. 1994. "The Deinstitutionalization of Conglomerate Firms in the 1980s." *American Sociological Review* 59:547–70.

Davis, Gerald F. and Suzanne K. Stout. 1992. "Organization Theory and the Market for Corporate Control: A Dynamic Analysis of the Characteristics of Large Takeover Targets, 1980–1990." *Administrative Science Quarterly* 37:605–31.

Davis, Gerald and Suzanne Thompson. 1994. "A Social Movement Perspective on Corporate Control." *Administrative Science Quarterly* 39:141–73.

DeAngelo, Linda. 1988. "Discussion of Evidence of Earnings Management from the Provision for Bad Debts." *Journal of Accounting Research* 26 Supplement:32–40.

Dechow, Patricia M., Richard G. Sloan, and Amy P. Sweeney. 1995. "Detecting Earnings Management." *Accounting Review* 70:193–225.

Defond, Mark L. and Chul W. Park. 1997. "Smoothing Income in Anticipation of Future Earnings." *Journal of Accounting and Economics* 23:115–39.

Donaldson, Gordon. 1994. *Corporate Restructuring: Managing the Change Process from Within*. Boston: Harvard Business School Press.

Donaldson, Lex. 1995. *American Anti-Management Theories of Organization*. New York: Cambridge University Press.

Dunlap, Albert J. (with Bob Andelman). 1996. *Mean Business: How I Save Bad Companies and Make Good Companies Great*. New York: Times Business.

Elayan, Fayez A., George S. Swales, Brian A. Maris, and James R. Scott. 1998. "Market Reactions, Characteristics, and the Effectiveness of Corporate Layoffs." *Journal of Business Finance and Accounting* 25:329–51.

Elliot, John A. and J. Douglas Hanna. 1996. "Repeated Accounting Write-Offs and the Information Content of Earnings." *Journal of Accounting Research* 34 Supplement:135–55.

Elliott, John A. and Wayne E. Shaw. 1988. "Write-Offs as Accounting Procedures to Manage Perceptions." *Journal of Accounting Research* 26 Supplement:91–119.

Ferris, Kenneth R. 1989. *Financial Accounting and Corporate Reporting: A Casebook*. Homewood, IL: Irwin.

Fligstein, Neil. 1985. "The Spread of the Multidivisional Form among Large Firms, 1919–1979." *American Sociological Review* 50:377–91.

———. 1990. *The Transformation of Corporate Control*. Cambridge, MA: Harvard University Press.

———. 1996. "Markets as Politics: A Political-Cultural Approach to Market Institutions." *American Sociological Review* 61:656–73.

———. 2001. *The Architecture of Markets: An Economic Sociology of Twenty-First Century Capitalism*. Princeton, NJ: Princeton University Press.

Francis, Jennifer, J. Douglas Hanna, and Linda Vincent. 1996. "Causes and Effects of Discretionary Asset Write-Offs." *Journal of Accounting Research* 34 Supplement:117–34.

Gordon, David M. 1996. *Fat and Mean: The Corporate Squeeze of Working Americans and the Myth of Managerial Downsizing*. New York: Free Press.

Hammer, Michael and James Champy. 1993. *Reengineering the Corporation: A Manifesto for Business Revolution*. New York: Harper Business.

Harms, John and Tim Knapp. 2001. "The New Economy: What's New, What's Not?" Paper presented at the Midwest Sociological Society Annual Meetings, St. Louis.

Harrison, Bennett. 1994. *Lean and Mean: The Changing Landscape of Corporate Power in the Age of Flexibity*. New York: Basic.

Harrison, Bennett and Barry Bluestone. 1988. *The Great U-Turn: Corporate Restructuring and the Polarizing of America*. New York: Basic.

Harvey, David. 1982. *Limits to Capital*. Oxford, England: Oxford University Press.

———. 1989. *The Condition of Post-Modernity*. Cambridge, MA: Basil Blackwell.

Healy, Paul and Krishna G. Palepu. 1995. "Challenges of Investor Communication: The Case of CUC International, Inc." *Journal of Financial Economics* 38:111–40.

Herman, Edward. 1981. *Corporate Control, Corporate Power*. Cambridge, England: Cambridge University Press.

Herzel, Leo. 1992. "Corporate Governance." Pp. 472–74 in *The New Palgrave Dictionary of Money and Finance*, edited by Peter Newman, Murray Milgate, and John Eatwell. New York: Stockton Press.

Herzel, Leo and Richard W. Shepro. 1990. *Bidders and Targets: Mergers and Acquisitions in the U.S.* Cambridge, MA.: Basil Blackwell.

———. 1992. "Regulation of Takeovers." Pp. 323–26 in *The New Palgrave Dictionary of Money and Finance*, edited by Peter Newman, Murray Milgate, and John Eatwell. New York: Stockton Press.

Hilferding, Rudolf. [1910] 1981. *Finance Capital: A Study of the Lastest Phase of Capitalist Development*, edited with an Introduction by Tom Bottomore. Reprint, London: Routledge and Kegan Paul.

Hirsch, Paul M. 1986. "From Ambushes to Golden Parachutes: Corporate Takeovers as an Instance of Cultural Framing and Institutional Integration." *American Journal of Sociology* 91:800–37.

Hirst, Francis W. 1931. *Wall Street and Lombard Street: The Stock Exchange Slump of 1929 and the Trade Depression of 1930*. New York: Macmillan.

Investment Company Institute. 1998. *Mutual Fund Fact Book*. 38th ed. New York: Investment Company Institute.

Jameson, Frederic. 1998. *The Cultural Turn: Selected Writings on the Postmodern 1983–1998*. London: Verso.

Jensen, Michael C. 1989. "Eclipse of the Public Corporation." *Harvard Business Review*, September–October.

———. 1992. "Market for Corporate Control." Pp. 657–66 in *The New Palgrave Dictionary of Money and Finance*, volume 2, edited by Peter Newman, Murray Milgate, and John Eatwell. New York: Stockton Press.

Johnston, Moira. 1986. *Takeover: The New Wall Street Warriors: The Men, the Money, the Impact*. New York: Belvedere Arbor House.

Kahlberg, Stephen. 1994. *Max Weber's Comparative-Historical Sociology*. Chicago: University of Chicago Press.

Kareken, John H. 1992. "Securities and Exchange Commission: Securities Fraud and Insider Trading." Pp. 417–24 in *The New Palgrave Dictionary of Money and Finance*, edited by Peter Newman, Murray Milgate, and John Eatwell. New York: Stockton Press.

Keynes, John Maynard. [1935] 1964. *The General Theory of Employment, Interest, and Money*. Reprint, New York: Harbinger.

Kose, John, Larry H. P. Lang, and Jeffry Netter. 1992. "The Voluntary Restructuring of Large Firms in Response to Performance Decline." *The Journal of Finance* XLVII:891–917.

Livingston, Joseph A. 1958. *The American Stockholder*. Philadephia: Lippincott.

Lowenstein, Louis. 1988. *What's Wrong with Wall Street: Short-Term Gain and the Absentee Shareholder*. Reading, MA: Addison-Wesley.

———. 1991. *Sense and Nonsense in Corporate Finance*. Reading, MA: Addison-Wesley.

MacNeil, Kenneth. [1939] 1970. *Truth in Accounting*. Reprint, Lawrence, KS: Scholars Books.

Manne, Henry G. 1992. "Insider Trading." Pp. 416–19 in *The New Palgrave Dictionary of Money and Finance*, edited by Peter Newman, Murray Milgate, and John Eatwell. New York: Stockton Press.

Markides, Consantinos C. 1992. "Consequences of Corporate Refocusing: Ex Ante Evidence." *Academy of Management Journal* 35:398–412.

Martin, John D. and John W. Kensinger. 1992. "Corporate Raiders." Pp. 477–80 in *The New Palgrave Dictionary of Money and Finance*, edited by Peter Newman, Murray Milgate, and John Eatwell. New York: Stockton Press.

Mautz, R. K. and Hussein A. Sharaf. 1961. *The Philosophy of Auditing*. New York: American Accounting Association.

McNichols, Maureen and G. Peter Wilson. 1988. "Evidence of Earnings Management from the Provision for Bad Debts." *Journal of Accounting Research* 26 Supplement:1–31.

Meigs, Walter B. 1953. *Principles of Auditing*. Homewood, IL: Irwin.

Meyer, John and Brian Rowan. 1977. "Institutionalized Organizations: Formal Structure as Myth and Ceremony." *American Journal of Sociology* 83:340–63.

Michel, Allen and Israel Shaked. 1986. *Takeover Madness: Corporate America Fights Back*. New York: Wiley.

Mill, John Stuart. [1848] 1909. *Principles of Political Economy*, new edition. Reprint, London: Ashley.

Mintz, Beth and Michael Schwartz. 1985. *The Power Structure in American Business*. Chicago: University of Illinois Press.

Monks, Robert A. G. and Nell Minow. 1996. *Watching the Watchers: Corporate Governance for the 21st Century*. Cambridge, MA: Blackwell Business.

Morck, Randall K. 1992. "Corporate Ownership and Management." Pp. 474–77 in *The New Palgrave Dictionary of Money and Finance*, edited by Peter Newman, Murray Milgate, and John Eatwell. New York: Stockton Press.

New York Stock Exchange. 1998. *Fact Book*. New York.

———. 1999. *Shareownership Survey*. http://www.nyse.com/public/thenyse/1e/1e9/1e9cfm.htm. Retrieved May 13, 1999.

Newman, Paul. 1988. "Discussion of an Explanation for Accounting Income Smoothing." *Journal of Accounting Research* 26 Supplement:140–43.

Nizer, Louis. 1944. *My Life in Court*. Garden City, NY: Doubleday.

O'Shea, James and Charles Madigan. 1997. *Dangerous Company: The Consulting Powerhouses and the Businesses They Save and Ruin*. New York: Times Business.

Pearson, Mark W. and Linda L. Okubara. 1987. "Restructurings and Impairment of Value: A Growing Controversy." *Accounting Horizons* (March):35–41.

Perry, Susan E. and Thomas H. Williams. 1994. "Earnings Management Preceding Management Buyout Offers." *Journal of Accounting and Economics* 18:157–70.

Piore, Michael and Charles Sabel. 1984. *The Second Industrial Divide*. New York: Basic.

Platt, Harlan D. 1994. *The First Junk Bond: A Story of Corporate Boom and Bust*. New York: Sharpe.

Pourciau, Susan. 1993. "Earnings Management and Non-Routine Executive Changes." *Journal of Accounting and Economics* 16:317–36.

Powell, Walter W. and Paul J. DiMaggio. 1991. *The New Institutionalism in Organizational Analysis*. Chicago: University of Chicago Press.

Prechel, Harland. 1990. "Steel and the State." *American Sociological Review* 55:648–68.

———. 1994. "Economic Crisis and the Centralization of Control over Managerial Process: Corporate Restructuring and Neo-Fordist Decision Making." *American Sociological Review* 59:723–45.

———. 1997. "Corporate Transformation to the Multilayered Subsidiary Form: Changing Economic Conditions and State Business Policy." *Sociological Forum* 12:405–39.

———. 2000. *Big Business and the State. Historical Transitions and Corporate Transformations, 1880s–1990s.* Albany: State University of New York Press.

Prechel, Harland and John Boies. 1998. "Capital Dependence, Financial Risk, and Change from the Multidivisional to the Multilayered Subsidiary Form." *Sociological Forum* 13:321–62.

Rappaport, Alfred. 1986. *Creating Shareholder Value: The New Standard for Business Performance.* New York: Free Press.

Rees, William P. and Charles M. S. Sutcliffe. 1992. "Creative Accounting." Pp. 514–15 in *The New Palgrave Dictionary of Money aand Finance*, edited by Peter Newman, Murray Milgate, and John Eatwell. New York: Stockton Press.

Robb, Sean. 1998. "The Effect of Analysts' Forecasts on Earnings Management in Financial Institutions." *Journal of Financial Research* 21:315–51.

Rock, Milton L. and Robert H. Rock, eds. 1990. *Corporate Restructuring: A Guide to Creating the Premium Valued Company.* New York: McGraw Hill.

Roe, Mark J. 1993. "Takeover Politics." Pp. 321–81 in *The Deal Decade: What Takeovers and Leveraged Buyouts Mean for Corporate Governance*, edited by Margaret M. Blair. Washington, DC: Brookings Institution.

———. 1994. *Strong Managers, Weak Owners: The Political Roots of American Corporate Finance.* Princeton, NJ: Princeton University Press.

Ronen, Joshua and Simcha Sadan. 1981. *Smoothing Income Numbers: Objectives, Means, and Implications.* Reading, MA: Addison-Wesley.

Roy, William G. 1997. *Socializing Capital: The Rise of the Industrial Corporation in America.* Princeton, NJ: Princeton University Press.

Sametz, A. W. 1992. "Financial Innovation and Regulation in the United States." Pp. 71–75 in *The New Palgrave Dictionary of Money and Finance*, edited by Peter Newman, Murray Milgate, and John Eatwell. New York: Stockton Press.

Samuels, J. M., R. E. Brayshaw, and J. M. Craner. 1995. *Financial Statement Analysis in Europe.* London: Chapman and Hall.

Schermerhorn, John R., James G. Hunt, and Richard N. Osborn. 1997. *Organizational Behavior,* 6th ed. New York: Wiley.

Schoenberger, Erica. 1997. *The Cultural Crisis of the Firm.* Cambridge, MA: Blackwell Business.

Schwartz, George P. 1995. *Shareholder Rebellion: How Investors Are Changing the Way America's Companies Are Run.* Blue Ridge, IL: Irwin.

Schwert, G. William. 1992. "Stock Market Crash of October 1987." Pp. 577–82 in *The New Palgrave Dictionary of Money and Finance,* edited by Peter Newman, Murray Milgate, and John Eatwell. New York: Stockton Press.

Scott, D. R. 1931. *The Cultural Significance of Accounts.* New York: Holt.

Shapiro, Alan C. 1992. "Leveraged Buyouts." Pp. 577–80 in *The New Palgrave Dictionary of Money and Finance,* edited by Peter Newman, Murray Milgate, and John Eatwell. New York: Stockton Press.

Singh, Ajit. 1992. "Corporate Takeovers." Pp. 480–86 in *The New Palgrave Dictionary of Money and Finance,* edited by Peter Newman, Murray Milgate, and John Eatwell. New York: Stockton Press.

Sirower, Mark L. 1997. *The Synergy Trap: How Companies Lose the Acquisition Game.* New York: Free Press.

Smart, Scott B. and Joel Waldfogel. 1994. "Measuring the Effect of Restructuring on Corporate Performance: The Case of Management Buyouts." *Review of Economics and Statistics,* p. 503–11.

Smith, Alexander. 1912. "The Abuse of the Audit in Selling Securities." *Journal of Accountancy* 14:243–53.

Sobel, Robert. 1987. *The New Game on Wall Street.* New York: Wiley.

———. 1993. *Dangerous Dreamers: The Financial Innovators from Charles Merrill to Michael Milken.* New York: Beard Group.

Srinivasan, Rangan. 1998. "Earnings Management and the Performance of Seasoned Equity Offerings." *Journal of Financial Economics* 50:101–22.

Stein, Benjamin J. 1992. *A License to Steal: The Untold Story of Michael Milken and the Conspiracy to Bilk the Nation.* New York: Simon and Schuster.

Stevens, Mark. 1987. *The Insiders: The Truth Behind the Scandal Rocking Wall Street.* New York: Putnam.

Stewart, James B. 1991. *Den of Thieves.* New York: Simon and Schuster.

Taggart, Robert A., Jr. 1992. "Junk Bonds." Pp. 553–55 in *The New Palgrave Dictionary of Money and Finance,* edited by Peter Newman, Murray Milgate, and John Eatwell. New York: Stockton Press.

Taylor, John. 1987. *Storming the Magic Kingdom: Wall Street, the Raiders, and the Battle for Disney.* New York: Knopf.

Teoh, SiewHong, Ivo Welch, and T. J. Wong. 1998. "Earnings Management and the Underperformance of Seasoned Equity Offerings." *Journal of Financial Economics* 50:63–99.
Tonks, Ian and David Webb. 1992. "Big Bang." Pp. 202–06 in *The New Palgrave Dictionary of Money and Finance*, edited by Peter Newman, Murray Milgate, and John Eatwell. New York: Stockton Press.
Trueman, Brett and Sheridan Titman. 1988. "An Explanation for Accounting Income Smoothing." *Journal of Accounting Research* 26 Supplement:127–39.
U.S. Bureau of Labor Statistics. 2001. *Statistical Abstracts Online*. (http://wwwcensus.gov/prod/www/statistical-abstract_.03html).
U.S. Census Bureau. 2001. "Money Income of U.S. Families." Electronic data available from *Statistical Abstracts Online* (http://www.census.gov/prod/www/statistical-abstract_.03html).
U.S. Federal Reserve Board. 1998. *Survey of Consumer Finances*. Washington, DC. Available from the Federal Reserve Board Web site, www.federalreserve.gov/releases.
Useem, Michael. 1993. *Executive Defense: Shareholder Power and Corporate Reorganization*. Cambridge, MA: Harvard University Press.
———. 1996. *Investor Capitalism: How Money Managers Are Changing the Face of Corporate America*. New York: Basic Books.
Vallas, Stephen P. 1999. "Re-Thinking Post-Fordism: The Meaning of Workplace Flexibility." *Sociological Theory* 17:68–101.
Veblen, Thorstein. [1904] 1932. *The Theory of Business Enterprise*. Reprint, New York: Scribner.
Wahal, Sunil. 1996. "Pension Fund Activism and Firm Performance." *Journal of Financial and Quantitative Analysis* 31:1–23.
Washburn, Watson and Edmund S. DeLong. 1932. *High and Low Financiers: Some Notorious Swindlers and Their Abuses of Our Modern Stock Selling System*. Indianapolis, IN: Bobbs-Merrill.
Waymire, Gregory. 1988. "Discussion of Write-Offs as Accounting Procedures to Manage Perceptions." *Journal of Accounting Research* 26 Supplement:120–26.
Weber, Max. [1930] 1998. *The Protestant Ethic and the Spirit of Capitalism*. Reprint, Los Angeles: Roxbury.
———. 1949. *The Methodology of the Social Sciences*. Translated and edited by Edward A. Shils and Henry A. Finch. New York: Free Press.
———. 1978. *Economy and Society*. Edited by Guenther Roth and Claus Wittich. Berkeley: University of California Press.
Weller, Jack. 2000. "Tests of Concepts in Herbert Blumer's Method." *Social Thought & Research* 23:65–86.

Wilson, G. Peter. 1996. "Discussion Write-Offs: Manipulation or Impairment?'" *Journal of Accounting Research* 34 Supplement:171–77.

Winter, Sidney G. 1993. "Routines, Cash Flows, and Unconventional Assets: Corporate Change in the 1980s." Pp. 55–98 in *The Deal Decade: What Takeovers and Leveraged Buyouts Mean for Corporate Governance,* edited by Margaret M. Blair. Washington, DC: Brookings Institution.

Wright, Mike and Steve Thompson. 1992. "Divestment and Sell-Off." Pp. 685–87 in *The New Palgrave Dictionary of Money and Finance,* edited by Peter Newman, Murray Milgate, and John Eatwell. New York: Stockton Press.

Wu, Y. Woody. 1997. "Management Buyouts and Earnings Management." *Journal of Accounting, Auditing and Finance* 12:373–89.

Zucca, Linda J. and David R. Campbell. 1992. "A Closer Look at Discretionary Writedowns of Impaired Assets." *Accounting Horizons* September: 30–41.

ARTICLES FROM BUSINESS MEDIA

Accounting Today. 1998. "Editorial: Can the Profession Cure Itself?" November 9–22.

American Banker–Bond Buyer. 1994a. "Stamping Out Fires: Task Force Tackles the Burning Issues." April 25, p. 5.

———. 1994b. "Restructuring Becomes All Day Event." August 1, p. 5.

———. 1994c. "Top of the Agenda: Accounting for Restructuring." August 1, p. 7.

———. 1994d. "EITF Hews to Tight Standards On Restructuring." October 3, p. 4.

———. 1994e. "Restructuring Put EITF on Alert." November 14, p. 5.

———. 1994f. "EITF Changes Its Mind On Restructurings." November 28, p. 6.

———. 1994g. "SEC's Chief Accountant Will Retire to Texas." December 5, p. 1.

Anand, Vineeta. 1992. "SEC Overhauls Proxy Rules to Foster Accountability." *Investor's Business Daily,* October 16, p. 4.

Anthes, Gary H. 1993. "Coalition Opposes FASB Decision." *Computerworld,* April 19, p. 123.

Bases, Daniel. 1998. "Cendant Insiders Recently on the Sell Side." *Reuters,* April 16, biz.yahoo.com/finance/980416/cendant_cd_10.html. Retrieved on April 20, 1998.

Bellinger, Bob. 1997. "Downsizing at 'Lowest Levels.'" *Electronic Engineering Times*, November 3, p. 137.

Berner, Robert. 1999. "Albertson's Says Purchase Charges to Hit $700 Million." *Wall Street Journal*, June 23, p. A11.

Berton, Lee. 1994. "Who's News: SEC's Controversial Chief Accountant, Schuetze, to Resign within Six Months." *Wall Street Journal*, November 23, p. B5.

Bigness, Jon and Karen Blumenthal. 1996. "Brand Central: Buying Avis Would Fit Unusual Business Plan of Growing HFS Inc.; Licensing, Vendor Fees Fuel the Franchiser of Hotel and Real-Estate Firms; A Dealmakers Latest Deals." *Wall Street Journal*, June 4, p. A1.

Binkley, Christina, David D. Kirkpatrick, and Steven Lipin. 1997. "Araskog's Latest: To Elude Hilton, ITT Agrees to Be Acquired by a Real-Estate Trust, Starwood Lodging. . . ." *Wall Street Journal*, October 21, p. A1.

Blackmon, Douglas A. 1997a. "Familiar Refrain: Consultant's Advice on Diversity Was Anything but Diverse; For Big Fees, Towers Perrin Gave Many of Its Clients Nearly Identical Reports; Nissan, Westinghouse Balked." *Wall Street Journal*, March 11, p. A1.

———. 1997b. "New Places: Worldcom's Massive Bid Shakes Up a Sleepy Town." *Wall Street Journal*, October 13, p. B1.

Bloomberg News. 1998. "Sunbeam Had a Profitable '97 after All." *Los Angeles Times*, November 13, p. C3.

Brooks, Rick and Matt Murray. 1997. "For Crutchfield, Persistence Unlocked Deal for Corestates; Undaunted First Union Chief Offered Not Only Money but Persuasive Incentives." *Wall Street Journal*, November 19, p. A3.

Browning, E. S. 1997. "Is the Praise for Worldcom too Much?" *Wall Street Journal*, October 8, p. C1.

Burrough, Bryan and John Helyar. 1997. "You Call This a Takeover?" *Wall Street Journal*, November 12, p. A22.

Burton, Lee. 1996. "Rule May Alter Accounting in Mergers." *Wall Street Journal*, May 1, p. A2.

Business Wire. 1998. "Cendant Corporation Sued by Investors for Securities Fraud." April 21. biz.yahoo.com/bw/980421/cohen_mils_3.html. Retrieved on April 21, 1998.

Byrne, John A. and Joseph Weber. 1996. "The Shredder: Did CEO Dunlap Save Scott Paper—or Just Pretty It Up? *Business Week*, January 15, pp. 56–64.

Chernoff, Joel. 1992. "Major Changes of SEC Proxy Reform Outlined." *Pensions and Investments*, October 26, p. 37.

Cole, Jeff. 1996. "Loral Corp.'s Schwartz to Get Bonus of $18 Million for Planning Unit's Sale." *Wall Street Journal*, January 15, p. A4.

Condon, Bernard. 1998. "Pick a Number, Any Number." *Forbes*, March 23, p. 124–30.

Dechow, Patricia M., Mark R. Huson, and Richard G. Sloan. 1994. "The Effect of Restructuring Charges on Executives Cash Compensation." *Accounting Review* 69:138–56.

Deogun, Nikhil and Stephen E. Frank. 1996. "NationsBank Deal May Prompt Seller's Market." *Wall Street Journal*, September 3, p. A3.

Dobrzynski, Judith H. 1992. "An October Surprise that Has Shareholders Cheering." *Business Week*, November 2, p. 144.

Dow Jones Investment Service. 1992. "Proxy Rule Changes Are More Likely." *Atlanta Journal and Constitution*, September 2, p. 3C.

Elkind, Peter and Rajiv M. Rao. 1998. "Garbage In; Garbage Out." *Fortune*, May 25, p. 130.

Evans, David. 1998. "CEO's Seldom Lose in Mergers; Executives Collect since They Get No Blame if Deal Goes Sour." *Plain Dealer*, September 6, p. H3.

"FASB Stock Option Proposal Blasted in Senate Testimony; FASB's Plan a 'Potent and Poisonous Job Killer.'" 1993. *Business Wire*, October 20.

"FASB's Stock Option Rule Threatens America's Entrepreneurial Culture, Technology Coalition Charges." 1993. *Business Wire*, April 7.

"Flaky Accounting on the March?" 1999. *Wall Street Journal*, February 5, p. A14.

Fox, Justin and Rajiv M. Rao. 1997. "Who the Hell Is Henry Silverman?" *Fortune*, October 27, www.pathfinder.com/fortune/1997/971027/hfs.html. Retrieved on April 22, 1998.

Franecki, David. 1998. "As Cendant's Drop Hits Mutual Funds, Some Managers See Buying Opportunity." *Wall Street Journal*, April 27, p. C3.

Frank, Robert. 1996a. "Corporate Focus: Huizenga Faces Challenge in Meshing Eclectic Empire; Republic Doesn't Plan to Stop at Solid Waste, Burglar Alarms and Used Cars." *Wall Street Journal*, July 3, p. B6.

———. 1996b. "Sunbeam's New CEO Begins to Revamp Management, Plans to Prune Products." *Wall Street Journal*, July 25, p. A4.

Frank, Robert and Joann S. Lublin. 1996. "Dunlap's Ax Falls—6,000 Times— At Sunbeam." *Wall Street Journal*, November 13, p. B1.

Frank, Stephen E. 1996. "Heard on the Street: In Bank Deals, Consider This: Buy the Buyer." *Wall Street Journal*, September 11, p. C1.

———. 1997. "Chase Chairman Saw '96 Income more than Double." *Wall Street Journal*, March 31, p. A4.

Granahan, Thomas and Greg Ip. 1998. "Mountainous Wave of Cendant Trading Ignites Debate on Big-Board Specialists." *Wall Street Journal*, April 17, p. A3.

Greenwald, John. 1996. "The Art of the Deal." *Time*, February 19, pp. 48–50.

Hager, Bruce. 1992. "Why Not Write Off 1991? Everyone Else Did." *Business Week*, March 16, p. 64.

Harlan, Christi. 1994. "High Anxiety: Accounting Proposal Stirs Unusual Uproar in Executive Suites; FASB's Stock-Option Plan Threatens Pay Packages; Lobbying Gets Intense; A Risk to High-Tech Firms?" *Wall Street Journal.*, March 7, p. A1.

Head, Simon. 1996. "The New Ruthless Economy." *New York Review*, February 29, pp. 47–52.

Holland, Kelley. 1998. "Messy Accounts at Waste Management." *Business Week*, March 9, p. 44.

Intindola, Brendan. 1998a. "Cendant Shares in Meltdown on EPS Restatement." *Reuters*, April 16, biz.yahoo.com/finance/980416/cendant_cd_3.html. Retrieved on April 20, 1998.

———. 1998b. "Cendant Stock Falls, Insurance Deal Imperiled." *Reuters*, April 16, dailynews.yahoo.com/headlin...16/business/stories/cendant_2_html. Retrieved on April 20, 1998.

———. 1998c. "Focus—Cendant Stock Falls, Denting Big Expansion Plans." *Reuters*, April 16. biz.yahoo.com/finance/980416/cendant_1s_4.html. Retrieved on April 20, 1998.

"Investors Unshaken by Huge Layoffs." 1986. *Chicago Tribune*, December 22, p. C18.

Ip, Greg. 1998a. "Big News on Your Stock? Hold on to Your Hat." *Wall Street Journal*, April 27, p. C1.

———. 1998b. "Some Analysts See Signs of Speculative Excess." *Wall Street Journal*, May 18, p. C1.

———. 1998c. "Abreast of the Market: Do Big Write-Offs Artificially Inflate Earnings?" *Wall Street Journal*, July 6, p. C1.

———. 1998d. "Big Board Considers Wider 'Collar' that Would Favor a Rising Market." *Wall Street Journal*, July 16, p. C1.

———. 1998e. "Why a Famous Bull Waved a Red Flag." *Wall Street Journal*, August 5, p. C1.

Ip, Greg and Raju Narisetti. 1999. "First Call May End Prerelease Peeks at Earnings." *Wall Street Journal*, January 27, p. C1.

Jenkins, Holman W., Jr. 1996. "Business World: To the Rationalizers Go the Spoils." *Wall Street Journal*, July 30, p. A15.

———. 1998a. "Before Chrysler, Daimler Was a Soap Opera." *Wall Street Journal*, Interactive Edition, June 10.

———. 1998b. "Business World: When CEO's Can't Add Up the Numbers." *Wall Street Journal*, August 19, p. A19.

Keller, John J. and Steven Lipin. 1997. "Wedding Bells: Worldcom, MCI Deal Could Rewrite Script for a New Phone Era; Ebbers Wins Bidding War With $37 Billion Offer; BT Exits With Big Gain; Madcap Manhattan Weekend." *Wall Street Journal*, November 11, p. A1.

King, Ralph T. 1999. "Scandal Fells McKesson's Top Executives; Chairman, CEO, 5 Others Quit Posts or Are Fired over HBO's Accounting." *Wall Street Journal*, June 21, p. A3.

Laing, Jonathan R. 1997. "High Noon at Sunbeam: Does Chainsaw Al Have a Truly Revived Operation—or Something Else?" *Barron's*, June 16, p. 29.

Linstead, John O. 1992. "Downsizing Is the Word of the Year." *St. Louis Post-Dispatch*, December 28, p. 10.

Lipin, Stephen. 1996. "Adviser Fees for Duracell Rile Buffett." *Wall Street Journal*, November 26, p. C1.

Lipin, Steven and Stephen E. Frank. 1997. "First Union to Acquire Corestates for Stock Valued at $16.3 Billion; Record Banking Deal Creates Powerhouse, May Spur Further Pacts." *Wall Street Journal*, November 19, p. A3.

Lipin, Steven and Leslie Scism. 1998. "Cendant's Acquisition Spree Continues; Ratings Agencies Warn about Pace." *Wall Street Journal*, March 27, p. C1.

Lisser, Eleena de. 1997. "Heard on the Street: Some Skeptics Wonder whether Nationsbank Is into One Deal too Many in Seeking Barnett." *Wall Street Journal*, September 9, p. C4.

Lohse, Deborah. 1997. "MCI–WorldCom Appears Headed for Nasdaq Listing." *Wall Street Journal*, November 12, p. C22.

Lowenstein, Roger. 1996. "Intrinsic Value: Republic Tender: In Huizenga We Trust." *Wall Street Journal*, July 11, p. C1.

Lublin, Joann. 1998. "Market Slide Ravages Value of CEO's Options." *Wall Street Journal*, September 1, p. B1.

Lublin, Joann S. and Martha Brannigan. 1996. "Sunbeam Names Albert Dunlap as Chief, Betting He Can Pull Off a Turnaround." *Wall Street Journal*, July 19, p. B2.

Lublin, Joann S. and Steven Lipin. 1995. "Scott Paper's 'Rambo in Pin Stripes' Is on the Prowl for Another Company." *Wall Street Journal*, July 18, p. B1.

Lublin, Joann S. and Elizabeth MacDonald. 1998. "Management: Scandals Signal Laxity of Audit Panels." *Wall Street Journal*, July 17, p. B1.

———. 1999. "More Independent Audit Committees Are Sought." *Wall Street Journal*, February 8, B1.

MacDonald, Elizabeth. 1997. "Worldcom Wants "Pooling' for MCI Deal." *Wall Street Journal*, October 8, p. B2.

———. 1998a. "Economy: FASB Renews Bid to Tighten Merger Accounting." *Wall Street Journal*, February 27, p. A2.

———. 1998b. "Proposed Deal Faces Rocky Due to Different Accounting Rules." *Wall Street Journal*, May 7, p. A10.

———. 1998c. "SEC Considers Limits on Acquisition Write-Offs." *Wall Street Journal*, August 21, p. A2.

———. 1998d. "SEC Chief Aims to Attack Abuses in Firm's Figures." *Wall Street Journal*, September 29, p. C18.

———. 1998e. "SEC Ready to Clarify Misconduct Rules for Auditors of Financial Statements." *Wall Street Journal*, September 23, p. A4.

MacDonald, Elizabeth and Robert McGough. 1999. "Stock Options Take Hidden Toll on Profit." *Wall Street Journal*, May 24, p. C1.

Maremont, Mark. 1997. "In the Money: Stock-Option Deals, Novel and Well-Timed, Bring CEO a Fortune; ADT's Chief Traded 3 Million Options for 8 Million Before Bid for His Firm; A Sale to Tyco International." *Wall Street Journal*, June 27, p. A1.

Mathews, Jay. 1994. "Accounting Board Drops Disputed Stock Option Rule; Companies Had Fought Proposal to Deduct Cost from Earnings." *Washington Post*, November 14, p. B17.

McCafferty, Joseph. 1996. "IBM Offs Write-Offs." *CFO: The Magazine for Senior Financial Executives*, May, p. 11.

McGeehan, Patrick. 1997. "Morgan Stanley, Dean Witter Have a Big Breakup Fee." *Wall Street Journal*, February 18, p. B12.

McGough, Robert. 1999. "Top Tier Banks in US Make So-So Matches." *Wall Street Journal*, June 4, p. C1.

Milken, Michael. 1999. "Prosperity and Social Capital." *Wall Street Journal*, June 24, p. A12.

Miller, Lisa. 1997. "Car Rental Companies Are Jacking up Prices." *Wall Street Journal*, February 4, p. B6.

Morgan, Bruce W. 1996. "Don't Sacrifice Value for Short-Term Gains." *American Banker*, April 25, p. 22.

Myers, Randy. 1995. "Much Ado About Write-Offs." *CFO: The Magazine for Senior Financial Executives*, March, pp. 61–64.

Nelson, Emily. 1998a. "Cendant Discovers 'Potential' Trouble in Its Accounting." *Wall Street Journal*, April 16, p. A5.

———. 1998b. "Cendant Dismisses a Senior Financial Aide." *Wall Street Journal*, April 20, p. A5.

———. 1998c. "Despite Its Problems, Cendant Is Bidding for a British Roadside-Service Business." *Wall Street Journal*, April 30, p. A4.

———. 1998d. "Manager Tied to Cendant Keeps Optimism." *Wall Street Journal*, April 27, p. C27.

Nelson, Emily and Leslie Scism. 1998. "Cendant Stock Plummets 46.5% on News that Accounting Woes Hurt Earnings." *Wall Street Journal*, April 17, p. A3.

"New Lieberman/Mack Stock Option Bill Counters FASB Rule, Promotes Broader Option Grants." 1993. *Business Wire*, June 28.

O'Connell, Vanessa. 1999. "Campbell Sees Profit Shortfall and Stock Gets Creamed." *Wall Street Journal*, January 12, p. A7.

Olster, Marjorie. 1998. "U.S. Stocks Weak; Tokyo, Cendant Shake Market." *Reuters*, April 16, dailynews.yahoo.com/headlin...16/business/stories/ stocks_76.html. Retrieved on April 20, 1998.

Petersen, Melody. 1998. "'Trick' Accounting Draws Levitt Criticism." *Financial Times*, September 29, p. C8.

Pope, Kyle. 1997. "The Market Bounceback: Nation of Financial Junkies Plugs In." *Wall Street Journal*. October 29, p. B1.

Pound, John. 1992. "Viewpoints: Freeing the Proxy Rules." *New York Times*, November 1, Section 3, p. 11.

Pulliam, Susan. 1996. "Heard on the Street: As HFS Calls Its Latest Buy a 'Rembrandt,' Some Question the Value of Overall Collection." *Wall Street Journal*, November 13, p. C2.

———. 1997a. "Heard on the Street: CUC-HFS Merger Draws Negative Reatction on Wall Street amid Doubts about Strategies." *Wall Street Journal*, May 29, p. C2.

———. 1997b. "Heard on the Street: Is Huizenga Losing His Magic Touch?" *Wall Street Journal*, July 10, p. C1.

———. 1999. "Lycos Insiders Sold off Shares Back in January." *Wall Street Journal*, February 10, p. C1.

Pulliam, Susan and Lee Burton. 1994. "A Restructuring of Write-Offs Is in the Making." *Wall Street Journal*, November 2, p. C1.

"Regulation of Communications among Shareholders." 1992. *Federal Register* 57, no. 205, part II, 57 FR 48276.

"Restructurings Put EITF on Alert." 1994. *American Banker–Bond Buyer*. November 14, p. 5.

Reuters. 1998a. "Ailing Cendant Fires Executive VP." April 17, dailynews. yahoo.com/headlin...17/business/stories/cendant_3.html. Retrieved on April 20, 1998.

———. 1998b. "Cendant Trading Volume Cracks NYSE Top 5." April 16, biz.yahoo.com/finance/980416/cendant_cd_6.html. Retrieved on April 20, 1998.

———. 1998c. "Growth Funds to Feel Pinch from Cendant." April 16, biz.yahoo.com/finance/980416/growth_fun_1.html. Retrieved on April 20, 1998.

———. 1998d. "Research Alert—Cendant Cut to Neutral." April 16, biz.yahoo. com/finance/980416/research_a_22.html. Retrieved on April 20, 1998.

Rudnitsky, Howard. 1996. "Henry the Magician." *Forbes*, September 9, pp. 98–99.

Rumbler, Bill. 1994. "Just Cutting Jobs Doesn't Impress Wall St. Anymore." *Chicago Sun-Times*, August 9, p. 43.

Ryan, Ken. 1998. "Sunbeam Eschews the Past, Outlines Growth Strategy Rescinds 2 Dunlap Decisions." *HFN*, August 31, p. 1.

Sandler, Linda. 1996. "Heard on the Street: Questions Posed on Huizenga's Used Car Plan." *Wall Street Journal*, April 9, p. C1.

Sandler, Linda and Oscar Suris. 1997. "Heard on the Street: Some Question Huizenga Deals With His Firms." *Wall Street Journal*, March 26, p. C1.

Schatz, Willie. 1993. "The Employee Stock Options Fight Enters Round No. 2." *Electronic Business*, April, pp. 26–27.

Schay, Alex. 1998. "Fool on the Hill: An Investment Opinion: D-Cendant." *Yahoo! The Motley Fool*. April 16, fnews.yahoo.com/fool/98/04/16/ dna_980416.htm. Retrieved on April 16, 1998.

Schellhardt, Timothy, Elizabeth MacDonald, and Raju Narisetti. 1998. "Behind the Buzz: Consulting Firms Get an Unexpected Taste of Their Own Medicine." *Wall Street Journal*, October 20, p. A1.

Schroeder, Michael. 1998. "SEC Accuses Grace of Fraud in Accounting." *Wall Street Journal*, December 23, p. A22.

Schwartz, Nelson D. 1999. "A Tale of Two Economies." *Fortune*, April 26, pp. 199–205.

Scism, Leslie, Elizabeth MacDonald, and Emily Nelson. 1998. "Live by the Sword: Cendant is Hammered, and Its Vaunted Plans for Growth Get Dicey, 'Accounting Irregularities' Cause 46% Drop in Stock, Its Currency for Expansion." *Wall Street Journal*, April 17, p. A1.

Serwer, Andrew. 1996. "Mr. Price Is on the Line." *Fortune*, December 9, pp. 70–81.

"Shareholders Decide to Alter the Way Board Is Elected." 1999. *Wall Street Journal*, May 29, p. A9.

Sherer, Paul M. 1998. "Timing Question Dogs Mattel, Coke, Too." *Wall Street Journal*, December 18, p. C1.

Smith, Hedrick. 1998. Transcript of *Surviving the Bottom Line*. Http://www. pbs.org/bottomline/html/e1_trans.html. Retrieved March 3, 2000.

Smith, Randall. 1994. "1993 Year-End Review of Markets and Finance." *Wall Street Journal*, January 3, p. R8.

Springsteel, Ian. 1998. "The SEC Decries Special Charges." *CFO: The Magazine for Senior Financial Executives*, November 1, p. 21.

Standard & Poor. 2000. *Report for McLeod USA, Inc.* July 22.

"Stock Option Reporting Rules Tightened." 1993, *Computerworld*, April 12, p. 6.

Storck, William. 1995. "U.S. Companies Must De-Emphasize Cost Cutting, Analyst Says." *Chemical and Engineering News*, February 6, p. 15.

"Sunbeam Adds Two. . . ." 1996. *Wall Street Journal*, August 8, p. B6.

"Sunbeam Shares Spurt after Perelman Accord; No. 2 Shareholder Gains the Right to Increase His Stake; Applances." 1998. *Baltimore Sun*, August 14, p. C3.

Tessler, Joelle. 1998. "As Amazon Turns." *Wall Street Journal*, December 18, pp. C1–2.

Tomsho, Robert. 1994. "Real Dog: How Greyhound Lines Re-Engineered Itself Right into a Deep Hole." *Wall Street Journal*, October 20, p. A1.

"Top of the Agenda: Accounting for Restructuring." 1994. *American Banker Washington Watch*. August 1, p. 7.

Tully, Shawn. 1996. "How to Make $400,000,000 in Just One Minute." *Fortune*, May 27, pp. 84–91.

———. 1998a. "Merrill Lynch Takes Over." *Fortune*, April 9. www.pathfinder.com/fortune/fortune500/mer.html. Retrieved on April 9, 1998.

———. 1998b. "Raising the Bar: Stock Options Have become even the Subpar CEO's Way to Wealth. Now Some Hot Companies Are Dramatically Toughening Option Plans—and Wall Street Loves It." *Fortune*, June 8, www.pathfinder.com/fortune/1998/980608/fea.html. Retrieved on June 5, 1998.

———. 1999. "The Earnings Illusion." *Fortune*, April 16, p. 206–10.

Wall Street Journal. 1997a. "Chairman's Pay Is Set at up to $21.7 Million as Part of Merger Plan." *Wall Street Journal*, January 9, p. B7.

———. 1997b. "HFS Says It Expects Expansion Will Come from Internal Growth." *Wall Street Journal*, October 13, p. B8.

Waters, Richard. 1994a. "Accountancy Column: Business School Winner Fails SEC Test—Why the Wider Use of Restructuring Charges in the U.S. Is Meeting Opposition." *Financial Times*, March 24, p. 12.

———. 1994b. "Accountancy: Tidying Up the U.S. Corporate Landscape—Proposals to Tighten Restructuring and Other One-Off Charges." *Financial Times*, November 24, p. 14.

———. 1998. "SEC in Attack on U.S. Accounting." *Financial Times*, September 29, p. 12.

Wessel, David. 1999. "U.S. Stock Holdings Rose 20% in 1998, Highest Percent of Assets in Postwar Era." *Wall Street Journal*, March 15, p. A2.

Wettlaufer, Dale. 1998. "Fool on the Hill: An Investment Opinion: More on Cendant." *Yahoo! The Motley Fool*, April 17, fnews.yahoo.com/fool/98/04/17/dna_980417.htm. Retrieved on April 17, 1998.

Whitford, David. 1998. "Becoming CEO? Call Him First." *Fortune*, June 8, www.pathfinder.com/fortune/1998/980608/the.html. Retrieved on June 8, 1998.

Wiggins, Phillip H. 1986. "AT&T Move Is Assessed." *New York Times*, December 19, Section D, p. 8, col. 3.

Wloszczyna, Chris. 1991. "Restructuring Rallies Often Short-Lived." *USA Today*, October 28, p. B3.

Ziegler, Bart and Gautam Naik. 1996. "Hefty Fees Set if Nynex Deal Comes Undone." *Wall Street Journal*, April 24, p. A3.

INDEX

Acampora, Ralph, 131, 133
Accounting and accountants. *See* financial accounting
Accruals, 23, 71–72, 102–5, 164, 170, 201, 223
Accumulation, 40, 62–63, 113, 262–63
Aglietta, Michel, 62
American Express, 106
American Stores, 232
Analytic Contingent, 129, 161
Annual meeting of shareholders, 48–49, 188–90
Annual Reports to Shareholders, 66, 69–70
Apple Computer, 116, 119
Arbitrageurs. *See* risk arbitrage
Arthur Andersen, 2, 99
AT&T, 179, 288n
Audit Committees, 100–1

Boeing, 229, 241
Bond market, 32–33, 40–44, 80, 139, 160
Bond rating agencies, 40–42
Bond-holder's interest in creditworthiness, 42–43, 47, 161–63
Bonds as a speculative security, 41–42
Borden, 215, 225
"bought deal," 36
Buffett, Warren, 44, 115
Burlington Northern, 47
Business media: rise of 7, 21, 62–66, 259–65; analytic contingent of 7, 80–83, 92–103, 123, 158–60, 186, 204, 209, 216, 246, 257–58; as social

intermediary 126–38; as cause of imperative for ceaseless speculative management 127–33; and security speculation 134–38
Business mobilization, 111, 117, 209, 233

Campbell, 97
Capital gains, 38, 50, 55, 113, 121, 123, 141–42, 154, 194, 266, 268–69
Capitalized earnings and speculative activity, 21–22, 82, 95–96, 142, 257
Cendant, 100
Certificates of deposit (CD's), 32–33
Chandler, Alfred, 65, 139
Chemical, 178, 210–11
Chevron, 206, 243
Chrysler, 167
Citicorp, 114
Clinton, President William, 118, 123
Coalition for American Equity Expansion (CAEE), 117–23
Coca-Cola, 27, 115, 134
Cohen, Abby Joseph, 131–33
Commodity speculation and business media, 136
Compaq, 117, 205
Conceptions of aggressively good management, 23, 66, 93, 128, 192, 214, 236, 245, 257, 264–65
Conceptions of corporate control, 140, 264–65
Conglomerates and conglomerateurs, 44, 57

Consulting firms and restructuring,
   196–200
Corporate governance structures, 24–28,
   66, 92–94, 123–26, 138, 144–47,
   150–65, 257–59
Corporate raiders, 38, 43, 58–59, 159–61
Corporate scandals. *See* scandals,
   corporate
Council of Institutional Investors, 116, 153
CPC International 248
Creditworthiness and bond-holder inter-
   est, 41–43, 43, 161–64, 195
CSX, 149, 164–65

Deindustrialization. *See* restructuring
Delegitimation of restructuring, 86–88,
   208–9, 236, 245–52
Deregulation of financial markets,
   31–35, 37
Derivatives and speculation, 111
Digital Equipment, 201, 220, 223
Discounted present value, 38. *See also*
   capitalized earnings
Discretionary write-offs, 104. *See also*
   financial accounting
Dow Chemical, 178, 210–11
Downsizing. *See* restructuring, internal
   reorganization
Dunlap, Al, 1, 114, 130. *See also* Sun-
   beam Corporation and Scott Paper

Earnings management, 73, 101–7\
Eastman Kodak, 149
Efficient Market Hypothesis, 64–66,
   160–61
Eisner, Michael, 114, 148–49
EITF. *See* Emerging Issues Task Force
Eli Lilly, 248
Emerging issues task force (EITF, 25,
   86, 95, 108–13, 176–78, 214–20, 227,
   259
Emerson Electric, 242–43
Enron, 2, 99–101, 106–7, 152, 269
Equity securities, 141, 147–48, 174, 195,
   245, 255–56

Equity valuation models, 95
European financial markets/systems, 26,
   32–34, 59, 63, 140
Event studies, weaknesses of, 172–74

FASB. *See* Financial Accounting Standards
   Board
Federal Funds Market, 33
Financial accounting: accounting for
   stock options 111, 113–23; accounting
   standards-setting 25, 111, 113; accruals v. transactions 72, 170; American
   Institute of Certified Public Accountants (AICPA), 218; as social intermediary, 92–124; audit as low profit-
   margin service, 235; balance sheet
   management, 175; big-bath charge, 73,
   102, 220; discontinued operations,
   218; discretionary accruals, 102–4,
   170, 176–78; earnings-management
   and accounting rules, 73, 101–7, 220;
   Generally Accepted Accounting Principles (GAAP), 94; Generally Accepted Auditing Standards (GAAS),
   96; goodwill and external/transactional
   reorganization, 71–72, 111–12; pri-
   macy of accounting data in equity valuation, 96–101; Financial Accounting
   Standards Board (FASB), 25–26, 86,
   96, 108, 110–14, 117–23, 158, 176,
   214–16, 235, 259; financial intermediaries, 24, 34; compared to social
   intermediaries, 92–93, 122, 139
Fleming, 241–42
Fligstein, Neil, 8, 30, 45, 64, 140, 264–65
Fordism: neo-Fordism, 63, 262; Fordist
   finance, 58, 61–64; post-Fordism, 63,
   67, 262–64, 277n; Fordist production,
   40, 263, 272n
Fortune 500 (Fortune Magazine), 67–69

GAAP. *See* financial accounting, Generally Accepted Accounting Principles
GAAS. *See* Financial Accounting, Generally Accepted Auditing Standards

General Electric, 104, 110
General Motors, 105–6, 125, 182–83, 231
Georgia-Pacific, 162–63, 166
Gillette, 179–80
Glass-Steagall Act, 35
Global Crossing, 2
Goodwill, 71, 111–12, 201, 239
Goodyear Tire, 171, 177, 180
Greyhound, 208

Halliburton, 203–4
Hammer, Michael and James Champy, 5, 13, 199
Hostile bid in corporate takeovers, 58

IBM, 60, 117, 168, 179, 202–3
Icahn, Carl, 125
Ideal type, 20–22, 24, 26, 31, 273–74n
Income-smoothing. See financial accounting, earnings management
Individual Retirement Accounts (IRA's), 50
Institutional investing, 148, 256
Institutional speculators more apt than institutional investors, 155
Interest rates and corporate restructuring, 39
Internal Reorganization, 22–23
Interpretive sociology, 174
Investing, retail, 50–57, 188–96, 256, 268–69
Investor capitalism, 22, 30, 138, 142–43, 153, 190, 200, 262

Junk bond market, 40–44, 160

Kahlberg, Stephen, 26, 274n
Kellogg, 231, 237
Keynes, John Maynard, 1, 267
Kimberly-Clark, 16, 226
Kmart, 231
Kohlberg, Kravis, Roberts (KKR), 195

Legitimacy and legitimation of restructuring as production management, 14,
88, 123, 157, 169, 180–81, 186, 194, 205–6, 231, 238, 260–61
Levin, Carl, 120–21
Levitt, Arthur, 91, 239
Lieberman, Joseph, 119
Lockheed Martin, 228–29
Lowenstein, Louis, 191–92

Management buyout (MBO), 151
Management stratification and consulting, 198
Managerial capitalism, 44, 59–60, 139–42, 264–65
Manpower, 201
Market for corporate control, 35–40, 160–61, 256
MCI, 108, 114–16, 169
McKesson, 101–2, 247–49
Mergers and Acquisitions, 39–40, 77, 80, 87, 184, 196, 232, 245–52
Merrill Lynch, 133
Milken, Michael, 40–43, 59
Mill, John Stuart, 268–69
Minow, Nell, 251–52
MLSF. See multilayered subsidiary form
Mobil, 209–10, 213, 231, 240
Money market, 31–35, 140, 256
Monks, Robert, and Institutional Shareholder Services, 46
Monsanto, 156, 202, 211–12
Morgan Stanley, 30, 36, 87, 131, 196, 236
Motorola, 164, 227
Multidivisional form, 247
Multilayered subsidiary form (MLSF), 8, 39, 61, 110, 157, 247
Mutual funds, 57

NASDAQ Index, 127–28

Occidental Petroleum, 228
Organizational restructuring. See restructuring, internal.
Outside directors, 151–53
Outsourcing of jobs, 18–19

Pacific Gas and Electric, 175, 194

PCS Health Systems, 248

Pecuniary Reorganization, 23, 29, 60, 156, 182, 184, 254, 261, 269

Pensions, defined-contribution plans, 50

Pfizer, 211

Philip Morris, 212–13, 230

Philips Petroleum, 162

Pooling of interest, 111–12

Prechel, Harland, 8, 12–13, 39, 110, 157, 247, 272n. See also multi-layered subsidiary form

Preferential treatment, 268

Primary financial markets, 92, 255

Production management, 272n

Promoter's profit, 23, 245–46

Proxy rules, 1992 changes in, 188–96

Reengineering. See restructuring, internal

Regulation school. See Fordism

Relationship banking, 33–34, 36, 40, 256

Reorganization, external. See restructuring, external

Reorganization, internal. See restructuring, internal

Reorganizer's Profit(s), 23, 37–38, 60, 231, 245–52, 254, 267

Restructuring charges or expenses, 70–74, 80–87, 105, 111, 114, 120, 123, 158, 170–78, 193, 201–4, 214–18

Restructuring, asset, 7, 71, 157

Restructuring, capital, 7, 157

Restructuring, corporate, 1–30, 50, 61–110, 131–210, 231–64

Restructuring, decline of: and speculative teams, 209–14; and financial accounting, 214–31, 233–36; and transactional reorganization, 231–33; and business media, 236–40; and delegitimation, 241–45

Restructuring, emergence of: and takeovers, 159–65; and speculative teams, 165–70; and financial accounting, 170–78; and legitimation in the business media, 178–83

Restructuring, external, 66, 74, 80, 82; linked to rise of internal reorganization, 159–83, linked to decline of internal reorganization 245–52, 274n. See also transactional restructuring

Restructuring, internal, 8–9, 22–28, 66–90, 70–71, 95, 138, 142, 146, 156–83, 217, 231–32, 253, 260, 274n

Restructuring, reign of: and speculative teams, 187–96; and consulting, 196–200, and financial accounting, 200–4; and business media, 205–6

Restructuring, wave of restructuring activity in late 20th century, 74–88, 258–61

Risk arbitrage, 36, 39, 146

RJR Nabisco, 195–96

Roach, Stephen, 30, 131

Rockwell International, 241

Roe, Mark, 140–41

Roy, William, 139

Scandals, corporate, 2, 99, 115, 130, 152, 168, 261, 269, 280n

Schuetze, Walter, SEC Chief Accountant, 110, 114, 201, 217, 233–34, 238

Scott Paper, 1, 16–17, 114, 120, 125, 130, 224–26

Scott Paper, 16–17

Sears Roebuck, 46–47, 49, 168–69, 204, 215

Secondary financial markets, 59, 60, 62, 64–66, 88, 92–93, 122, 126, 147, 153, 181, 186, 207, 255–57, 263

Securities and Exchange Commission (SEC) Staff Accounting Bulletin 67 (SAB 67) 158, 176–78, 201

Securities and Exchange Commission (SEC), 25, 66, 91–100, 108–14, 150–58, 175, 187–90, 233–37

Security analysts and security analysis, 97–99, 105, 129–31, 191

Serial restructuring, 237–38

Sharedata, Inc., 120

Shareholder activism, 44–47

Shareholder stratification, 146–47, 190–93

Shareholder value, 44–47, 209–10, 213

Shareholding, by masses, 50–57. *See also* retail investing.

Simulated restructuring, 71, 193–94

Smith, Adam, and the "invisible hand," 65

Social intermediaries: defined, 24, 28; role in shaping corporate restructuring, 62–66, 91–94, 126, 138, 145, 170, 209, 234, 257

Sociologists and the study of markets, 64, 277n, 278n

Southern, 193–94

Speculation, 65

Speculative capitalism, 60, 128, 248, 256, 266–69

Speculative management: introduced, 1; defined, 22; in late 20th century, 153, 187, 192–96, 209, 245, 255–58, 264–65; and internal reorganization, 82–86; and external reorganization, 86–88

Speculative teams, 63, 127–29, 150, 165–70, 181, 186, 199, 209–21, 241–46, 257–69

Speed-up of restructuring due to 1994 EITF rule change, 224–27

Stock market and speculative capitalism, 2, 17, 22–28, 43–44, 50–53, 60–66, 74, 90–94, 104, 123–26, 137–59, 172–78, 201–5, 211–20, 245–66

Stock options, 15–16, 86, 91, 100–5, 113–23, 147–50, 166–68, 186, 210, 234, 259

Stock touting by business media, 134–38

Sunbeam Corporation, 1–2, 13–14, 120, 125

Takeover Defenses, 163–64, 166

Takeovers, corporate. *See* transactional reorganization

Taxes, 17–18, 43, 96, 114, 121, 203, 229

Tenneco, 244–45

Textron, 165

Transactional finance, 31–39, 50–61, 92, 123–27, 137, 245, 255–56, 263–66

Transactional reorganization, 31–40, 57–59, 112, 157–71, 205–14, 229–49, 256, 261. *See also* external reorganization

TRW, 70, 244

Underwriting, 34, 36

Unearned Income privileged over other earnings, 268–69

Unisys, 206, 242

United Technologies, 180

Useem, Michael, 5, 8, 30, 142–44, 146–48, 153–54, 189, 191, 262

Veblen, Thorstein, 60, 245, 267

W.R.Grace, 70, 98–99, 108

Walt Disney, 114

Warner Lambert, 177

Weber, Max. *See* ideal type

Weller, Jack, 21, 274n

Whirlpool, 1, 268

Winchell, Walter, as stock tout, 137

WMX (Waste Management), 99–100, 249–51

Woolworth, 49

Worldcom, 2

Worldcom, 99

Writeoffs. *See* Financial Accounting, Discretionary Accruals)

Xerox, 128